My Story

My Story

Elizabeth Smart

with Chris Stewart

St. Martin's Press ❦ New York

MY STORY. Copyright © 2013 by Elizabeth Smart. All rights reserved. Printed in the United States of America. For information, address St. Martin's Press, 175 Fifth Avenue, New York, N.Y. 10010.

www.stmartins.com

Design by Steven Seighman

Library of Congress Cataloging-in-Publication Data

Smart, Elizabeth.
    My story / Elizabeth Smart, Chris Stewart.
      pages cm
    ISBN 978-1-250-04015-2 (hardcover)
    ISBN 978-1-4668-3540-5 (e-book)
    1. Smart, Elizabeth, 1987–   2. Kidnapping victims—Utah—Salt Lake City—Biography.   3. Kidnapping—Utah—Salt Lake City.   4. Missing children—Utah—Salt Lake City.   5. Mormon children—Crimes against—Utah—Salt Lake City.   I. Stewart, Chris, 1960–   II. Title.
    HV6603.S63A3 2013
    364.15'4092—dc23
    [B]

                                        2013024888

St. Martin's Press books may be purchased for educational, business, or promotional use. For information on bulk purchases, please contact Macmillan Corporate and Premium Sales Department at 1-800-221-7945, extension 5442, or write special markets@macmillan.com.

First Edition: October 2013

10 9 8 7 6 5 4 3 2 1

This book is dedicated to the safe return of missing children everywhere.

Acknowledgments

My parents, Ed and Lois Smart.

My immediate and extended family.

People who searched and prayed for me everywhere.

Chris Stewart.

And my wonderful husband, Matthew Gilmour.

The power of choosing good and evil
is within the reach of all.
—Origen Adamantius

For we are troubled on every side, yet not distressed;
we are perplexed, but not in despair; persecuted, but not forsaken;
cast down, but not destroyed.
—2 Corinthians 4:8–9

My Story

Prologue

November 2001

We had just walked out of the ZCMI store in downtown Salt Lake City. The heavily tinted windows, with their grated iron accents, were at our backs as we waited to cross the street. Traffic was light. I remember it was cold. The Mormon temple and visitor center was just a block away and high-rise buildings rose on every side. Salt Lake City was getting ready for the Winter Olympics and there was construction all around. The sky was gray and clear, and the sun was moving quickly toward the western horizon. There weren't a lot of pedestrians—winter was coming on—so the beggar was hard to ignore, standing among the well-dressed crowd.

He didn't seem to notice as we walked by. I was on my mother's right, my little sister on her left, holding my mother's hand. We had been shopping, and I carried a couple of little bags. I was a teenager, but just barely, with blond hair and blue eyes. As we walked, I remember glancing at my mother. She was very pretty. I liked being with her. She was one of my best friends.

Salt Lake City was not a dangerous place, and I had the luxury of growing up with a mother who was open and unassuming. Her demeanor was friendly yet careful.

Standing by the beggar, waiting to cross the street, I looked and made eye contact with him; my brothers had already seen him and had come back to ask my mom if we had any work for him.

Mom glanced at him warily, not wanting to stare. I don't remember a lot about him, but I do recall that he was clean-cut and well groomed. No beard. No robes. No singing or talking about prophets or visions or being the Chosen One. All of that would come later. For now, he appeared to be nothing more than a normal guy who had hit a rough patch in his life. He certainly didn't seem to be dangerous or threatening.

"I thought he was a man down on his luck," my mom would later testify. "He just lost his job, looked young enough that maybe he had a family, people he was responsible for."

So she walked toward him, five dollars in her hand.

I held back, my hair blowing in the autumn wind.

He glanced in my direction, seeming to take me in from the corner of his eye. I gave him a quick smile. I felt sorry for him and was happy when my mother handed him the money.

What I didn't know—but would later learn—was that he had been watching me very carefully as we walked toward him. He had taken the opportunity to study me further as my mother searched through her purse. He remembered everything about me: the clothes that I was wearing, my blond hair, the way I looked up at my mother, the color of my eyes.

And though he was very careful not to show it, he decided at that moment that I was the one.

1.

Elizabeth

———

It's funny, some of the things that I remember, many of the details forever burned in my mind.

It's as if I can still smell the air, hear the mountain leaves rustle above me, feel the fabric of the veil that Brian David Mitchell stretched across my face. I can picture every detail of my surroundings: the tent, the washbasin, the oppressive dugout full of spiders and mice. I can feel the cut of the steel cable wrapped so tightly around my ankle, the scorch of the summer heat lifting off the side of the hill, the swaying of the Greyhound bus as we fled to California. I can still see the people who were around me, their blank expressions, their fear of how we were dressed, my veil and the dirty robes, the looks of confusion in their eyes.

I remember so many overwhelming feelings and emotions. Terror that is utterly indescribable, even to this day. Embarrassment and shame so deep, I felt as if my very *worth* had been tossed upon the ground. Despair. Starving hunger. Fatigue and thirst and a nakedness that bares one to the bones. Intruding hands. Pain and burning. The leering of his dark eyes. A deep longing for my family. A heartbreaking yearning to go home.

All of these memories are a part of me now, the DNA inside me. Indeed, these are the things that have moved and shaped me, sometimes twisting, sometimes wrenching me into the person I am today.

Sometime long before I was taken, I had been told that when someone dies, the first thing you forget is the sound of their voice. This thought terrified me. *What if I could no longer remember my mother's voice, a sound I had heard every day of my life!* I started to think of her, and other members of my family and their voices. I started to think of all the things my mom used to tell me every day: *Have a good day at school. I love you. Have a good night.* I would have given anything to hear her at that moment.

Every morning she used to sing at the top of her lungs, *"Oh what a beautiful morning . . ."*

I used to hate it.

What would I have given to hear her voice again!

Over the first few weeks of captivity, I forced myself to think of things like that. I remember sitting in the heat of the summer, the sun baking on my back, forcing myself to think of my mom's voice, her laugh. How beautiful she looked in her black skirt and gold top. The shape and the color of her eyes.

But there were other feelings too. And though it might be hard to understand, a few of them were good, for they show the things you cling to when everything is gone.

I remember the pure rush of gratitude for any time that I could sleep. The realization that I would live another day! Relief when the sun went down and the heat gave way to the cool of the night. Gratefulness for food or water. A few minutes when I might be left alone. The ability to slip into a state of pure survival, a state of blankness, a quiet and painless place where I could shut the world down.

Looking back, I realized that at one point, early on the morning of the first day, something had changed inside me. After I had been raped and brutalized, there was something new inside my soul. There was a burning now inside me, a fierce determination that no matter what I had to do, *I was going to live!*

This determination was the only thing that gave me any hope—the realization that as long as I could survive one more day or one more hour, I might find a way to get back home.

I also discovered something that is harder to imagine, and much more difficult to explain.

Sometime during the first couple of days, I realized that I wasn't alone. There were others there beside me, unseen but not unfelt. Sometimes I could picture them beside me, reaching for my hand.

And that is one of the reasons I am still alive.

When I think back on those dark days of my capture, I realize my story didn't start on the night that David Brian Mitchell slipped into my bedroom and held a knife at my throat. In an odd way, my story began a few days before. Sunday afternoon. In my home. Just a few days before my world was torn apart.

Over time, I have gained an enormous appreciation for what I experienced on that Sunday. It has helped me to keep perspective. It helped to give me hope. And it helped me understand a little better why things might have happened the way they did.

2.

Sunday School

Two days before I was taken, I was sitting in my Sunday school class, surrounded by a group of other fourteen- and fifteen-year-olds. There were maybe seven or eight of us, a mix of boys and girls. Some of the kids were listening, but not everyone, for we were teenagers, you know. Looking around me, I was comfortable, for these kids were my friends. I had grown up with them, gone to school with them, eaten snacks at their houses, giggled with them on the playground. We knew one another well.

Though there was some horseplay among the class, for the most part I was quiet. I don't know if I was shy, but I guess I was. I just didn't feel a need to stand out. It surprises some people when I tell them that. Most of them picture me as an outgoing teenager. A cheer-leader type, I think. But I wasn't. I was kind of quiet. A very obedient child. A 4.0 student. I played the harp, for heaven's sake! How un-cheerleader is that!

Some people say I'm pretty. Blond hair. Blue eyes. But I promise, I've never thought of myself that way. As a fourteen-year-old girl sitting in my Sunday school class, I certainly didn't think of myself as beautiful. Honestly, I don't think I ever thought about it at all. Some of the girls I knew were boy-crazy, but I never thought about those kinds of things. I didn't wear makeup. I had never had a boyfriend. The thought had never even crossed my mind. My favorite things were talking to my mom and jumping on the trampoline with my best friend, Elizabeth Calder. We just liked to have fun together. But our idea of fun wasn't chasing boys, or prank calling other kids in our class. In almost every way, I was still a little girl.

And one thing that I can say for certain is that I didn't understand the world.

I remember pressing my white cotton dress—printed tulips with light-green edging—with my hands while listening to my teacher. To most of us kids, he seemed to be about a hundred years old, with his gray beard and white hair. But we liked him. I felt he cared about us, even if we didn't listen to him all the time.

That morning, my teacher said something that hit me in a way that few things ever had before.

"If you will pray to do what God wants you to do, He will change your life," he said.

I pressed my dress again, my head down. I was listening carefully to him now. I don't know what it was, but there was something in the way he said it, the intensity of his voice, that made me realize that what he was saying was important.

"If you will lose your life in the service of God, He will direct you. He will help you. So I challenge you to do that. Commit to the Heavenly Father, and He will guide your way."

But what can I do to serve God? I asked myself. I'm just a little girl. I don't know anything. I can't do anything. What path could He even guide me on?

I didn't know the answers to these questions. But I felt that, whatever it might be, I had to do what my teacher had challenged me to do.

Later on that day, I went to the bedroom I shared with my little sister, Mary Katherine, and shut the door. I went into the bathroom and locked it. On the other side of the bathroom was a walk-in closet. I went into the closet and shut that door too. I have three younger brothers, a younger sister, and one brother who is a year and a half older than me. With six kids, our house was always chaotic. Full of life and voices. But there, in the closet, I was as alone as anyone could be in a home with eight people.

Kneeling down, I closed my eyes.

I didn't know how to say it, but I did the best I could. "God, I'm here," I said. "I'm only fourteen. I know I'm just a little girl. But I'll do whatever it is that you want me to do. I really do want to serve you. But I'm not sure that I know how."

I waited a moment. Maybe I was waiting for something to happen. A vision. A revelation. Some kind of sign from God.

But nothing happened.

So I got up and didn't think about it again.

At least not until two days later, when Brian David Mitchell took me from my house and forced me to start climbing up the mountain in the middle of the night.

Struggling up the side of the hill, breathless and terrified, a bearded man behind me and a long knife to my back, with scratched arms and my silky red pajamas clinging to my legs, I couldn't help but wonder, *God, is* this *what you had in mind?*

I was so confused and so afraid.

I don't understand! I did what you have asked me! This can't be what you wanted!

And it certainly wasn't. I know that now. Being taken captive was not part of some great, eternal plan.

But the confusion was overwhelming. My mind tumbled in sheer terror: *This doesn't make any sense! I've never done anything wrong!*

And though it would take a while, the answers to my confusion eventually settled in my mind.

I don't think what happened to me was something that God intended. He surely would not have wished the anguish and torment that I was about to go through upon anyone, especially upon a child.

But since that time, I have learned an important lesson. Yes, God can make some good come from evil. But even He, in all His majesty, won't make the evil go away. Men are free. He won't control them. There is wickedness in this world.

Which left me with this: When faced with pain and evil, we have to make a choice.

We can choose to be taken by the evil.

Or we can try to embrace the good.

3.

Brian David Mitchell

———

Brian David Mitchell began his journey to my bedroom many years before he actually found himself standing beside my bed in the middle of the night.

Indeed, the evil that grew inside him was planted very early in his life.

But before I go any further, I'd like to make it very clear that Brian David Mitchell's life isn't something that I want to understand. It's not something I have studied, or spent even a moment trying to figure out. Knowing him and his background is like learning about the devil. But I wasn't given any choice. I had been thrust into his life. Because of the situation in which I found myself—the abduction and then the seven-year trial—I have been forced to come to know him in ways that no else could.

I know about his teenage conviction for pedophilia after exposing himself to a child. I know about his three marriages. The thirteen children and stepchildren. More charges of child abuse. I know about his various stages of activity in his church, just enough to help him get the vernacular and religious customs down. More charges of abuse from his stepchildren. Threats of violence against his family. An urgent marriage to Wanda Barzee on the very day that the divorce from his second wife had been finalized. Barzee giving up all parental rights to her six children in order that they could marry. The growing realization that religion could be used to get what he wanted, whether from Barzee or someone else. The transition from a relatively quiet man to a controlling and abusive husband. Twisted relationships with other women, including invitations for them to become polygamous wives. An intense and sudden interest in Satan. Barzee feeling rejected because of his constant invitations to other women. A sudden surge of religious revelations that told him that he was chosen. Barzee accepting his lustful eye. The emergence of the Davidic king. Separation from, and then the eventual severing of his relationship with, other members of his family. His own mother having a restraining order placed against him. Drugs and alcohol and pornography. The prophet Immanuel taking to the city streets. No more jobs. No more money. He and Barzee hitchhiking across the country with nothing but what they had in their backpacks. The writing of the Book of Immanuel David Isaiah (a compilation of Mitchell's spiritual revelations). The decision to take me and make me his second wife.

These are the defining moments of Brian David Mitchell's life.

For me to have to wander through this web of darkness is very difficult. And to crawl inside his head can be terrifying, for it is a closed and evil place.

But again, I had to understand him. I wasn't given any choice.

It's also important to realize that understanding Brian David Mitchell is made very difficult by the fact that he is a master manipulator.

To this day, he will rant and rave in gibberish, then suddenly pull into himself, holding his cards very close to the chest. It's as if he's always evaluating his next move, weighing the odds, trying to figure out the best way to control the situation. Even when he isn't ranting, meaningful conversation is utterly impossible unless you are a prison guard or someone else who can give him something that he wants. He is selfish and angry. But he's also very smart, far more intelligent than most want to give him credit for. That is important to remember. This is not a foolish man. Some say that he is brilliant. Indeed, this proved to be part of his power, the ability to appear harmless and unassuming, even while he was plotting and demeaning and raging inside.

Throughout the ensuing investigation, his family has cast very little light upon my capture, perhaps partly because they don't want to talk, and perhaps mostly because they simply don't understand him. He's had very few friends, and those few people he was ever close to were forced to abandon him as they realized what a wicked man he was.

But though he has always refused to talk to the authorities, and his background is depressingly convoluted, Brian David Mitchell has not hidden everything beneath his deceptions and his lies.

Indeed, the trial of Brian David Mitchell for my kidnapping and criminal sexual assault left few stones unturned. Though I would happily have withdrawn myself from the process, I couldn't, for I was the central figure in the case, the most important witness, *the* reason for it all. Everything that was said or done during the trial had to be focused to some extent on me.

But I also understand that thousands of hours have gone into building the prosecutor's case. Dozens of investigators, police officers, attorneys, doctors, judges, psychiatrists, mental-health officers, criminal forensic specialists, jurists, and advocates helped to pull the various pieces together, each of them having a bit of the story to tell.

Press reports provide thousands of pages of additional information. Indeed—and I say this with very mixed emotions—few stories have so captured the nation's attention as did my case, the abduction and trial being covered extensively among the local, national, and international press.

But while these sources may be helpful in understanding Brian David Mitchell, the real story can only be told by those of us who were there.

Mitchell's wife, Wanda Barzee, is one of those. And she wasn't an innocent bystander. She is a wounded and evil woman—a mother who once secretly fed her daughter her own pet rabbit, watching her eat it with a smile—who must accept her share of the blame. But at least she has been somewhat willing to discuss the events that took place.

Of course, there is also Brian David Mitchell. But once he was finally captured, he went from incessant talking to not speaking at all.

Which leaves the keys to the story lying in my hands.

I am the one who lived through nine months of hell. I am the one who was forced to lie beside Mitchell every night. I am the one who had to listen to his stories, including long and wandering tales that revealed some of the most intimate details of his life. I am the one who felt his hot breath on my face, hiked with him atop the mountain, washed with him, ate and napped with him, hid behind Dumpsters and in the mountains with him, hitchhiked and rode on a cross-country bus with him. I am the one who was forced to watch things between Barzee and him that no one should ever be forced to see. I am the one who witnessed Mitchell turn away Barzee's jealous rage with nothing but a soft word about his weaknesses and a blessing upon her head. I am the one who had to listen to his incessant talking, sometimes interrupted only long enough that he could rape me before going back to sharing his insights once again. I am the one who saw him play other people like a fiddle, watched him deal with police and investigators—people who were trained to spot deception—as if they were nothing but children in a game of hide-and-seek. I saw his calm. I saw his cool. I saw him constantly pull the wool over other people's eyes.

I saw all this, and more. Which is why I know Brian David Mitchell better than any other person in the world. Believing I would be his wife forever, he told me about it all.

I know his comings and goings in the months leading up to the night when he snuck into my room. I know what he did on the day he came to take me. I know how he planned it, where he walked, and what he ultimately had in mind.

I know that he decided to take me after seeing me on that November afternoon, when I had been shopping with my mother in downtown Salt Lake City. I know that he plotted from the beginning, offering to rake leaves and repair my father's roof in order to find out where I lived. I know he manipulated his way into my home in order to note the location of my bedroom and my sleeping arrangements. I know what he did to prepare for the kidnapping, staking out the mountains high above the city in the months and weeks before that fateful night in June. I know that he bought the hardware he would need: steel cable, bolts, a couple of padlocks and orange-handled bolt cutters. I know he moved his and Barzee's summer camp, trudging higher up the mountain, where it would be more difficult to be found. There, at the upper camp as they called it, he expended enormous effort to excavate a dugout among the trees, cutting thick logs to make a roof and leveling the hill in order to provide a shelter where he intended to spend the winter with Barzee and his new wife.

I know he didn't spend all his time living like a hermit on the mountain. He told me how he frequently walked the streets of Salt Lake City, bumming for alcohol, looking for a party, stealing from the local market, begging for food. I know that he was lazy; feeling too entitled to really work, preferring to hang out on the streets. He liked to call it "ministering," but his life was bumming and nothing more.

I also know that, as time went by, he slipped deeper and deeper into his caricature of a prophet. But none of it was real. Brian David Mitchell is not insane. The professional analysis is clear.

He is a manipulative, antisocial, and narcissistic pedophile. He is not clinically psychotic or delusional. He is just an evil man.

Brian David Mitchell slipped too easily in and out of prophecy for it to ever be his actual state of mind. He simply used the culture and language of religion to manipulate people in order to get what he wanted. I witnessed it again and again. When he really needed something—knowing that prophets were difficult to take seriously—he could turn the switch off and act very rational. When the situation required it, he could act very sane.

Still, as the night of the kidnapping grew near, he decided that the persona of a modern-day prophet was the way to go. Way less work. Way more opportunities for mischief and manipulation. And the ability to claim that he was a man who spoke to God was pretty exciting. It carried a little punch. A bit of power. It got him attention and helped to explain some of his unconventional behavior. So he lost the Levi's and started walking around in robes and leather sandals. But even then, his intentions were only to manipulate. For example, when running around the mountain in sandals and dirty sheets proved to be impractical, he started stashing his sandals in a hollow oak he called the shoe tree. When he went down into the city, knowing that other people were going to see him, he'd bring out the sandals. Hiking back up to the mountain, knowing that no one else would be around, he'd stop at the shoe tree and put his hiking boots back on.

As I have already testified in court:

He was his number-one priority, followed by sex, drugs, and alcohol, but he used religion in all of those aspects to justify everything.

Nine months of living with him and seeing him proclaim that he was God's servant and called to do God's work and everything he did to me and my family is something that I know that God would not tell somebody to do. God would never tell someone to kidnap her at knifepoint from their bed, from her sister's side . . . never continue to rape her and sexually abuse her.

Nor would God tell him to kill me. But that's what he was prepared to do.

4.

Dark Night

June 4, 2002
The mountains east of Salt Lake City, Utah

Having walked the trail many times now, I know that Brian David Mitchell must have moved very quickly down the mountain, which is surprising, given the fact that it was a very dark night. I remember even now how the heavy trees that lined the narrow path sucked up most of the moonlight. The mountains are full of coyotes—I heard them almost every night once we were in the upper camp—and it is likely that some of them watched him from the ridge as he made his way toward the city. The maples and oaks along the trail are very thick, with occasional outcroppings of granite that drop into narrow depressions where the winter snows melt off, but it was early summer when he came to get me, and the ground was dry and packed. A gentle stream, hardly more than a trickle, ran through the bottom of the canyon and he would have been forced to move among the peppermint and watercress in order to follow its path.

As he moved down the mountain, no man saw him pass.

Behind him, high up on the mountain, the other one was waiting to receive me with a dirty bed and clean linen robes.

Coming down the mountain is pretty easy, and can be done in as little as an hour. You follow a narrow canyon that drops sharply from the east to join a well-established trail that runs for about half a mile toward the city. But although you can come down from the mountain fairly quickly, going back is much more difficult and the going is always slow. The mountain is very steep and the way is not well marked. So Brian David Mitchell was in a hurry, for he knew that on that night, it would take us many hours.

For one thing, it would still be dark. And he would have to guide me, knowing I would be looking to escape. He knew that he could make me hold the flashlight, allowing him to keep the knife at my back, but it would be awkward to move together, keeping his hands gripped tightly around my arm. Worse, he knew we could not go back up the same trail that he had used to come down. We'd have to go on the backside of the mountain. There, the mountain was very steep and, without a trail to follow, the brush and trees would be so thick we'd end up crawling on our hands and knees.

Yet it was absolutely essential that we make it back to camp before the sun was up. Before the darkness gave way to the summer light, he would have to have taken me up to where I could be hidden and no one could hear me if I screamed.

A little after one A.M., Mitchell neared the bottom of the mountain. There, the trail widened, allowing him to move more quickly.

Everything he wore was black: black sweats, black gloves, black stocking cap and beard. All of this allowed him to blend into the darkness like the shadow of a ghost.

He balanced two military-green sacks across his back. I remember them very clearly. They were tied together with a strand of material and bounced uncomfortably as he moved. As he came off the Wasatch Mountains, the lights of Salt Lake City would have slipped into view. From my house, the valley spreads south and west, neat rows of streetlights that line up in an almost perfect grid. Brigham Young was nothing if not a visionary, and the city is designed along streets that run in neat north-south and east-west rows. To the north, an edge of the mountain to the west hides the northern portion of the valley. As he hiked down, Mitchell surely had to stop to take a break. He was not a young man. And though he seemed to be a fanatic about exercise, he suffered from poor nutrition and inferior hygiene. He and Barzee had skipped many meals, leaving him a little thin. And the alcohol and drugs he had pounded into his body would not have helped him catch his breath. But as tiring as it was to come down from the mountain, it would be much worse climbing back up. It seemed we would stop every few minutes so he could urinate and rest.

Breaking from the streambed, he would have been able to quicken his pace. Here, the lights of the city would have helped illuminate his path, and the moon wouldn't have been so obscured by the thick trees. Just before two A.M., he stood on the empty streets above the city.

He was almost to my house.

I lived on the east bench of the city, almost as high as any of the houses were allowed to be built. My neighborhood—beautiful homes, some new, some older—looked down on the University of Utah, the capital and downtown buildings, and the Mormon temple and towering skyscrapers situated around the city center.

In the darkness, it must have taken him a moment to get his bearings. But he had studied the scene many times before, and even in the darkness he knew exactly where to go.

Breaking from the foothills, the terrain is bare, with only June grass, rock, and weeds. The first of the houses lie just below the trail. A ribbon of asphalt winds down toward the city. Streetlights line the road. But at two o'clock in the morning, there would have been few, if any, cars. Mine was a quiet neighborhood. A quiet city, even. No one saw him as he hunched beside the road.

He crossed Tomahawk Drive, then dipped through an empty lot to avoid another house before turning north again, bringing himself to look down on my backyard. It backed up to a steep part of the hill and was heavy with bushes and trees. A small storage shed was positioned along the hillside, nestled among the brush. He hid his bags in the weeds, then crept down a narrow path of flat stones to step onto the grass of my backyard.

My house was dark inside. He first circled around, looking for a point of access. Finally, after making sure no doors had been left unlocked, he moved across the patio, past a row of empty windows toward the patio door. Stopping at a narrow window on the left side of the patio, he took out a knife. Long. Deadly. A serrated blade. He carefully cut the screen and pushed against the glass. Earlier in the evening, my mother had burned something on the stove and my dad had left the window open just a crack to air things out. The window pushed back on its hinges. He was able to get into the house!

Mitchell later told me that for a moment he had hesitated.

"If God wants me to do this, He will allow it," he said to himself.

Mitchell knew that once he climbed through the window, he would be treading on very dangerous ground. From where he was on the patio, he was looking at trespassing. Criminal mischief. Attempted burglary, if the prosecutors really got on a roll. He would have claimed, of course, that he was nothing but a hungry beggar desperate to find a little food. If he'd been caught outside on our patio, he'd spend a few days in jail and nothing more.

But once he crawled through the open window, everything would change. If he was caught inside the house, especially with the knife, that would be impossible for the prosecutors to ignore.

And once he made his way toward my bedroom . . . that would be a *completely* different deal.

Yes, he understood the repercussions.

But he did not turn away.

The window was too high, so he leaned an iron patio chair against the wall. Standing on the chair, he shimmied through and dropped onto the kitchen floor.

The house was quiet.

No barking dog. No sounding alarm. Again, he was surprised.

If God wants this . . . rolled around inside his head again.

Somewhere in the house, a clock ticked. Maybe in the kitchen? Maybe somewhere down the hall?

He moved through the kitchen and into the hallway.

The front door was on his right. A wide stair on his left. He turned. The stairway rose before him. He moved up the stairs and headed down the hall. Which bedroom was I in? In the darkness, he couldn't tell! He reached out for the nearest door and slowly pushed it open. Soft light fell upon the bed along the wall. My little brother was sleeping there.

He quietly shut the door, then moved a couple steps farther down the hallway until he stopped outside my bedroom door.

5.

Taken

I woke up with my little sister sleeping beside me, a dark man standing over me, and a knife to my throat. Rough hands were pressed upon my body as the stranger leaned over, his dirty beard against my face. "I have a knife to your neck," he whispered. His voice was soft but very serious. "Don't make a sound. Get out of bed, or I'll kill you and your family."

For a fraction of a moment, I was not fully awake, caught in that fuzzy place between wakefulness and sleep where your body may be reacting but your mind has not realized what is happening yet. Was I dreaming? Was this real? My mind was like molasses. Slow. Caught in uncertainty and fear.

Then I felt the pressure of the knife, cold and sharp against my throat.

"I have a knife to your neck," he repeated. "Don't make a sound. Get out of bed, or I'll kill you and your family."

I was jolted awake. I felt the sharpness of the knife as he pressed it against my skin. My heart began to race, exploding in my ears.

I fought the urge to scream, glancing at my little sister in the dark. The words he had spoken seemed to echo in my ear.

I will kill you and your family!

I wanted to reach out for my little sister, to hold her, to protect her from this horrible thing. I *needed* to protect her. I froze in fear.

Seeing the shadow of evil on his face, hearing the determination in his voice, and feeling the strength of his hands, I knew that he would kill us if he had to.

From that moment forward, I never doubted what he would do. Let me be clear about that. I spent more than nine months under his control. Every day that I spent with him made me more and more convinced that this man was capable of killing. He would have stuck me in an instant. There is no doubt and never was.

I quietly slipped out of bed.

The man grabbed me by the arm. There was enough light that I could see his knife. It wasn't a pocketknife. This was much more than that. It was long and black and serrated. Maybe eight inches long. It looked like it could cut right through me, right through my heart and bone.

I can't describe the terror! It is simply impossible to express. Here I was, a little girl, in the middle of the night, being taken from my bed, from my own home, from what I thought was the safest place in the entire world. It was an unimaginable intrusion! Everything that I had thought, every feeling of safety or comfort, every assumption of protection, was stolen in that instant. My world spun on its head.

My mind began to race. Had he already killed my parents? Were other members of my family dead? What about my little sister, sleeping beside me in the bed? Would he harm her? Would he kill her? What could I do to keep her safe?

His hands were large and powerful as they pulled me from my bed. Holding the knife at my back, he pushed me toward my closet. All of the lights were turned off. On the way, I stubbed my toe.

"Ouch!" I whispered, and he threatened me again. We passed through the bathroom. Holding me very close, the knife always at my back, he pushed me inside the closet. One of us turned the light on, but I don't remember if it was me or him.

"Get your shoes," he whispered in my ear.

I bent toward a pair of slippers.

"No!" he spat, pushing me toward my white running shoes. "Get those!"

My heart sank in utter horror. Was he taking me outside?

Sensing my hesitation, he leaned toward me again. "I'm taking you hostage. For ransom."

I felt myself deflate. It seemed the very life was ready to leave my body. My throat tightened up with fear.

The light was on now and I could see his face. His long beard. His dark-brown hair. Everything he wore was dark. The terrifying knife. In every possible way, this was a very dark man.

"Grab your shoes!" he barked again. His voice was low but deadly. He was holding tightly to my arm, his fingers digging into me. I hardly noticed the pain. My body was flushing with adrenaline. I was trembling with fear.

I picked up my white running shoes, the same ones that I had worn when I had gone jogging the night before. Bending over, I started to put them on.

"No! Not now. Bring them with you," he ordered.

He pushed me toward the bedroom door. We slowly moved out into the hall. He stayed right behind me, never more than a fraction of an inch away. The long knife was always close. "Not a sound!" he told me. "I'll kill you and your entire family!" My heart pounded in my chest. I felt the itch of his beard against my neck. He led me toward the stairs. It was dark and quiet. None of my family was awake. Deadly quiet. Deadly darkness. I could hear the grandfather clock ticking from downstairs. He led me down the hall and pushed me past the stairs. Realizing his mistake, he forced me to backtrack, then led me down to the main hall.

Dad, please wake up! I was praying in my mind. *Mom, can you hear me? Please wake up and save me!*

"What is the quickest way out?" he whispered as we stood in the main entry.

I hesitated, feeling sick with utter fear.

He is going to take me outside, I thought. He is going to hurt or kill me!

I felt the knife against my back. Cold. Hard. I imagined the cut of the blade into my body. "The sliding-glass door behind us," I answered, afraid that I was going to cry.

He acted like he didn't hear me. Pushing me forward, he directed me through the kitchen, past the pantry, toward the back door. Out we went. We were on the patio now. He was always very close, controlling everything I did. He directed me across the backyard and up the hill to the side yard near the top of our property. I felt his arms tighten up around me as he pulled me to a stop. "Put on your shoes now," he said.

"Why are you doing this?!" I cried.

He looked at me in anger. "I'm taking you hostage."

I knelt down and pulled my shoes on. I wasn't wearing any socks. I glanced back toward my house. It was still completely dark. I felt a yearning to rush back there. Then I felt the knife again. He pushed me up the hill. We were walking through the empty lot. Scrub oaks. Lots of dry brush and grass. He suddenly stopped me, reaching down among the weeds. Picking up the two green bags that had been tied together with a rag, he slung them over his back and chest.

The road behind my house runs up against the mountain. Reaching the top of the empty lot, we hit the road. He pushed me to the left. The road sloped gently downhill. A hedge ran along the front of the nearest house. Headlights illuminated the side of the mountain as a car came winding down the road. Immediately, he thrust me behind the bushes, pressing me toward the ground. The grass was damp. The night was cold now. As he held me close, I realized how powerful he was. Peering through the hedge, crouched just a few inches off the ground, I watched the car approaching. I saw the lights on top of the roof, then the markings on the door. A police car! It was a miracle! It was going to be okay.

"If this is the work of God, then let this police car pass without finding us," the dark man said as he held me to the ground.

The car drew nearer, its headlights illuminating the winding road.

"If you move, I'll kill you. If you make a sound, I'll kill you." He held the knife against my chest.

I watched the car pass in front of us, no more than ten feet away. The stranger seemed to hold his breath. I felt the tension in his body. The car was moving slowly. I didn't know what to do. He seemed to sense what I was thinking and held me tighter.

"Move and I will kill you!" he said again.

The police car passed. The man waited only a second before he pulled me up again, directing me across the road. On the other side was a trailhead that led up the side of the mountain. We started climbing up the trail.

The reality finally hit me. It was like a jolt to my heart, a stabbing pain in my chest: This isn't a joke. This isn't a nightmare. This is real! I've got to run!

But he was always right behind me, the knife always at my back. He held on to me with a tight grip that hurt my arm. The trail was steep around us, thick trees and rock on all sides.

If there had ever been an opportunity, that time had passed.

As we started climbing, I gathered courage. "Who are you?" I begged. "Why are you doing this? I have never done anything wrong."

He continued pushing me up the mountain.

"Why are you doing this?" I begged again.

"I'll explain to you later. When we get to where we're going."

We continued climbing. The night was dark. He forced me to hold a flashlight to illuminate our way. He held the knife in one hand, his arm always at my waist or shoulder.

"Do you realize what you are doing?" I pleaded.

"Of course," he seemed to huff.

He had told me that he intended to hold me for ransom, but I didn't believe that anymore. "If you let me go, I won't press charges. I won't let my father press charges on you," I said with as much conviction as I could muster.

He huffed again. The trail was getting steeper. "You don't need to make me any promises," he said in a sarcastic tone. "I know what I'm doing. I understand the consequences of my actions." He didn't sound crazy. He only sounded mean.

Up and up we climbed. The trail grew narrow and more difficult. Farther up, there were trees on every side. We climbed and climbed. I was getting tired and very thirsty. He stopped to drink, pulling a canister of water out of one of his bags. He didn't offer me any. Not this time. Later he would, but I didn't want to drink from his water anyway. He urinated, then we kept on climbing. A streambed joined the trail on our right. "Turn up the streambed," he commanded. Though the trail continued, we left it and headed up the rocky streambed. The going became even more difficult. Boulders. So many trees. So much thick brush. Yet he was always right behind me, matching my every move.

I thought of the story of Moses and the parting of the Red Sea. I thought, *Okay, God, this isn't the Red Sea. This is just some scrub oak. Could you please just part it so I can run away?* I kept looking for an opening, for any means to escape. But the man was right behind me. He had a knife on me. And if he wasn't right behind me, he was in front of me and always holding tight.

So I kept on climbing.

It got colder. It was the middle of the night. I was praying and pleading for a way to escape, but there were steep slopes along the stream bed, walls of scrub oak on each side. It was hopeless and I knew it.

By then, I'd had enough time to consider another option that I hadn't thought about before; something just as terrifying but not as likely to enter into the mind of a little girl. "Please," I begged. "If you're going to rape and kill me, please do it here. That way someone will find my body."

"Keep moving," he replied.

We kept on climbing. It was painfully slow. So dark. So steep. So many obstacles.

"Stop," he commanded. I stood there in the dark. I listened as he urinated once again. He mumbled to himself. "We're going to wait here until daylight." He seemed to be thinking to himself. Was he getting tired? Were we really just going to sit there on the rocks until the sun came up?

I turned around to look at him. He was not very tall, with narrow shoulders and a slim chest. It was too dark to see much more than just the outline of his body, and his beard hid most of his face, but I could see his cheeks and eyes. Then it hit me. I remembered him! I had seen him once—no, twice—before. Once when I was shopping downtown with my mother. Sometime in the fall. She had given him a little money. She had given him my dad's name and cell-phone number so that they could help him more. My father had hired him to do some handiwork. Just before Thanksgiving, I thought. I also remembered watching him from the upstairs railing that looks down on our front hall. He had looked up to see me watching him while he was waiting to get paid.

"Why are you doing this?" I pleaded. "My parents were only trying to help you."

"You are my hostage," he replied. "You'll learn. I'll tell you what you need to know when we get where we are going."

"My parents never hurt you. Why are you doing this?"

"All will be made known in due time."

"Where are we going?"

He didn't answer.

"My parents will pay any amount of money to get me back. Anything you ask for."

Again, he didn't answer. Though he claimed I was his hostage, he showed no interest in talk of ransom or any money. He stood there in the darkness without responding in any way, the long knife in his hand. He gestured farther up the mountain. "My wife is waiting up there," he said.

Might he only want a daughter? I wondered. The idea tumbled inside my head.

I soon discovered that being taken to be his daughter was an enormously optimistic hope.

He pointed up the mountain. It was steep. So rough. Looking at it, I realized we'd have to crawl in places. Dawn was getting closer now. The sky was still dark, but the eastern horizon was turning a hint of gray. Moving closer to me, he repeated, "If you try to run, I will catch you. Do exactly what I say, or I will kill you. I have friends. They will kill your family. Your little sister. All the others. If you try to escape . . . if you do *anything* that I don't tell you, I will kill you and your family."

I felt his breath upon me.

"Do you understand?"

I understood. And I believed him. He stared at me, then grunted. "Let's go."

I turned and started crawling up the mountain once again.

6.

Mary Katherine

My younger sister, Mary Katherine, remembers being wakened by a nudge. But she figured it was just me and drifted back to sleep. Seconds later, she was jolted fully awake when she realized that I was climbing out of bed. Opening her eyes, she saw a stranger standing there! Taking her older sister. Holding a long knife to my chest!

A large, uncovered window let some light into the room, shadows of darkness cast by the stars and the moon. Mary Katherine watched what was happening through half-open eyes, pretending to be asleep, her heart racing in her chest. The man stayed very close to me, pushing me toward the bathroom.

"What are you doing?" she heard me ask. The answer was too muffled to really understand. *Hostage?* Maybe "hitchhike"? She didn't know what he said. But she did pick up on "kill" and "your family," and was even more terrified. She watched as I moved toward the bathroom, the stranger right beside me. The door shut. Light seeped into the bedroom from underneath the door. Very muffled voices. A few minutes passed. The light went out. The door opened. Quiet footsteps. A floorboard creaking. The sound of muffled movement in the hall.

And then quiet. Deadly quiet.

Mary Katherine was utterly petrified, frozen stiff with fear. And how could she not be! She was a nine-year-old girl who had just witnessed her older sister being taken from her bed by a stranger with a long beard and a knife, a man who had hissed and pulled and held her so close that she could not get away!

It was just too much to manage.

My nine-year-old sister lay underneath her covers, too terrified to even move. She hardly dared to breathe. She was in a deep state of shock, completely numb with fear.

An agonizing amount of time passed. She didn't sleep. The grandfather clock chimed downstairs. Still, she didn't move. More time passed. How long, she didn't know. The shadows traced the movement of the moon across her bedroom wall. The clock chimed again. She poked her head out from the covers. Starlight and moonlight filtered into the room. Yellow. Dull. She reached across the blankets to the left side of the bed. The sheets were flat and cool. I was not there.

Finally, in a moment of courage, she grabbed her baby blanket, pulled it over her head, and bolted toward my parents' room.

It was a few minutes before four in the morning.

I had been gone for hours.

Some question how Mary Katherine could have delayed telling our parents that I had been taken. What could she have been thinking! It was the obvious thing to do!

And yes, it might be obvious . . . *if* you are an adult and have the benefit of understanding the situation. And yes, it might be obvious if, at this moment, you don't feel overwhelming fear.

But Mary Katherine was a child who had just had the most traumatic experience of her life. She thought that her own bedroom, inside her house, with her parents and brothers sleeping all around her, her older sister at her side, was the safest place in the world that she could be. She knew that her father always locked the doors and windows before he went to bed. She knew they had a security system. Yet a stranger had overcome all of these safety measures and gotten into their house. Then he had found his way into their bedroom. *How did he even know where they slept?* Once inside their room, he had pulled her older sister from her bed! He had threatened to kill her. Threatened to kill their entire family. He was holding a long and terrifying knife! Her older sister had gone without fighting!

How could any of this be?

Was someone with him? Were other killers inside the house?

It didn't make any sense!

The only thing she knew was that she feared for her life.

And we have to keep in mind that she was *just a little girl*!

Adults think differently. We are rational. And we now have the benefit of hindsight, knowing what really happened on that night. We know that Brian David Mitchell had already taken me from the house, that he could no longer threaten my little sister. We know my parents had not been killed or injured, that they were sleeping in their bed.

But these things Mary Katherine didn't know.

Lying underneath her covers, she had to wonder: Was the bad man still in the house? Was he lurking in the hall? He had said that he would kill our entire family. Were they dead already? If she ran into our parents' bedroom, what horrible thing might she find there? Had he killed other members of our family? Was she alone inside a house where everyone else was dead?

It is impossible for us to appreciate the terrible fear she must have felt.

We also should remember that she was hardly the first one to go into shock after having experienced an overwhelming crisis. It is common. There are even examples of men in combat who have frozen up in fear, unable to do the task that they were trained to do. Sometimes they shut down, losing their ability to function in almost every way; mentally, emotionally, physically. Which is why their training is so important. Chaos leads to panic. Panic leads to fear. Fear can be debilitating to the point where the mind and body may shut down. During these times of gut-wrenching panic, a soldier's training and preparation is supposed to kick in to protect them.

But Mary Katherine had not been prepared for such a life-and-death situation.

She was just a little girl.

Having gathered her wits about her, Mary Katherine finally raced into our parents' bedroom, running to my father's side of the bed. She spoke but didn't manage to wake him, so she moved to my mother's side.

"Elizabeth is gone," she said in a quiet voice, her baby blanket still draped over her head. My mother opened her eyes. Mary Katherine had said it so softly, so matter-of-factly, that my mother didn't know what to think. It wasn't unusual for me to move into another room to sleep. Sometimes I would sleep downstairs on the couch or maybe on the floor in one of my brothers' rooms. Surely they would find me there.

Hearing their voices, my dad sat up on his side of the bed.

"Elizabeth is gone," Mary Katherine said again.

Mother sat up now, her face growing concerned.

"You won't find her. A man came and took her." She hesitated. "He had a gun," she mistakenly concluded.

Both of my parents were instantly terrified. Something in the simple way Mary Katherine had said it made them realize that something was very wrong. And neither of them could ignore the look of utter fear upon her face.

My father raced to check the other upstairs bedrooms. Not finding me, he ran down the stairs to the main floor. My mother followed. Mary Katherine stayed right next to her, unwilling to leave her side. They searched frantically, my father running through the rooms in the front of the house. Hoping to find me sleeping on the couch, my mother turned on the lights in the family room. Of course I was not there. She fought a building panic. Turning to her right, she moved into the kitchen. Mary Katherine ran along beside her, never more than a step away. Mom turned on the kitchen lights and looked around. The smell of burned potatoes still lingered in the air. But there was something more now. Other smells. Damp grass. Canyon winds. The smells of the outdoors. Her eyes went straight to the cut screen.

Then she stopped, moving her hand to her mouth. Looking at it, she felt her heart freeze like a brick of ice inside her chest.

She knew instantly what it meant.

She let out a scream, yelling, "Call 911!" My dad came racing into the kitchen. My mom's face showed nothing but fear and utter disbelief. Dad stopped in the middle of the kitchen and followed her eyes. He saw the open window. He saw the knife cut in the screen.

Mary Katherine's words seemed to hang in the air between them.

Elizabeth is gone. You won't find her. A man came and took her. He had a gun.

7.

Morning Light

———

We climbed all night. It was a terrible struggle, going up the back side of the mountain without the benefit of any trail. It was climbing and crawling and moving through rough patches of weeds and thick trees. As the sky changed from black to gray to pink to light blue, the man became more and more agitated. More in a hurry. More anxious to get out of sight. As the sun broke, we were just crossing the highest ridge on the mountain. The sky was clear, with not a single cloud, and I suppose that you could see for miles. I was wearing a pair of red silk pajamas that I had been given by a friend of my mother's. The man looked at my bright clothing in the growing light. "Someone is going to see you," he said in anger.

I looked down at my pajamas. They were very bright.

He said something more about a runner seeing me, something I really didn't understand—what kind of runner would be up here on top of the mountains?—then reached into his bag and pulled out a gray shirt. I don't remember if I put it on or not, but I do remember that he made me hurry. By this time, the man had put away his knife. He figured I couldn't get away from him now. Still, he always stood beside me, ready to grab me if I ever made a run for it.

Over the top of the ridge we moved, dropping onto a steep canyon on the other side. There the trees were not as thick, seeming to grow in patches of scrub oaks and small pines, with a few quakies scattered in, most of them nearer to the bottom of the canyon. There was thick grass and weeds, and the mountain dropped steeply toward the south. Above the treeline, there was a large basin of barren terrain we had to cross. The man almost made me run, so worried was he that I might be seen. I was exhausted by then. I'd been climbing all night. I was terrified and thirsty and dreading whatever lay ahead. But I moved quickly with him, too terrified to resist.

We hiked across a barren patch of grass, thistle, and weeds. Then he pulled me toward a grove of mountain oaks that was about a third of the way down the ridge. Approaching the trees, he stopped and called out. "Hephzibah!"

A woman's voice answered from the trees: "Immanuel."

He seemed relieved and moved faster toward the voice.

The old woman was waiting for us near the trees. I studied her hopefully, but her hard stance and cold eyes told me she was anything but a friend. She had a wild look about her, emotional and tense, like a strand of wire that was being pulled too tight. She had straggly brown-and-gray hair, a broad face, and brooding eyes. She looked older than she was, and it was obvious that she had lived a hard life. Her eyes were dull, but grew excited now, an ember of fire beneath her drooping lids. She had rough hands and a rough manner that was all-business and curt. She was dressed in a linen robe, not the kind you tie at your waist, but those you have to slip over your head. It shocked me to see her dressed like that, up there on the mountain.

That turned out to be one of the first clues as to what lay in store for me.

The first thing she did was walk up and put her arms around me, pulling me into a strong embrace. But it was not a warm thing. Not an act of kindness, and certainly not an act of love. No, it felt more like an act of dominance than any sort of welcome. *I am stronger than you are. And don't ever doubt it—when it comes to you and me, I am number one.*

I felt dangerously out of place, standing there in my red pajamas. Though my top had a collar, sometime before, to be more modest, I had taken a safety pin and pinned it a little higher. I touched the collar, then thought of my mother, knowing she had a set of pajamas the same as mine. Thinking of her, I wanted to cry.

I glanced quickly around the camp, trying to take it in. It was primitive but well stocked. Tents. Tarps. Other things. They had obviously been up there for a while.

I don't really know what time it was, probably close to midmorning. It had been something like six or seven hours since I had been taken. I don't remember feeling tired any longer, but I remember feeling very scared.

Immanuel (I didn't know his real name yet) nodded, seeming to signal to the older woman. Hephzibah (again, I didn't yet know her name was Wanda Barzee) nodded back. Without any explanation, she took me by the hand and pulled me toward the large tent. It was obvious they had planned out what was going to happen before I had been brought into the camp.

As she pulled me by my arm, I knew that my world was about to come apart.

8.

Rape of a Child

Stopping outside the tent, I had a better chance to look around. It was a big tent; maybe six people could sleep inside it. A large tarp had been placed on the dirt in front of it, with another tarp hung from the trees, making a roof of sorts that hung over the camp. There were several blue Rubbermaid plastic containers. Lots of kitchen utensils were out. It was a very well-stocked camp. On the far side of the tent there was a large mound of dirt where part of the mountain had been shoveled away. More than a dozen logs were piled on one another. Thick and heavy. It would have taken a lot of power to move them into place. I didn't know yet what it was, some kind of dugout or winter bunker, but it was imposing and depressing to look at it and I had to turn away.

Opening the flap, the woman pulled me into the tent, which was filled with bedding. She had a blue basin already set up, the kind that hospitals give to young mothers to wash their brand-new babies in. She had already filled it with clean water. She pushed me toward an upside-down bucket and told me to sit down on it. She took off my running shoes and placed my feet into the hot water and washed them.

Then she told me to take off my red pajamas. I pulled back in horror. "No!" I cried. She scowled, her dark eyes hard. I could see even then that I was not going to be able to tell her no. But she forced herself to be patient. I didn't know it yet, but this was to be my wedding day. It was supposed to be a beautiful occasion. So the woman forced herself to be patient, showing a little leniency, at least for now.

"I need to bathe you," she said through a tight smile.

I recoiled even further, pressing against the fabric of the tent. "I took a shower last night," I whispered, somehow thinking I could convince her to leave me alone.

She hesitated, then yelled toward the zippered flap. "She says that she had a shower last night. Is that okay?"

Both of us looked toward the tent door, my stomach crawling into my chest.

There was a moment's hesitation as he considered. The absurdity was surreal. It was as if she were asking, *Is she clean enough for you?*

"Yeah, that's okay," he answered. His voice was very close. He was waiting just outside the tent. Anxious. A starving animal ready to devour.

She turned to me again, my feet still inside the basin. "Take your clothes off," she repeated.

"No," I said again.

"Take them off, or I'll have him come in and rip them off you," she rasped in anger. I knew that she would call him. And I knew that he would indeed come and do exactly as she said he would do.

Pulling away, I started crying. I couldn't stop it. My heart seemed to break inside me. The tears left my face wet, my eyes stinging and red.

"Take your clothes off, or he will rip them off you!" she repeated.

She then handed me a white robe. Again, it wasn't the kind you can wrap around your body, but one you have to pull over your head. I quietly slipped it on. And wiggled out of my pajamas underneath.

She waited, and then pointed. "Take off your underwear."

I choked on more tears. "No," I stumbled simply.

"I'll have him rip them off your body." Her voice was firm, and certainly not kind.

Lowering my eyes, I slipped them off.

She looked at me with satisfaction, then crawled toward the opening of the tent.

I sat on the bucket, sick with dread, huge tears rolling down my cheeks. My body was so tight I felt I couldn't breathe. I shivered, my feet still wet. I waited, crying softly as he came into the tent. He had changed his clothes and was now dressed in a linen robe just like mine, except his had a sash tied around the waist.

I waited on the bucket, my head low. Tears of horror filled my eyes. I choked in order to keep on breathing. He started talking, but through my sobbing it was difficult to understand what he was saying. Then I caught some of his words: "I seal you to me on this Earth, and what is sealed here on Earth will be sealed in the afterlife, and I take you to be my wife. Before God and His angels as my witnesses."

"No!" I screamed, unable to contain my horror.

He reached out as if he was going to slap me, moving suddenly very close. "If you ever scream again, I'll duct tape your mouth shut!" he sneered.

Then he forced me off the bucket and onto the dirty bedding. I fought him as best I could. "I'm just a little girl," I begged in desperation. "I haven't even started my period. I'm still a child!"

He stopped, his face tight, as if he were suddenly unsure of what to do.

He yelled outside to the woman, telling her what I had said. "Is it still okay?" he asked.

My heart leaped in hope. *I was a child!* Might there be a miracle? Might he let me be?

The woman didn't hesitate. "It's okay," she answered.

He turned to me again.

I fought and kicked and struggled. I did everything I could. But he was a powerful and driven man. There was nothing I could do.

When it was over, he got up and crawled out of the tent, leaving me crying on the floor.

Over the next nine months, Brian David Mitchell would rape me every day, sometimes multiple times a day. He would torture and brutalize me in ways that are impossible to describe, would starve and manipulate me like I was an animal. Many times I would think, Okay, this is the bottom. Things *couldn't* get any worse.

But whenever I began to think that way, I would quickly find out that I was wrong.

9.

Broken

After he crawled out of the tent, I lay alone. The sun was up, but it was still early and the thick trees provided heavy shade, keeping it cool inside. I lay on the dirty blankets, curled in a fetal position, the linen robe pressed against my waist.

I felt disgusting. I felt sick. I felt like someone had crushed my very soul.

I thought about my family and what they were doing. Did they realize that I was gone yet? Were they looking for me? Was there a chance I might be found? I thought about my sister, Mary Katherine, and what she must be feeling. I thought about my brothers. I thought about my mom and dad. Then a terrible idea seeped into my soul: If they knew what the man had done to me, would they still want me?

The question cut me to the core.

Would they still love me? Would they want me? Or would they feel like, "We don't want her anymore"?

I know that sounds crazy, but that's exactly how I felt.

I didn't feel like a whole person anymore. I felt like I was . . . like not even half, like I was just a portion of a human being. I just felt filthy and disgusting. I felt like, Who could ever want me back? Who could ever want to talk to me? Who would ever be my friend?

I don't know what the exact definition of despair is, but if it is feeling as if your life is over, as if there's no point to continue because no matter what happens, you will never be accepted or happy again, then despair is what I felt.

Part of the reason I felt so bad was that my family was very religious. I had lived a sheltered life. In my faith, and in my family, a great deal of emphasis is placed on sexual purity, waiting until you're married for those kinds of relationships.

Another was the fact that I was so young and so I didn't have the tools yet to deal with what had just happened to me. But I now understand that what I felt is not uncommon among victims of rape or abuse. Rape is such a violation; the feeling of worthlessness is almost universal. In addition, some women feel like they might have asked for it or deserved it in some way. They think it might have been their fault because of a low-cut shirt, or maybe they were flirting, or somehow they had communicated that they wanted it and then they didn't want it anymore. There are lots of reasons why they might feel responsible.

But I was not confused. I knew what had just happened to me wasn't my fault. I didn't ask for this! I didn't run away with this stranger. I didn't marry him. None of this was my choosing.

But I still felt completely broken.

Imagine you have a beautiful crystal vase. Then imagine that you accidently knock it off the table and it shatters into pieces on the floor. We all understand it isn't the vase's fault that it was pushed off the table and shattered. But still, it is broken. It is worthless. You don't want it anymore. So you sweep it up and throw away the pieces.

That is how I felt.

It wasn't my fault. But I was broken. No one would want me anymore.

So even though I knew the bearded man could kill me at any time, I had already reached a point where I no longer cared.

I thought about other children I'd seen on the news, children who'd been kidnapped and didn't come back. I thought they were the lucky ones. They were in a better place. I began to realize that there were some things worse than death.

I believe in a God who loves me. I'd never pictured Him as mean or vindictive or anything like that. I'd always pictured Him as a beautiful person, glowing with love and kindness, someone who understood exactly how I felt all the time, someone who loved me as one of his children. I think of Him as someone who comforts and loves everyone.

Even after I had been raped, I still thought of Him that way. He loves us all. Even me. Even still.

I would have happily gone to Him if I could have left that place of pain, if I could have left behind all those feelings of worthlessness and fear, if I could have left behind all of the feelings of darkness. I wanted to go home to this person who loved me, who would take care of me and protect me and never let me feel the hurt and pain again.

But even in the midst of all this emotion, it never occurred to me to take my own life. I knew I could never do that. If someone with a gun had said, "I'm going to shoot you," I might have said, "Okay." But if they had handed me a gun and told me to shoot myself, I would have recoiled at the thought. I could simply never do that, no matter whatever else I felt.

So I just closed my eyes and curled up into a tight ball of despair. I pushed toward the corner of the tent and cried myself to sleep.

The last thing I remember thinking before I drifted off was, To-night I'm going to run.

I slept lightly for an hour or so, never really slipping away, always aware in the back of my mind where I was and the situation I was in.

There was no rest in my brief sleep, no comfort, no solace. It was a weary sleep. Hard ground. Dirty blankets, sheets, and pillows. The horrible linen robe bunched around my body. I was in pain. I was bleeding. But it was infinitely better than being awake.

I woke up feeling something being wrapped around my ankle. I jolted awake. The sun was high and it was getting hot inside the tent. The man was kneeling over me, wrapping a steel cable around my ankle. The cable was stretched to near its limit. I followed it with my eyes. It extended out the tent door and disappeared.

I turned back to the man as he jerked the cable tight around my ankle. "What are you doing!" I cried in disbelief.

"Shearjashub, I just want to take away any temptations," he replied sarcastically.

I felt the cable being cinched against my skin. I felt its tautness. I felt its strength.

My heart sank.

"Shearjashub, you've got to be a good girl now," he said.

Shearjashub! Who was Shearjashub? *What* was Shearjashub? I didn't know.

I watched in horror as the man finished his work. He used a crimper to clamp the cable tight, then gave it a tug to test it. Satisfied, he crawled out of the tent, leaving me alone again, leaving behind the taint of his smell. Just when I thought it couldn't get any worse!

I picked up and studied the cable. Steel wrapped inside a plastic cover. It seemed strong enough to hold a car. I adjusted my leg, relieving some of the pressure.

Earlier that morning, even as the man had forced me out of my bed, then throughout the long hike up the mountain and the horrible nightmare in the tent, I always thought that he would kill me. I thought he would hurt or kill my family. That scared me even more. And I absolutely knew what he was capable of doing now.

If you haven't been in such a situation, if you haven't felt the kind of stone-cold fear that cuts you to the core—and few people really have—it's impossible to imagine what it does to your thinking, to your emotions, to the way your heart and brain begin to work.

I had always been afraid that he would kill me. But now I realized that wasn't his plan. He wouldn't have gone through all the trouble to bathe me, dress me up and marry me, and then to trap me with the steel cable if he were going to kill me. My nightmare was not ending. It was just getting started.

Then I had the most horrible thought of all.

What if this goes on forever?!

Is this to be the only life that I will ever know?

10.

Tender Mercies

Most of us believe in miracles. Not everyone, I understand that, but most of us are pretty comfortable with the thought that there are good things in our lives that come to us as special gifts from God. I don't mean everything, of course. Sometimes these intersections of fate are really just coincidences. But I think there are far more miracles in our lives than we may ever realize. Like flickers of light among the darkness, they remind us that God is there and that He cares.

One of the miracles that I experienced on that first brutal morning was the fact that, in the midst of all the torment, I was able to find a tiny ray of hope.

Nothing that had happened to me so far was fair. No one knows that more than I do. It was brutal and violent and the greatest intrusion on one's person that can happen in this world. And the suffering was just beginning. Nine months of pain and fear and the greatest humiliation still lay ahead.

And like I said, I was just a little girl.

Remembering what happened makes me think of a song that I know. It is beautiful, I think, and the lyrics are powerful: "Consider the Lilies" by Roger Hoffman. The third verse asks the listener to think about all the beautiful children who have suffered throughout the history of the world. It goes on to say:

> *The pains of all of them he carried*
> *From the day of his birth.*

I'm probably not the only one who wonders about that sometimes: *The pains of all of them he carried?*

How could that be? I mean, looking around us, it doesn't seem real. In fact, quite the opposite, it seems completely impossible! And in one sense it is. You would have to be blind not to see that there is so much suffering in the world today, much of it heaped upon children. That has always been the case. Maybe it always will be. The fact is, many times children suffer for the sins of others. I was not the only child to have suffered. And the list of ways in which children can be hurt is depressingly long. Fear. Abuse. Pain. Starvation. Slavery. Hunger or sexual exploitation. Being separated from or losing the people they love. In many cases, they are put in absolutely impossible situations where they can't even begin to protect themselves.

Are their pains eliminated? Are they saved from all this suffering?

In some cases they aren't, at least not in this world.

Yet if their pains are not eliminated, how then are they comforted? How are their burdens lifted? How are their pains "carried"?

I don't have all the answers. But this much I know.

Sometimes there are miracles—"tender mercies" some have called them—that comfort us in ways that other people may not see. Sometimes things are offered that we may not know about. Things that give those who suffer strength. Things that give them hope. Things that help them to hang on.

That certainly was the case with me.

I felt some of these miracles along the way.

My grandfather Francon died a few days before I was kidnapped. In fact, that was one of the memories that I tried to lock inside my brain after I had been captured; how beautiful my mother looked on the day of his funeral.

I was very close to both of my grandfathers, so Grandpa Francon's passing was a very sad day for me, but kind of sacred, too. He had dedicated pretty much his entire life to helping others. He was a good man, a good father. He served in many positions in our church, including about twenty years working in the Salt Lake City temple as a volunteer. He worked in various positions right up until the time he got sick.

One of the great memories that I have of when I was young was going to his home for summer picnics. Grandpa and Grandma had a huge backyard, and my cousins and I could play there for hours. They would flood the backyard from the irrigation ditch. We'd have little bonfires and roast hot dogs and marshmallows and have water fights. I remember this old tin basin where we used to bob for apples. Then when the apples were gone, Grandpa would throw in candy, which would, of course, sink to the bottom of the basin. Still, I'd go in after it, getting completely soaked. They had a big garden in the back. He spent a lot of time working there. He was always very active, very healthy. I don't think he ever took any medicine a single day in his life.

But not long before I was kidnapped—it was about the same time that the Winter Olympics were being played in Salt Lake City—Grandma noticed that Grandpa was starting to slow down. Then he started having trouble getting up once he had sat down. When Grandpa went to see doctors, they discovered a massive tumor in his brain, strands of sinewy fingers stretching in all directions. They operated on him immediately. It seemed like he was getting better for a while. He started to eat again; he seemed to be a little more alert, a little stronger. But it wasn't real. The fingers were too deep. They couldn't get out all of the cancer inside his head.

My mom was going to their house almost every day to help Grandma and to spend some time with her dad. Sometimes I'd go with her. They didn't live far away, maybe twenty minutes to the south, their house nestled up among the Wasatch Mountains. I had a small harp that was a little easier to move around than my big one, and I took it to their home so I could play for him. Sometimes I'd rub his feet and talk to him. Sometimes I'd just sit and hold his hand. I wanted him to know that I loved him, that I wanted to help him if I could. "He knows you are there," my grandma would tell me. And I know that he did. Right after his surgery, I remember kissing him on the cheek and telling him I loved him. I put my hand in his, and he held it very tight.

He died on May 28. He was seventy-eight years old on the day he passed away.

The funeral took place the day before I was kidnapped.

Which brings me to one of the tender mercies that helped me to carry the horrible pain.

God knew what was about to happen to me. I think that's why He brought my grandpa home. He knew that Grandpa Francon could be more helpful to me from the other side of the veil. Grandpa was one of my guardian angels. He was sent to comfort and inspire me in the very darkest hours, to help me find reasons for hope or encouragement when I felt the most despair. There were many occasions during the time that I was captured when I felt his spirit near.

During the darkest days that I was captive, it helped me to think that someone I loved, someone who loved me, *someone who was a good man,* was standing at my side. It helped me remember that God still cared for me, that He hadn't forgotten or forsaken me, that He was doing everything He could to help to carry my pain. It brought me comfort to think that Grandpa was helping me too, giving me a little strength when I had nowhere else to turn, nothing else to hope for, nothing in my life but pain and fear.

> *Consider the sweet, tender children*
> *Who must suffer on this earth*
> *The pains of all of them he carried*
> *From the day of his birth.*

Yes, I believe that God helped to carry me. In fact, I know that He did.

Which is why, as I lay in the tent that morning, wounded and confused, my emotions as jumbled as a jigsaw puzzle, I found the strength to search for something that would help me to go on.

11.

Family

I thought back on my family. As I did, I remembered something that had happened to me just a few months before. I had come home from school really upset. My mom asked me what was wrong. I told her I'd been sitting at a table with my friends, and this popular girl came up and said, "I'm having a party this weekend and all of you are invited." We were all excited. This was a pretty big deal. To be invited to a party with the popular crowd. That's the top of the mountain to a junior-high girl.

But then she turned to me. "Except you," she said. "You're not invited to my party."

My friends didn't even seem to notice. I felt so bad. I was embarrassed and hurt.

After I told my mom what had happened, she tried to make me feel better. "It won't be that bad spending another weekend at home," she said.

That didn't help much.

"You can spend some more time with your family."

No help at all.

My mom kind of smiled. "You know that 'popular' is just another word for rude."

Now, that I could agree with.

Then she asked me something that added to my hurt: "Do you really think those girls sitting at the table with you are your friends? Are they really friends if, at the first offer, they abandon you?"

I didn't want to answer that question. I mean, what did it say about my social life? That it was nonexistent. What did it say about what I and every junior-high girl more or less aspired to—being one of the popular ones? Worst of all, what did it say about the girls I thought were my friends? Not one of them had stood up for me. None of them had said, "Don't worry, Elizabeth, we'll have our own party this weekend. We'll hang out with you."

My mom continued. "Elizabeth, you're going to meet lots of people in this life. Some of them will like you. Some of them won't. But of all the people you'll have to deal with, there are only a few people that matter. God. And your dad and me. God will always love you. You are His daughter. He will never turn his back on you. The same thing is true for me. It doesn't matter where you go, or what you do, or whatever else might happen, I will always love you. You will always be my daughter. Nothing can change that."

As she spoke, I realized that she was right. How many times had she picked me up when I felt down? How many times had she talked to me when I needed her or helped me understand a problem or sat through my harp lessons (which weren't always pleasant) or done a million other things that moms do? She had always been there for me.

Thinking back on this conversation, I realized that my mom would accept me back home again. The fear of rejection was still raw in my mind, but I knew that she wouldn't reject me for what had happened. She still loved me. She would always love me.

The more I thought about it, the more I realized that my dad would accept me back as well. I mean, how many times had I crashed one of our snowmobiles into a snowbank? How many other things had I done that he could have gotten mad at me for? But he hadn't. On the other hand, how many times had he tucked me into bed and told me stories or sang me songs at night? He had always loved me.

Yes . . . my parents would always love me. My siblings would love me too. They would still accept me, no matter what the man had done.

Which meant I had something still to live for.

I took a breath and held it, a shudder moving down my spine. In that moment, the world seemed to tip ever so slightly toward the normal. It was as if, in the midst of all the blackness, I saw a ray of light. My mind focused in on it, grasping toward it as a falling man might grasp for a rope.

The realization that my family would still love me proved to be the turning point. In fact, it proved to be the most important moment throughout my entire nine-month ordeal.

It was at this moment that I decided that no matter what happened, I was going to find a way to survive. The conviction was crystal clear. I would do whatever it took to live. No matter what it took, no matter what I had to do, I was going to survive.

And then I thought of something else.

It was desperate, I know that—sometimes I laugh about it now—but it shows how frantic I was to think of some kind of plan.

I pictured my horrible captor. I thought of his long beard and salt-and-pepper hair. He had to be at least as old as my father. The woman looked as old as he.

Which meant I could outlive them.

The thought was like a lightning bolt inside my mind.

It might be twenty years, or maybe thirty, but one day they were going to die.

And when they did, I would be free of them. And I could go back to my life.

12.

Without Me

About the same time that I came to the determination that I was going to fight to survive, my parents were being interrogated by the local police.

Their morning had been nearly as terrifying as mine. After being woken by my younger sister with the simple words "Elizabeth is gone," they had frantically searched through the house. Not finding me, but seeing the open kitchen window and the cut in the screen, my father had called 911.

Their ordeal had begun.

After calling the police, my parents started calling other members of our family, friends, neighbors, people in our church, anyone who might help them. It was a series of very difficult calls to make, full of the most desperate words a parent may ever have to utter. "My daughter has been taken! We need your help!"

The police arrived at 4:13. Our neighbors and close friends were right behind, some of them arriving by 4:15. News of my abduction quickly spread throughout our neighborhood. It was panic and chaos, with people starting to jam into our house. The police made the mistake of not declaring our home a crime scene and closing off the premises, thereby contaminating any evidence that might have been left behind. Shortly after arriving, the police separated my parents, keeping them from talking to each other. They took Mary Katherine up to the second floor, making her repeat her story again and again. Not wanting her memory to be tainted by other sources, they kept her isolated and alone. It bothered my parents a great deal that she had been cut off from our family. After my mother had insisted, they finally allowed my grandmother to sit with my sister through the questioning.

Meanwhile, my dad continued calling family and friends, asking for their help. All of them were willing. But what were they to do? No one really knew. For hours, there was no direction on how to proceed, no real movement toward organizing a search, notifying the media, putting out any kind of alert. At one point, my dad called our neighbors across the road who had young daughters, warning them that they might be in danger and to check on them too. He thought maybe someone had taken me for ransom and that he might have taken other children too.

Eventually there were so many people coming to volunteer that the police forbade any more of them from entering our house. Finally, the police secured the scene.

By six o'clock, small groups of volunteers were canvassing the neighborhood, knocking on doors, talking to neighbors, explaining what had happened, asking if any of them had seen or heard anything. Apparently, no one had.

My mother was in shock. Someone offered her some kind of sedative, but she pushed it away.

By six-thirty, my parents and older brothers were taken to the police station for questioning. Mary Katherine was taken to the Children's Justice Center. My parents and my brothers, who were twelve and sixteen years old at the time, had to travel to the police station in separate cars. All of them were suspects. As were my uncles and other members of my family. Everyone was guilty until they could prove that they were not involved.

Separated and alone, their reactions caught on video and observed by who knew how many people, my parents and older brothers were interrogated. "What kind of girl is Elizabeth? Is she promiscuous? Into drugs? The occult? How does she do in school? What about your friends? What about a boyfriend? Does she sneak out at night? Did you kill Elizabeth? Do you know who did? Did one of your friends kill her?"

It was a terrible ordeal, brutal and humiliating. After living through the shock of losing their daughter and sister, it's horrible to think that my family was treated this way. But the truth is, the police had no choice. More than half of all middle-class abductions are carried out by someone who is a family member or close friend. They would have been derelict if they had not looked at every possibility. But that didn't make it easier or alleviate the pain. Nor did it help to bring me back, which is what my parents were fighting to do. My dad was going crazy, wanting to get home to organize a search, talk to the media, and get my name and picture out there—anything to help find me.

By nine-thirty, the police allowed my parents to go to my grand-parents' house. The questioning of my brothers had also ended. But it would be a long time before my family would be together again. My younger siblings ended up staying with my grandparents for almost a month. My older brother had to bounce around. It seemed there was nowhere for him to go. All of my family were considered suspects, their routines utterly torn apart. For weeks, our home remained a crime scene, my bedroom coated in fingerprint dust and other hall-marks of an investigation. (Months later, in an effort to make it easier for Mary Katherine to feel comfortable in our room, it was redeco-rated with new wallpaper, paint, and bedding.)

After being questioned by the police, one of my older brothers, along with an adult friend from our church, immediately started searching throughout our neighborhood for any clues. Other search parties started combing through other neighborhoods and the foothills around my home. More and more people showed up, many of them strangers. But still, there was little organization to their efforts.

By early morning, an alert had gone out to the media. Information regarding my abduction began to crawl across the bottom of the local television screens. Radio stations began to relay the information. Soon after, the media were camped in our front yard. Many of them were to stay there a very long time. The national media soon picked up the story. Hundreds of volunteers were searching for me now. I suppose that most of them didn't understand how crucial the first twenty-four hours of an abduction always is. Law enforcement could have told my parents that if an abductor intends to kill his victim, they usually do it within the first three hours. If a child is taken for ransom, they usually make contact within the first day. I don't know if they shared this information with my parents. I hope they didn't. I don't think it would have helped.

By the end of the first day, several family members and friends were working on a Web site with my picture and information about the search parties that were being organized. Within a short time, it was getting more than one million hits a day. A $10,000 reward was offered for any information that led to my rescue. Within a week, it had grown to $250,000, all of the money contributed by private donors. On the second day, hundreds more volunteers showed up to look for me. The search expanded beyond my neighborhood to the city and the state. Over time, this number swelled to thousands. Individuals and businesses contributed food and supplies for the effort: flashlights, food, water, maps, batteries, coffee, doughnuts, communications gear. Volunteers with bloodhounds came down from Montana. Helicopters were used to search the mountains around my home. Hundreds of posters with my picture on them were distributed to law enforcement officers throughout the inter-mountain region.

On the afternoon of the second day, my father faced the media for the first time. It was an incredibly stressful and emotional experience, but one he would be forced to repeat on an almost daily basis as my parents struggled to keep the search going. Thousands of posters were placed around the city. Eventually, hundreds of thousands were distributed nationwide. Light-blue ribbons and buttons with my picture began to appear from California to Maine.

My abduction was to become the most publicized case since baby Charles Lindbergh had been taken from his crib.

I don't know what it was that drove so many people to try to help me. It's beyond my ability to comprehend why so many good people were willing to work and to sacrifice for me, a little girl they didn't even know. All I know is that I am more grateful than words can express. And to this day I remain the luckiest girl in the world!

13.

A Nice Girl

I don't remember being thirsty on that first morning in the camp. I don't remember being hungry. During the first week, I don't remember feeling anything at all. Well, that's not quite true. I felt pain. And I felt fear. But those are the only feelings I remember during that time.

I hadn't yet begun to accept what had happened to me. If fact, it took a long time to accept it. It was just too crazy. I mean, I had gone to bed just like every little kid, only to be wakened with a knife at my throat. I had been taken from my home, which was supposed to be the safest place on Earth. How did this happen? How had this man been able to break into my impenetrable fortress and steal me?

I couldn't quit thinking about my family. I couldn't imagine how they were feeling. Were they okay? What was going on at home? I particularly worried about my mom. I pictured her driving around our neighborhood, looking for any clues. I loved my mom so much and couldn't imagine how worried she must be. I thought back on the time when my little brother had dislocated his arm (it really wasn't my fault, family legend aside) and my poor mom, who had just returned home from running errands, became almost overcome with worry and rushed him to the hospital. My brother was fine once the nurse popped his arm back into its socket. But thinking back on that, I knew she wasn't going to handle my disappearance very well.

I felt deeply homesick. I tried to remember what our living room looked like, with its decorated walls and intricate rug. I knew my parents had been thinking of putting our house up for sale. What if they moved? How would I find them if they were gone?

But surely, I thought, my parents were looking for me by now. Others were probably looking too. Someone had to be close. I mean, it wasn't like we had hiked to Wyoming. I wasn't that far away! Maybe they would rescue me! *Surely* they would find me. Eventually I would be found.

But they hadn't found me yet.

And since they hadn't, I had to find a way to live.

I looked at my surroundings inside the tent. Thick pads for the man and the woman, a thinner pad for me. Horrid flower-print sheets. A dirty plum-colored comforter with dark fabric on one side and a lighter shade on the other. (I decided then and there that I didn't like the print one bit.) Two feathered, poufy pillows. Two hard cot pillows stuffed along the top of the tent.

This was my new home.

The thought made me feel sick.

It was getting very hot now, the tent holding in the sunlight like a greenhouse. Lifting up the cable to keep from tripping, I followed it out of the tent. My two captors were there. I looked around. No one spoke to me. I was still dressed in the linen robe. Still bleeding and in pain.

I examined the steel cable, looking for any means of escape. Unlike the night before, I wasn't waiting any longer for God to part the trees or move the mountain. Given the slightest chance, I was going to run. But the steel cable was now tight around my ankle. I examined it more closely. Wound steel. Tight. Strong. Thin as a pencil. The cable was tethered to another steel cable that had been bolted between two trees, allowing me a little bit of movement around the camp, just enough to stretch between the fire pit on the up-canyon side and the depressing dugout on the other. Maybe twenty feet of movement in any direction. In that space there was one tent. A couple of rubber basins. Buckets. A couple of coolers filled with food and containers filled with water. The cable wasn't long enough to reach more than a few feet into the dugout. There was a hole in the ground on the other side of the fire pit that a bucket, used as a latrine, was dumped into.

Twenty feet. One tent. This was now my world.

My captors continued to ignore me. Moving carefully, I walked over to another upside-down bucket and sat down in the sun. I was crying again, huge tears running down my face. Neither of them tried to comfort me. I cried on.

"This is your time to cry," the woman eventually said. "This is your wedding day. So go ahead and get it out. But know this: you can't go on and cry forever. Pretty soon, you'll have to stop."

So I sat on the bucket and cried all morning long.

At one point, I remember looking at a tiny branch of a mountain oak. Sometime before, the man had taken an ax to clear the campground, cutting back a couple of small trees and branches. A stump had been left jutting out of the bare ground and the man had used it to tie down one of the corners of the tent. A small sapling had started to grow out of the side of the stump. A few leaves. A single branch, smaller than my pinky finger. I stared at the sapling as it struggled to find a place to grow. Over the summer, I would stare at that tiny tree for hours, admiring its determination. Its mother tree had been cut away, leaving it as the only spot of green surrounded by bare dirt and plastic tarps and tents. Its bed was hot and dry and dusty. Yet it kept on fighting to survive.

I resolved once again: *Whatever it takes to survive!*

Eventually, the man looked at me. "You will call me Immanuel," he said. He nodded to the woman. "You will call her Hephzibah." I turned to look at her. It was an ugly name. Harsh and unnatural. It seemed to fit.

"Shearjashub," he called me, pointing in my direction.

"My name is Elizabeth Smart," I answered.

The man ignored me and started talking. Soon I was to learn a couple of things. First, my captor had many names. Second, he liked to talk. A lot. About his life. About his writings. About his purpose. Anything about himself. He and Hephzibah had kept extensive records of "the path they had taken," and it became obvious that I was going to hear it all.

I didn't know who he was, I didn't know his real name, but I recognized him. I remembered he had come to our house to help with some repairs. My parents had tried to help him. Over time, I learned that my captor had changed his name from Brian David Mitchell to David Shirlson and finally to Immanuel David Isaiah. Although I was told to simply address him by Immanuel. The woman had gone from Wanda Barzee to Elladah Shirlson to Hephzibah Elladah Isaiah.

During most of my captivity, I called them Immanuel and Hephzibah. But I have a hard time thinking of them by these names anymore. Too loaded with ugly baggage. Brian David Mitchell and Wanda Barzee are more comfortable to me now.

"You are her handmaiden," Mitchell then told me as he pointed to Barzee. "You are the second wife."

I looked at them. The word *crazy* rolled around my head.

"She is your mother wife. You are her handmaiden."

I couldn't wrap my mind around it. *Mother wife! Handmaiden!* I had no idea what that meant.

Soon I was to learn. To him, a handmaiden was a sex toy. To her, it was a slave.

———

Lunchtime approached. The woman got up and started fixing food to eat. I watched her for a moment through puffy eyes.

I knew that the man could kill me anytime he wanted. He certainly had the physical capability. He could kill me with nothing but a twist of his hands. No one would ever know. Nobody was there to protect me. Nobody was there to take care of me. I had to watch out for myself.

My mind started turning. Okay, I thought to myself, I can't fight them all the time. If I do, they'll keep me cabled. I'll never have a chance to escape.

I thought back on a girl I knew in junior high. She was a friend to the Polynesian kids, the Mexicans, the Caucasians. She was friends with everyone. She was just so nice. So I thought, Okay, I can be like her. I can make this situation the best that I can for myself. Nobody wants to be around a crybaby. Nobody wants to be around a sad sack. If I am miserable and whiny and don't carry my weight, then he will be far more likely to kill me. What was there to stop him? If I'm going to survive this, then I have to step up. I have to try to help myself.

I continued thinking.

If I did as they told me, if I didn't always fight him, then maybe it would be harder for him to hurt me. If I could get them to trust me just a little, maybe they would let me off the cable. Maybe they'd realize how much they were hurting me. Maybe they would come to like me, maybe even come to care about me. Then maybe they would let me go.

So I got up and walked over to where they were seated in the tarped area in front of the tent. They had set a tablecloth on some of the plastic containers. She had started to grate carrots and cut up onions. He was just sitting there, waiting for his lunch.

"I can help," I said. "What do you want me to do?"

She hesitated. I think she was surprised. Then she passed me a cutting board and grater, careful to keep the knife out of my reach.

(Not that it mattered. I never could have hurt them, even in the most desperate times.) I started grating carrots, helping to prepare the food. They had onions, raisins, and carrots mixed with mayonnaise and rolled in tortillas for lunch. They ate like they were starving. I ate next to nothing at all.

When they were finished, I asked if they wanted me to help clean up.

"It's okay," Barzee said. "It's your wedding day. You don't have to help me anymore. You can go and cry again for now. But you're gonna have to stop soon. You can't cry your life away."

That started it all over again. *My wedding day!* Any composure that I had captured was immediately lost at that thought.

"Please don't hurt me again," I begged him. "Please, please, just leave me alone."

Mitchell shook his head. "We're man and wife. That's a part of what we do now."

"No, no, please don't do it again. Please . . . I'm begging you . . . you don't have to do it. Please . . ."

He was instantly angry. "It's what we do!" he seemed to hiss.

I kept on begging and crying. I couldn't seem to stop.

Watching me, he suddenly grinned in a menacing way. "Tomorrow we are going to be as Adam and Eve in the garden," he said. "We'll be his little children. Tomorrow, we're all going to go naked. Then Hephzibah and I are going to demonstrate . . ."

He went on to describe what they were going to do. Things I didn't want to know about. I thought I was going to be sick to my stomach. The image was so disgusting. So humiliating. I couldn't even think.

I spent the rest of the day crying by myself.

I don't remember if we ate dinner. All I remember is sitting there, alone. Night fell, and it grew cool. The mountain was dark. I could hear coyotes and crickets, the wind blowing through the tops of the maples. But that is all I heard. No voices calling out my name. No airplanes or helicopters. Nothing good at all.

That night, we all slept in the tent. The cable wasn't long enough and I couldn't stretch out my leg. I curled in the fetal position against the side of the tent, not even on my pad. Mitchell curled up next to me, his arm around my shoulder. I recoiled at his touch. I pulled away as far as I could. He moved against me again. I was pressing so hard against the tent that I thought it was going to tear. I curled tighter into a ball. My rejection didn't bother him. In fact, it seemed to urge him on, being able to dominate me like that. Domination and power. That was always his intent.

The night wore on. I prayed as long and as hard as I had cried the day before. I was so scared and lonely. So afraid of what was coming.

But never was I angry. Never did I blame God. I never thought, Why me? This isn't right! This isn't fair! I knew that He didn't want these things to happen to me. This wasn't an expression of His will. But I also understood that Brian David Mitchell had his free will. He had the freedom to choose. He could choose to be a good man or a devil. To be a devil is what he had chosen. And I also knew that God wouldn't leave me to suffer through this alone. I just knew that was true. In fact, I never felt closer to God than I did throughout my nightmare with Mitchell. He did not leave me without comfort. I always felt Him near. And I felt the presence of my grandpa. I knew that he was near as well.

As I felt a little of their comfort, exhaustion finally overcame me, taking me to a place where my captors couldn't hurt me anymore.

14.

Adam and Eve

———

There was only one time when I woke up in the middle of the night and thought that I was home. It didn't happen on that first night. In fact, it didn't happen until several months after I had been taken, when I woke up searching for my alarm clock. For a moment, I was confused. When I couldn't find it, I finally remembered where I was.

But this only happened once.

On the morning of June 6, I woke up and knew immediately where I was.

It had been a long night. For one thing, it had rained. The sides of the tent were dripping with condensation. But Mitchell had dug a small trench around the outside to funnel the water away, so at least our bedding was not wet. Another thing that made it a long night was the fact that Mitchell kept getting out of bed. He'd get up, unzip the tent, and go outside. I could hear him out there, huffing and puffing through some kind of exercise. He did this every night. Get up. Go outside. Work through a series of stretching exercises, puffing as he bent and stretched and worked his muscles. I don't know if he did it because he was nervous or if it was part of his fanatical exercise routine, but I don't think he ever slept through the night for the entire time that I was with him.

When I woke up, the sun was just beginning to break over the top of the mountains. It was only a few weeks from the summer solstice, the longest day of the year, and it was very early. Mitchell, always anxious to begin talking or drinking or getting naked or whatever else he had in mind for that day, apparently didn't like to lie around. He and Barzee got up with the sun. Which meant that I got up as well.

My mouth was dry. I ached from sleeping on the ground, pressed against the side of the tent, trying to put some space between my captor and myself. And my stomach was already churning as I remembered Mitchell's words: *We're going to be like the children of Eden. We're going to go naked.*

As daylight broke, the birds began to chatter from above us. Then the wind began to stir, moving down the canyon to the valley floor below. Mitchell and Barzee crawled out from underneath their bedding. I grew tight, afraid to move. If I kept my eyes closed, maybe they would go back to sleep. If I didn't move, maybe they would leave me alone. If I pretended I was asleep, maybe they would just go away.

The cable was tight against my leg and I felt cramped and claustrophobic. It was a bright morning. We were a long way up the mountain and the air was still cool.

A few minutes passed until Mitchell announced, "Okay, let's get naked now."

I was instantly mortified. I am a very bashful person. I always have been. And, being so young, I was very self-conscious about my body. So I pretended I didn't hear him and didn't move.

Mitchell started to grow anxious. "Take it off! You have to take it off," he said.

I looked down at my linen robe. The day before, I thought it was the most disgusting piece of clothing that I had ever seen. Now it was my shield. I wanted to keep it on more than anything I had ever worn before. I longed for my red pajamas with the high collar and wondered what Mitchell had done with them. (A few months later, I would learn that he had very weird plans for the clothing I had been wearing on the night that I was captured.)

Seeing that I was not responding, Mitchell started growing angry, his dark eyes darting here and there. He had a cool way about him. Evil. Calculating. He stroked his beard without thinking, as if he were . . . I don't know, trying to calm himself. His lips curled back in agitation and I thought of his knife. Barzee was also getting anxious as she looked at me in anger.

"Take it off," he sneered a final time.

I knew I couldn't defy him any longer. Moving as if in slow motion, wanting to delay the moment for every fraction of a second that I could, I slipped out of the robe. Sitting in a corner of the tent, I grabbed a pillow and held it in front of me, grasping it as if it were a life preserver and I was drowning.

Mitchell and Barzee quickly took their clothes off too. Then Mitchell started the anatomy lesson. He was the instructor. Barzee was the object. I closed my eyes. "Look at this," he commanded. I opened one eye and peeked. He went on. Barzee was utterly compliant. I could hardly keep my stomach from turning. I didn't understand most of what he was saying. I shouldn't have *had* to understand what he was saying. I was still so young. And I certainly should not have had to learn it *this way*! I closed my eyes again. "Look!" Mitchell commanded. "You have to look!"

Mitchell knew what he was doing. He understood my upbringing, my family, my religious and personal beliefs. He knew I had been taught about modesty (a quaint word, I know, old-fashioned and outdated, but that was who I was then and I still hold such values dear).

Everything I had treasured was being robbed. And he was taking it from me with such pleasure.

He was the master. I was the slave. That was the real lesson of the day.

"You think you're so perfect!" he would later say. "You're so prideful. You're so self-righteous! But you're not perfect. Not at all! You're no better than the prostitutes out on the street. You're no better than the homeless people. That's why I have to do this. That's what I have to teach you. You're no better than any trash on the street. And remember this: the Bible says that before you can rise above all these things, you have to descend below them all. You have to experience everything. That is why I am doing this. God commands me to show you all the low things of the world."

I was soon to learn that was how he justified everything he did. And it didn't matter what it was. Pornography. Drinking. Drugs. God wanted—no, God demanded—that all of us partake. Mitchell. Barzee. Me. Just like them, I had to *descend below all things.* It was a phrase that he would use all the time. *Descend below.* Get in the gutter. I had to sink to the lowest level before I could be cleansed. I had to experience all of the evil in the world before I could be worthy of being Mitchell's chosen wife.

But in that moment, on that second morning in the tent, Mitchell wasn't there to teach me about being humble. He wasn't there to tell me God's will. He wasn't there to tell me about the path that they had taken or about the ways of the world. That morning in the tent was just for him. Just for his pleasure. It was about hurting me. Trying to destroy my beliefs. Cutting off all the ties to my family and my previous life, to my church and my values. It was about diminishing me as a person. That's what this lesson was about. His love of power and control. All of it was terribly exciting to him. And Barzee was his willing partner. Later in the day, they would fight like cats and dogs, something they always did, but at that moment she wanted to reinforce the idea that they were a team, and that they were strong together.

This went on for an hour or so. After the demonstration, he raped me. Then I guess that he got hungry because he went out to get some food. By that time, the summer sun had started drying the ground from the rain and it was damp but not wet. We ate breakfast while still naked. We hung around all morning, Mitchell and Barzee walking around like a couple of wild animals.

We remained without clothing all day, Mitchell always the proud one. I sat crying on the bucket, the steel cable around my ankle.

I grew firm that day. Committed. The determination grew like a hard stone inside me. *Whatever it takes to survive. I will do what he tells me. I will not endanger my family. I will not endanger myself.*

I realize that I am not a perfect person. During the nine months that I was in captivity, there were times when I may have failed or made mistakes along the way. But in this one thing, I never wavered. In this thing, I was strong until the very end.

I lived in fear that he was going to rape me again. I kept trying to convince myself that he wouldn't do it. Okay, I thought, it happened twice. Maybe that's all it needs to be. Maybe it can end now. But I knew it wouldn't. So I begged him to leave me alone, to not do it again. I begged and I cried. I said everything that I could.

He was having none of it. "We're man and wife. It's an important part of the relationship. If you're sick or something maybe we won't do it, but otherwise, plan on it."

Throughout all of these conversations, Barzee never intervened to save me. She never tried to soften the pain I endured in any way. I find that interesting. She is a very jealous person. She didn't want to share her husband. But at the same time, she believed in him and allowed herself to be manipulated. Who was she to say that it was a bad idea to steal a fourteen-year-old girl from her bed, take her up to the mountains, cable her to a tree, and rape her every day? God had spoken. Her husband acted. Apparently, it sounded like a good plan to her.

Throughout the day, Mitchell talked. And talked. It seemed he never would shut up.

"You know, Shearjashub, you are a *very* lucky girl," he would say. "I have taken you out of the world and saved you. God has chosen you. You are so blessed!"

I didn't feel very lucky.

He went on (and on!) to explain.

The end of the world was coming. Maybe not that month, or that year, but it was coming soon. Maybe fifteen years, at the outside. (I guess he didn't realize that I felt like my world had already come to an end.) In preparation for the end of the world, God had called him into the wilderness. God had purged and cleansed him. He was now a clean and holy vessel. (As I looked at his dirty clothes, stringy beard, and small black eyes, the words *clean* and *holy* didn't come to mind.) As part of God's plan, before the end of the world, the Lord had commanded him to take seven wives. All of them had to be young girls. All of them virgins (of course)! And yes, I was the lucky one. I was the first. But have no fear, the day would soon come when all of his new wives would truly love him. We would have children with him. We would be so happy. And when the time was right, all of us would go out and testify to the world that he was the Immanuel. We would tell of his greatness and holiness. We would testify that he was indeed the holy one, the chosen vessel from God. Then we would stand against the authorities and beg for Mitchell's life. By then, the Antichrist (yeah, who else) would have come and conquered the world. The evil Antichrist would sit among the holy of holies in the temple. After taking the house of God, the Antichrist would claim it for his throne, sitting upon it as he ruled the world with blood and war and horror.

Having been called out of the wilderness with his seven wives and their children, Immanuel would stand before the world in all his glory, ready to reclaim the throne of righteousness for God.

Now, I was just a little girl, and not wise to the ways of the world, but all of this seemed unlikely to me.

Yet all day long he talked. And talked. And talked. Over the coming months, he would continue to talk and talk. Eventually, I'd heard it all so many times that even now I can remember it almost word for word. I can hear his voice in my mind, the structure of his phrases, his intonations and verbal tics. I can remember all of the scriptures that he quoted. His explanation of how God had taken him and made him clean by telling him and Barzee to get rid of their home and live in their RV, then to sell their RV and live in a small trailer, then to sell the trailer and everything else that they owned. Eventually, they ended up hitchhiking around the country with nothing but a handcart and the packs on their backs. Modern-day pioneers, Mitchell and Barzee and their god against the world.

Of course, I knew it was ridiculous. He was a dirty old man who wanted a bunch of young girls for his wives. That's the only thing he cared about. Sex and drugs and alcohol. That was the only thing this was about. He could do all of the preaching that he wanted, but there was never any doubt in my mind. He was an evil man who had taken me and held me captive. He threatened to kill me. He raped me every day. He threatened to kill my family.

That seemed to take God out of the equation for me.

Sometime that afternoon, Mitchell explained that from the first time he had seen me, he knew I was the one. He had chosen me. God intended us to be together. He then explained how he had started his preparations to take me, how he had implemented a plan to talk to my parents. Get into my home. Gather up the needed supplies. Convince Barzee it was finally time for him to take a second wife. Prepare their camp way up on the mountain, where he could hide me. All of it was well planned. And certainly it was justified. He *had* to kidnap me to save me from all of the wickedness in the world. The wickedness of my church. He had to save me from it all. Everyone around me, the entire world, was carnal and sensual and devilish. Which was kind of ironic news, coming from a naked man standing in the middle of the forest with his "new wife" cabled to the trees.

Mostly, I just cried through it all. It was just so humiliating. So painful and so crazy.

I remember thinking my life was over. I'd never make it back home. I'd never see my family. I'd never grow up and go to high school. I'd never date or have a boyfriend. I'd never play my harp again. Never see any of my friends. No high school football games or prom. I'd never go to college. I'd never learn anything more than what I already knew. I'd never get married—really married—to someone I loved. I'd never be free or happy. I'd never know anything beyond the cable and the trees.

I don't remember saying anything out loud, but I must have mumbled something and he heard me. "You're worried about going to college," he sneered. It obviously made him angry I wasn't grateful. He seemed to grow a bit darker, a cloud passing in front of his face. "You're in the Lord's university now." His voice was sharp and indignant. "He will teach you what you need to know. You will have a degree from God, a degree that is higher than any the world is going to give you."

I knew all of it was brainless junk. But at that point, all I could do was nod. I was starting to grow a shell, the beginning of my defensive mechanism. Soon I would be like a hardboiled egg. On the outside, he could roll me whatever way he pleased, but I was only going through the motions. I was only being rolled. Nodding my head, I never argued.

Whatever it takes to survive, I thought.

Later on that afternoon, we sat in silence for a while. "Shearjashub is your name," he said after a rare moment of silence.

I looked at him, dumbfounded. "What?" I answered. Then I remembered he had called me that a couple of times the day before.

"Your name is Shearjashub," he said again. "He was the first son of Isaiah."

I stared at him. "You're giving me a man's name?"

"It means *a remnant will return.*"

I didn't care what it meant; I thought it was completely stupid. I was going to be called by a man's name. Some unknown offspring of Isaiah. I wondered again if he even knew my real name. "My name is Elizabeth Smart," I said.

"Your name is now Shearjashub."

I thought for a while. This was terribly distressing. I realized it was nothing but another of his manipulations, another way to cut me off, another way to separate me from my previous life. I thought for a long time. "Can I choose a middle name?" I asked him.

Mitchell looked at me.

"You and Hephzibah have middle names," I continued. "You're Immanuel David Isaiah. She is Hephzibah Elladah Isaiah. I'm just Shearjashub Isaiah. I would like a middle name too."

He hesitated. "All right," he finally said. "You can choose a middle name." He seemed kind of happy. Maybe I was starting to get it now.

I thought in silence. It was hot. My bare skin was dry and dirty. I heard a dull sound way above me—an airplane or something else? I turned back to look at him. "I want my middle name to be Elizabeth."

His smile turned instantly into a frown. "No! Not Elizabeth. Nothing like that! Not Elizabeth. And not Ann . . ."

Ann! That was my real middle name. He did *know who I was!*

"You can choose your middle name, but it can't be anything like your old name," he instructed.

It was my turn to be disappointed. He watched me with suspicion as I thought. It seemed he could almost read my mind. "Your middle name has to be from the Old Testament," he then added.

"Anna was a prophetess in the Bible."

"It will not be Anna!" he commanded for the final time. He was getting angry with me now. Impatient. Hadn't he been kind enough already? Did I really want to test him? His anger was always boiling, getting ready to burst through.

I knew that I had pressed as far as I could.

They had a Bible in the camp and I walked over to pick it up. Barzee watched me. She was curious to see what I would do.

Thumbing through the Bible, I kept considering. I wanted my new middle name to start with an "E." I wanted it to have some connection, even if just a tiny one, to my real name. I let the pages slide through my fingers. One of my heroes in the Old Testament was a queen named Esther. She was strong. She was courageous. I thought about it for a moment. It was a big decision, after all, choosing a new name for my new life. Laying the Bible down, I said, "I want my middle name to be Esther."

Mitchell seemed to scowl as he thought, trying to find a reason to disagree. He glanced toward Barzee, seeing if she had some kind of objection that he hadn't thought about. If she did, she didn't show it. "Okay," he said.

"I want you to call me Esther. Not Shearjashub. Esther is a girl's name. It's from the Bible. Will you call me that now?"

He reluctantly agreed. And for a while they did. But after a few months, they went back to Shearjashub. I don't know why. They just did.

But for a short time, I had a tiny victory. Did it make me feel any better? Not really. Did it bring me any hope that I might be able to manipulate my situation? Again, not really. It was a victory, but such a hollow one; it didn't change a lot of how I felt.

15.

The Voice

My captors and I were sitting in the tarped area outside the tent. It was the third day since I'd been taken. The sun was starting to drop toward the horizon. Soon it would be cool. Barzee was standing near the containers with the food. In a few minutes, it would be time to eat. Food was the last thing that I wanted. My stomach was always tied in knots. The trees provided shade, but it was June, and the sun was burning through the leaves. There was no breeze. We had little water and I was thirsty. Mitchell was reading from the Book of Immanuel, the fascinating tome that he had written. I was learning more about his church, the Church of the First Born in the Last Days, and how he was the prophet of the world. Then he started reading scripture. When he talked of God, it was the creepiest thing you can imagine; the words of God coming from the face of the devil. It was the scariest thing I had ever seen.

I shifted on the bucket. It was early afternoon and the day was very calm. I was dressed in my robe. It was already filthy and only getting worse. Though it'd only been three days, it already seemed like years. I looked up at the sky as the sound of an airplane filtered through the trees. It seemed there were a lot of them now. I could hear them almost constantly. I searched for the aircraft through a break in the leaves but it was too high to be seen. Way too high to see me. A couple of times that morning some helicopters had flown over the ridge, but none of them had been very close. At least, I didn't think they were, although it was hard to tell for certain as the sound of their rotors reverberated up and down the canyon walls. Although it was terribly disappointing that none of them came close enough to see me, at least I knew that they were out there looking.

I pulled against the steel cable that held me. *If I could just get free! If I could run into an opening! If I could signal them in some way!*

The sun was high now, almost at its apex in the sky. Hot. Dry. I felt like I was going to die of thirst. We were getting very low on water. A few cups was all that remained in the plastic containers. I was sitting in my usual place, on the bucket by my tiny sapling, when I heard it. Far away. So far away. My heart instantly jumped into my throat.

Mitchell heard it too. He fell silent. His eyes grew wild in fear and anger, his face growing hard as stone. Barzee was sitting right beside him. She didn't seem to hear. Mitchell reached out and grabbed her shoulder, commanding her to hold very still.

Elizabeth . . .

The sound drifted through the trees.

Elizabeth . . .

The voice was faint as a breeze, soft as a whisper in the night. I strained my ears to hear it, praying it would come again.

Nothing.

I held my breath.

Nothing.

Mitchell slowly stood.

I continued straining.

Elizabeth . . .

It was drifting through the trees from the bottom of the canyon.

It was so faint. So far away. I wondered if I had imagined it. But I know that it was real. And Mitchell knew it too.

I thought I had recognized my uncle's voice. I wanted to scream! I wanted to cry! I wanted to jump up and down and wave my arms. I wanted to yell and shriek.

Mitchell moved toward me like an animal on the attack. He knelt down right beside me, his face just a few inches from my own. "I have my knife." His breath was hot and foul. "One tiny peep, and you know what I will do."

I stared at him in terror. Yes, I knew.

"If you make a sound, I'll tape your mouth shut."

I glanced in fear toward the bottom of the canyon, tears of frustration burning my eyes.

Elizabeth . . .

The sound drifted through the trees again.

"If he comes into our camp, if he even gets close, I'm going to kill him," Mitchell sneered. "Do you understand that? If you call him and he hears you, if he comes up here, I'm going to stick him with my knife! He's alone. He won't be ready. If you call out and he finds us, I will kill him right here and now. So you better pray he doesn't find you unless you want him dead!"

I turned in terror toward the sound of the voice. I couldn't hear it any longer. I listened, tilting my head to the side. Yes . . . yes . . . there it was again. Was it really my uncle David? I couldn't tell for sure. I peered through the trees. The mountain oaks were thick with leaves. I found a gap in the branches and looked down the side of the canyon. It was much too steep and thick with trees to see more than a few yards. I could look across the canyon at the mountain on the other side, but I could not see anything when I looked down. None of us had set so much as a foot outside of the camp and I had no idea what was down there. I didn't know how far down it was to the bottom. I didn't know if there was a trail, a road, a stream?

Mitchell was as taut as wire. He didn't move. He hardly breathed. He stood there listening, tense and ready to spring. I didn't know where he kept his knife, but I knew that it was always close. It seemed that he could make it appear out of nowhere. I pictured it again in my mind. Long. Black. Serrated on one side. A cutting knife. A deadly knife. And if I had learned anything about Brian David Mitchell, it was that he was evil enough to kill.

So we waited there together, listening for the sound of someone calling out my name.

I was being torn apart inside. My heart beat with both terrible excitement and utter fear. Someone was looking for me! Someone was very near! Calling my name. I might be rescued! He might find me! But if he did, would Mitchell kill him? If I screamed, the man might hear me. He might try to climb up the side of the mountain. But would he find me? I could picture Mitchell, this crazy man jumping out from behind a tree and slitting his throat. My uncle would be dead. I would still be captured. Nothing would really change. Then would Mitchell kill me too? Would he move me somewhere else? Somewhere worse? Somewhere more dangerous? Someplace much farther away from my family and my home? I remembered how hard it had been to climb the mountain. There had been times when we had been forced to crawl on our hands and knees. It might take, what . . . an hour for my uncle—if it was my uncle—to climb up the mountain to the camp? Plenty of time for Mitchell to kill me. Plenty of time to get ready to attack whoever came into the camp.

For a moment, a fantasy flashed into my mind, the dream of a desperate little girl. I imagined lots of men. Maybe twenty. Maybe more. They knew where the camp was without me screaming. They surrounded the camp. There was nothing Mitchell could do. He couldn't hurt me. He couldn't attack them all. He might turn to me in anger, but he would know that it hadn't been my fault that they had found me! I had not even made a sound. He couldn't be mad at me. He couldn't blame me. I had done everything he had told me to do. But the men had found me anyway.

I wanted it so badly that I could hardly breathe. I wanted to be away from there. I wanted to be away from him. I wanted to go home. I wanted to see my family. I wanted to be safe and not hurt anymore.

But I knew it wasn't real. There was no group of men. They weren't going to surround us. There was only one man. And Mitchell was going to kill him if he came into the camp.

I glanced at Barzee. Her face was mean and hard. Mitchell moved closer to me. His eyes were as deadly as the steel of his knife. *You will die here*, his eyes seemed to say. *You and whoever is down there in the canyon. There's no way this ends well if he starts climbing toward our camp!*

My heart fell into my stomach. I wasn't just brokenhearted. I was shattered. Simply shattered. I had lost my only chance! I started shaking. My knees turned to rubber, my throat grew so tight I couldn't breathe. The bitter disappointment seemed to crush my soul.

We waited, all of us listening intently. The voice called again a time or two but then faded. A long time passed. We didn't move. The voice was never heard again.

That night, I cried myself to sleep again. And though I didn't know it, four or five miles to the west my mother cried herself to sleep as well.

16.

Wind and Noise

———

Early the next afternoon. I was sitting on my appointed seat—the bucket had become the only object to which I could lay claim within the camp—when I heard a faint noise and vibration. I immediately looked up. It grew closer. Louder. The thump of helicopter blades echoed down the canyon. They slapped the air like gunshots, coming at me before the sound of the engines could reach my ears. Without even thinking, I stood up and moved toward the sound, my head up, my eyes searching, the blue sky obscured by all the trees.

Mitchell froze. He was only a few feet away from me. Barzee was on the other side of him, her face turned toward the sky. The sound was getting closer. Her eyes were growing very wide.

The helicopter seemed to be moving down the slope of the mountain. And it was moving very slow. It grew louder. So low. So slow. This helicopter was obviously searching. And it was moving directly toward the camp.

We had heard the sound of airplanes before, but they had always been far away and so high that they could never have found me. And we'd heard a few helicopters, but they were just the sound of beating

rotors and noisy engines in the sky. Most times I never even saw
them, only heard them as they moved across the top of the ridges on
the mountain. But this one was different. It sounded like it was moving directly toward us. The sound grew louder. The roar of engines.
The sound of rushing air. I started to feel it now. The trees began
to move, blowing toward the bottom of the canyon. The helicopter
was coming right toward us. And it was *so* close.

Instinctively, I pulled against the cable around my leg. My eyes
darted here and there, looking for an opening, any break in the trees
where I could be seen. I moved toward a spot of sunlight breaking
through the branches, my eyes always toward the skies.

Mitchell was frozen in uncertainty and fear. Barzee seemed to be
made of stone. I expected Mitchell to spring into action, but he seemed
incapable of doing anything. For the first time, a thought crossed my
mind: Maybe he doesn't have all the answers. Maybe he doesn't even
have a plan.

I lifted my hands toward the skies. I almost started screaming,
"I'm here! I am here!"

They were going to find me! My nightmare was nearly over!

It's impossible to describe how powerful the helicopter seemed to
be. The noise filled my ears. Jet turbines. The power of the rotors. I
couldn't see the helicopter yet, but the trees were bending down around
me. Frantically, I searched above me, reaching out toward the wind.

Suddenly, I felt a vise grip on my arm. Mitchell pulled, his hand
like cold steel on my skin as he forced me toward the tent. Barzee was
already there, tugging frantically at the zipper. We piled in, almost
tumbling onto the floor. I made a move toward the opening, but
Mitchell was already standing in my way. I slid toward the corner of
the tent and waited. They might not see me, but they would see the
tent. There were blue and gray tarps all over the ground. They *had* to
see our camp. They *had* to be looking for me! Why else would this

helicopter be hovering down the side of the mountain? They would send someone up to investigate. Surely I would be found. . . .

It seemed the helicopter was right above us. The branches on the trees were being beaten down. I looked up through the air vent in the top of the tent, but I could only see a tiny slit of sky. But I could see the branches blowing all around us. Dust and dry leaves were in the air.

Seconds passed. And then a minute.

Surely they will see us. . . .

Truthfully, I wasn't certain that all of this effort was part of the search for me. It seemed a little bit extravagant. But why else would a helicopter be hovering right over our camp?

The chopper didn't move. They must have seen the tent, the camp, all of our utensils scattered here and there. I looked anxiously toward my captors. Fear showed on their faces. I wanted to scream with joy. I imagined that maybe the pilots on the helicopter had heat-seeking equipment that would allow them to see through the fabric of the tent.

Mitchell's face was taut, his eyes wide, his lips tightly drawn against his teeth. Barzee was huddled in the tent beside me.

They know it's over, I told myself. They're going to catch them. They will be in prison and I'll be free!

More seconds passed. The helicopter remained directly above us, the wind blowing the tent like a flag in the wind.

Mitchell was peering through the vent in the roof, the same as me. His expression looked like a bomb was about to fall on his head. I wanted to cry with relief. I wanted to scream in pure joy.

Then the helicopter started moving away.

I followed the sound with my eyes. The helicopter didn't dart away but moved slowly, inching down the canyon as if it were . . . still searching for something! The wind began to decrease, the branches blowing with much less force. The dirt began to settle. We all waited.

Another minute. The sound faded. A couple of minutes. The helicopter was gone.

I stared in disbelief. Had they not seen the tents? The tarps? The dugout and our camping gear? Had they not seen anything? I wanted to cry with frustration! They had hovered directly over us. I expected them to . . . I didn't know . . . drop a sheriff from a cable? Yell out over some loudspeakers, circle around and fly back over the camp? Anything to give me a signal that help was on the way.

But nothing. They did nothing.

The sound of the helicopter was completely gone now, leaving only the quiet of the mountain and the gentle summer breeze.

I thought that maybe they would return. I thought maybe someone would come hiking up the mountain. Police. Someone prepared to save me. But no one did. The afternoon dragged by. All the time I waited, alert, my ears straining to pick up the sound of someone hiking up the canyon, calling out my name. All afternoon I waited. All night. All the next day. I tried to keep my hopes up, but I realized that no one was going to come.

Another heartbreaking moment. Another bone-crushing defeat.

We spoke little of the disappearance of the helicopter, but I could see that Mitchell took it as another sign from God. *If it is God's will that I do this, let the helicopter fly away.* I don't know that he ever said those words, but it was just too easy for him to interpret it as another sign from heaven. However, after the helicopter, he also became more cautious. He realized that they were still searching for me—making a real effort to locate me—and he was going to have to be more careful.

So while he took it as another sign, I took it as nothing but another opportunity lost. And I struggled to explain it to myself. It was so frustrating trying to understand how the helicopter could have missed seeing us. Maybe they thought it was a homeless camp. But we were so far up on the mountain, that wouldn't have made any sense. Maybe they thought we were some hikers. But if we were, and they were looking for me, wouldn't they have wanted to talk to us to see if we had seen anything?

I thought back on the other opportunities lost: tiptoeing down the steps in my house, just a few feet from my parents' bedroom; crouching behind the bushes as the police car had driven by; the first morning, after he had raped me and then left me alone inside the tent. That was before I had been cabled. The voice calling me from down the canyon. The helicopter hovering right over my head.

17.

Tracks in the Mud

Water was a big deal. It was precious. It was rare. Mitchell and Barzee rationed it closely. It took a lot of work to get and we conserved it carefully. We kept a small bowl to wash our hands in, but that is all the washing we ever did. The rest of the water we drank. It was warm and tasted of plastic, but I didn't care. Getting my share of water was a really big deal.

Mitchell hated going down to the spring at the bottom of the canyon, which meant that every couple days we'd run out of water. He'd usually make us go a day or so before he'd finally gather up the plastic containers and head on down the canyon. These waterless days were miserable. I was already hot and dry and filthy. Going a day without any water while enduring the summer heat only made it worse.

When he'd go for water, I'd beg him to let me go with him. His reply was always the same: "You're not ready." Which was an interesting thing to say. Already, he was starting to manipulate me. *Be good and I will reward you. I can be generous and kind. But you have to earn it. And you will owe me once I have given some freedoms to you.*

It's ironic that by letting me off the cable, he was trying to reel me in. Even then, he was trying to get me to love him. But it certainly didn't work. Never did I develop any feelings for him or Barzee. All I ever felt was fear and repulsion.

When it came to the possibility of letting me go down with him to get some water, I don't think he was worried that I would escape. For one thing, he could always hold on to the other end of my cable. And it was two adults against a child, hardly an even fight. But trying to get away wasn't what motivated me. I was simply desperate to relieve the boredom. I was so tired of being cabled that I wanted to scream. Watching as he headed down the mountain, I longed to be free of the cable that held me in its narrow cage.

Looking back on it now, I think that might have been the beginning of my subjection to him.

Soon I would be walking around the city with Mitchell and Barzee and not telling anyone who I was. Soon, I would be questioned by a policeman in the Salt Lake City Library, and not dare to answer when he asked me my name. People wonder how I could have done that. Why didn't I cry out for help? Why didn't I scream to escape when, finally, I had the opportunity?

The answer is difficult to explain, but it comes down to fear. Fear for my life. Fear for my family. Fear of the pain and humiliation. Part of it too was the constant intimidation. Part of it was the feeling that I had already lost my life and everything worth having—the feeling that I had gone too far to be saved.

All of these emotions were going to overwhelm me. They were going to make it possible for Mitchell to take me into the city and lead me around like a dog. Every ounce of energy and courage I had was used on maintaining my drive to survive; nothing was left to use on plans of escape . . . yet.

And I think most of that started when I was raped and chained up every day.

One morning, Mitchell and Barzee had a big fight. They were constantly at each other's throats, always nagging and poking and getting on each other's nerves, but this one was a big one. Lots of screaming and yelling and calling bad names. Barzee was tired of all the attention I had been getting. "You're just being lustful!" she screamed at her husband. "Just because she's young and beautiful. You're being lustful! You're being carnal. It's not right!"

I sat on my bucket and listened to them fight about me, wishing I could be somewhere else.

They screamed at each other for a while but eventually settled down. After they had a chance to cool off, Mitchell approached his wife, all humble and submissive. He never said that he was sorry, but he was certainly groveling and acting like a child.

Then I saw something I had never seen before, but would see again.

In an act of contrition, Mitchell asked if she wanted him to give her a blessing, kind of a special prayer that is anointed on her head. Her body language seemed to soften and she nodded yes. Mitchell put his hands on her head and started to pray. Using his authority as a prophet, he reminded her that he was God's servant. He had been called by God. But just like Moses needed Aaron, he needed her as well. She was his strength and wisdom. She was smarter and more worthy than he. While he was forced to go into the world, she was to be his rock and salvation, his source of his spiritual strength. He told her that she was the one who made it possible for him to lead the world out of sin and oppression. He needed her. God needed her. She was the great one, not he. He told her that she was a friend and companion to Mary, the mother of Jesus, and Mary Magdalene. She was a friend to all the great women in the history of the world. Her position in heaven was assured. Finally, he reminded her that she needed to be patient when he was weak. He would try to be better, but she would always be greater than he. She needed to show that by her patience when he did wrong.

When the blessing was over, I stared at them, dumbfounded. Barzee was beaming. She was eating it up.

I thought it was the strangest thing that I had ever heard—and I had heard a lot of strange things over the past few weeks.

Sometime during the second week, I begged him once again to let me go with him to get some water. It seemed that he and Barzee had already talked about it and made a decision. Without saying anything, he walked to where my cable was padlocked to the longer cable anchored between the trees. He pulled out the key that he kept on a string around his neck and unlocked my cable. Holding tightly, he gave it a brutal tug to remind me that I was still under his control. I didn't care. I was overjoyed at the prospect of getting out of the camp. And I hadn't entirely given up on the idea of trying to get away. I knew there might be an opportunity to run.

And I had another secret plan.

I used to read Louis L'Amour Westerns all the time. It seemed the old trackers could track a rattlesnake across a rock. I suspected there would be mud around the spring and I intended to leave as many footprints as I could. If I could leave some trace behind, the searchers might track me back to the camp. At least, that was my hope. It wasn't a lot, I know that, but when you don't have a lot to cling to, you hang on tight to what you have.

We started down the side of the mountain. There was no trail and we had to cut our way back and forth between the scrub oaks and pines. It was steep and difficult to travel. The weeds were high; thistle, dyer's-weed, June grass, an occasional patch of dying sunflowers. Mitchell held the cable and walked in front of me, Barzee always just a few steps behind. Whenever we were about to break out of the cover of the trees and move into the open, Mitchell would stop and take a look around, listening and looking, his head cocked to the wind. Standing on the edge of the trees, he always pulled the cable short, forcing me to stand beside him. We'd stand there until he was satisfied, then he'd continue to lead me down the mountain.

Halfway down, he turned to cut across the mountain at an angle instead of heading straight down.

A small meadow spread before us, and for the first time I had a chance to really look around. I realized that we were in one of the canyons that cut east of my house. Looking west, way down to where the sides of the canyon came together, I could see a small portion of the Salt Lake Valley. I was startled for a moment. We weren't that far from my home! Looking down on the valley, I could see the dark out-lines of tall buildings, roads, and freeways. Though all of the details were lost in the distance, the city didn't seem that far away. I looked up at the blue sky. Not a hint of clouds or rain. The sides of the mountains were mostly dry now, though there were occasional patches of weeds that dotted the canyon with spots of green. The south face of the canyon—the one opposite me—was scattered with trees and out-croppings of rock.

Looking at the rocky slope that lay below us, I realized a couple of things. First, it was going to be very hard to climb back up the mountain, for it was steep and hard-going. Second, Mitchell had been very smart in where he had placed his camp. Because it was halfway up the side of the canyon, there was no easy way to get to it from either the top or the canyon floor. And it was high enough up in the moun-tains that no one was going to stumble upon it unless they knew exactly where it was.

Turning, I looked back toward our camp, but it was completely hidden among the trees. In fact, I saw no trace of any human passing, for Mitchell had been careful not to ever walk the same path so as not to make a trail.

I only had a minute to look around before Mitchell tugged on my cable to get me moving again. We continued down the mountain. The ground turned bare and started to get very rocky as the terrain became steeper and more exposed. We continued at an angle, the slope far too steep to hike straight down. After a while, we had to use our hands to keep from sliding. It was treacherous and we were going very slowly. Eventually, it got so steep that Mitchell had to let go of my cable. He wasn't worried. It was obvious I could not escape, and he needed both hands to keep from sliding. Afraid that I would trip on my cable, I coiled it up and held it in my left hand, using my right to keep from falling as we slowly worked our way down.

Over the coming weeks, I would learn that they called this part of the trail the crucible. And that's exactly what it was: a severe test created by a miserable and exhausting trail. The crucible was steep and dangerous. It was on the side of the mountain that faced south, directly into the summer sun. No trees to provide any shade. Steep and rocky. It was difficult for any man to hike along the crucible, let alone a fourteen-year-old girl, let alone a girl who was dragging a steel cable and carrying a thirty-pound container of sloshing water.

I grew to hate the crucible. And I hiked it many times.

Eventually, we scratched and clung our way down to the bottom of the canyon. Here, there was a small spring that seeped out of the canyon floor. For a moment, Mitchell seemed to take a look around, listening for the sound of any voices. He stared up and down the stream as he listened, then looked around the soft earth for any signs of any footprints. Barzee waited patiently while he did his security review.

It was cool in the shade, and the stream was tucked inside a pretty glade. It flowed gently downhill, gathering a little more water out of the aquifer as it descended, but it was never more than a trickle meandering across the soft ground. Along the stream, the trees were green and full, lots of hardwoods, pines and oaks. The grass along the stream was thick, with peppermint and watercress mingled in.

"We're going to bathe," Mitchell told me. I had mixed feelings about this. On the one hand, I was so filthy that the thought of getting clean was more appealing than I could imagine. On the other, the thought of getting undressed in front of him sent a sickening shiver down my spine. Mitchell lifted up one of the rubber containers we had carried with us and nodded at me. "Take your clothes off," he commanded. I froze, the words cutting me to the core. I flashed back to the first morning in the tent when Barzee had commanded me to take my pajamas off. When I didn't move, Mitchell took a step toward me, the bucket in his hand. Knowing I couldn't fight him, I pulled the linen robe over my head and dropped it on top of the nearest shrub. Mitchell moved me toward the center of the little stream where the mud was thick and squished between my toes. I stood naked as he dipped the bucket in a pool of standing water and poured it over my head. I nearly went into shock, it was so cold! The water washed over my hair and down my body. He handed me a rough bar of soap and a squirt of all-natural organic shampoo and told me to wash up. He only gave me a couple seconds. Another bucket of ice-cold water and that was it. My weekly bath was through.

Shivering, I moved to a spot in the sun to dry off while he and Barzee washed themselves. When they were finished, we put our dirty robes back on, then I helped to fill the water containers, working carefully to leave as many footprints in the soft mud as I could. Above the spring, on the north side of the mountain, there was a dusty patch, and I tried to leave my footprints there as well. But we only stayed at the stream for a couple of minutes. Mitchell was anxious to get back up to our camp. So we quickly filled our water containers, then headed up the side of the mountain again.

It was hot, exhausting work. The summer sun bore down. A hundred yards up, I was already dirty and exhausted. I held two one-gallon plastic containers of water and they sloshed heavily in my arms. Up we climbed, my cable dragging behind me. I don't know if Mitchell had decided I wouldn't run off or if he was only getting sloppy, but after a while I picked it up and carried it myself. Up we climbed, then we turned to our right. The crucible lay before us. Steep mountain and sharp rocks. I didn't know how I would do it. Climbing. Slipping. Barely catching my fall. The water felt like a load of heavy sand in my arms. It grew heavier and heavier. We stopped every five or ten minutes to rest. Across the crucible. Farther up the mountain. As we climbed, I looked ahead of us, not knowing for certain where our camp was. Late that afternoon, we finally stumbled into camp.

Before I even had a chance to sit down, Mitchell walked over and locked my cable with the padlock again.

I was thinking that, you know, maybe he would leave me un-cabled for a while. Maybe he trusted me, at least a little. Maybe he would give me a few minutes without being cabled to the trees. But that wasn't to be the case.

At least I can dream, I thought as I listened to the click of the pad-lock being snapped again.

18.

Food and Wine

A little more than a week into my captivity, we ran out of food. Up to that point, we hadn't eaten well, but we had enough to get by. And I hadn't given a lot of thought as to where our food had come from, or where any more food was going to come from in the future. I just didn't think about it. It was obvious Mitchell and Barzee had been in the camp for a long time. They hadn't starved. They had to continue eating in the future. Surely they had a plan.

But then we ran out of food. The coolers were completely empty. Nothing in the plastic containers. No raisins. No tortillas. No crackers or apples. Nothing at all to eat.

In my church, on the first Sunday of the month, we fast for twenty-four hours, then take what money we would have spent on food and give it to the poor. It's a day of fasting and prayer and giving, which is a good thing. But I guess I'm just a baby. It was always really hard for me to go hungry.

So even though I was used to going a day without eating, it was very discouraging to be trapped in the camp without any food. I'm the kind of person who has to eat every three hours or I feel miserable and become a little cranky. And I don't think I'm alone. Most of us don't realize, or we forget because we don't have to do it very often, how quickly we feel hungry and how badly we want to eat.

We went a morning without eating. And then a day. And then another. I was getting really hungry. All of us were. It was miserable. My belly hurt. Then I started to wonder, What's going to happen? Is he going to go and get us some food? How is he going to get it? How long is it going to take?

About midmorning, Barzee and I were in the tent. She was teaching me how to patch our robes, which was a good wifely duty and one I had to learn. To do this, she had brought out new robes for us to wear while we mended the linen ones. (Initially they had been a whitish light-beige color but now they were more brown than beige.) The new robes were made from gold sheets that we had to pull over our heads, then secure with a clasp and tie with a sash. The material was cheap and flimsy, but the sheets were not well worn, making them the finest clothing in the camp. They were awkward and ugly, though, with sleeves that fell to our sides in huge triangles, giving them the appearance of an African muumuu. All morning we sewed and patched away, getting the linen robes into fine shape. But it was hot and miserable. And I was getting so hungry. It was the only thing that I could think about.

Finally, Mitchell poked his head into the tent and announced, "I'm going to go down to Babylon to plunder."

At first I didn't know what he meant. *Babylon? Plunder?* But then I got really excited. *Going down to Babylon.* I was smart enough to figure that one out. He was going down into the world. He was going to get us food.

But that wasn't the only thing that made me happy. This meant an entire day without him. I wouldn't get raped. I wouldn't get abused. I wouldn't have to listen to him tell me how he was going to kill my family. I wouldn't have to listen to him tell me how grateful

I should be that he had saved me from the world. I didn't know which was more exciting, a day away from him or the possibility of getting food.

Watching him get ready to leave, I felt like a little girl on Christmas morning. My mouth began to water at the prospect of finally having something to eat. My heart raced as he put on his boots and picked up his pack. *Yes*, I wanted to say. *Go down to Babylon and get me food!*

But how was he going to get it? What did plunder really mean? I looked at him, confused. But Mitchell didn't offer to explain, which was unusual, for he was always searching for something new to talk about. It turned out that it didn't matter. I would learn about plunder soon enough.

Then another thought popped into my mind. Maybe he would bring me some news of what was going on with my family. Maybe he would tell me about the search efforts. I could picture him using the news to torment me: *Esther, they were so close. So close. And yet so far away.* Maybe he would bring me news of the world, anything at all to break the boredom. Or better yet, maybe someone would follow him when he came back to our camp. Maybe someone would stumble upon us while he was gone. Maybe someone would catch him while he was down in the city. I knew all of these things were extremely unlikely, but I couldn't keep the thoughts out of my mind. He was going to the city. He was exposing himself to society, other people, maybe even the police. That had to be helpful, I just couldn't figure out how.

Then my heart seemed to jump with a terrifying thought. What if he did get caught? What if he didn't come back? He had the key to the lock on my cable. No key, no freedom. I'd be trapped forever. If he got caught and didn't come back, what would Barzee do? She'd take off and leave me, that's what she'd do! She'd run as far and as fast as she could go if that's what it took to protect herself. She'd leave me there, cabled to the trees in the middle of the mountains. I would die, alone, starving, and out of water. It was a terrifying thought.

As he got ready to go down into the city, he talked excitedly to himself. For someone who was convinced the world was nothing but a den of sinners, he sure seemed to be in a good mood. Then it occurred to me that he was planning on doing a little "descending below all things" of his own. Maybe even a lot of descending. He was going down to eat and drink and party, leaving me cabled to the trees.

Mitchell was gone all day. It got hot. A little bit of water for lunch was all we had. The sun moved toward the western horizon. I was getting pretty good at estimating the time by watching as it marched across the tops of the trees. The mountain shadows were growing long. The sun faded behind the highest ridge line and evening came on. It started to get cooler. I started to wonder how Mitchell was going to get us any food. He didn't have any money. Nothing he could trade for. He might be able to steal a pocketful of something, but how could he possibly get enough to feed us all? What if he came back with nothing? Then I started to get angry. He'd been gone a long, long time. What if he was down there eating and came back with nothing for the rest of us to eat?

I kept looking down the mountain, expecting him to walk out of the shadows of the trees. I listened carefully for the sound of branches snapping or the crunch of boots upon the leaves. I was getting really hungry. I couldn't wait for his return! *Come on . . . come on,* I was praying inside my head.

It grew dark. We waited in the darkness. No fire. No flashlights. It grew colder. Finally, Barzee said it was time to go to bed. We climbed into the tent. I tried to sleep, but I couldn't. I was too hungry. And I was worried now that he was not coming back. But Barzee seemed unconcerned. She knew how far it was down into the city. She knew it was a long and tiring hike. But I had also seen the way she kept her eyes toward the canyon, the way she listened too, hoping to hear the sound of his footsteps across the dry leaves.

After a while I feel asleep.

Around eleven, I felt her shaking me on the shoulder. He was back.

We scrambled out of the tent. I was so excited to see what he had brought. He pointed his flashlight at the sacks of food as he placed them on the ground, then set the flashlight on a limb so it would shine between us. He seemed very pleased with himself. The great hunter-gatherer had returned. Barzee seemed very pleased as well. Her husband had provided. What more could she ask? Now it was time for the women to stand in gratefulness and awe.

Truth was, I would have kissed the ground he walked on if he would have given me something to eat. I mean, talk about the natural animal coming out! "Where's the food?" is all I could think about.

The grocery sacks were from an expensive boutique food store on the east side of the city. How could he possibly have afforded it? "How did you get this?" I asked.

"I ministered and plundered for it."

"What does that mean?"

Stupid of me to ask a question. With Mitchell there were plenty of simple questions, but no such thing as a simple answer. He started to explain, telling me how in the Old Testament the Lord would lead the children of Israel into battle and then tell them that they could take whatever they had conquered as a reward for the fight. If they wanted it, they could take it. But only the Lord could designate when and where they were allowed to take from others, it could never come from man. So when you're fighting for a righteous cause, and when the Lord commands you to take something, that is plunder. It isn't stealing. It is different, because you're doing it for God. And the Lord had commanded him to plunder. And obeying was how we showed faith in Him. He was only doing God's will when he stole from the grocery store.

Okay. I got it. Plundering was stealing. I really didn't care. All I knew was, I was hungry. But I was also curious. "What do you do when you are ministering, then?"

He smiled. This was his territory and he was happy to explain. "When I'm on the street, in a store, wherever the Lord may take me, the true disciples of Christ recognize me as their true prophet. When they do, they give me money. That is how God provided for us."

I thought back on the first time I had seen him, that long-ago November afternoon in downtown Salt Lake City. So he called it ministering when he was panhandling (which was where he got most of the money we needed to buy food). His elaborate explanation didn't change how I felt. He was a panhandler then and was still a beggar now.

He then explained why it had taken him so long. The ministering hadn't gone as well as he had hoped it would. Not so many folks, apparently, recognized him as the prophet he really was. The good news was that the plundering had gone a little better. But after all the ministering and plundering, he had to go down to Pioneer Park, where some of his people liked to hang out, so he could rest awhile. Which meant he had to drink a little, smoke a little, whatever it took to gather up his strength for the long hike back up the mountain.

Turns out he had spent most of the afternoon drinking, then had to sleep it off before he had the energy to make it back to camp.

"Guess what I saw down there," Mitchell then announced with great pride.

I didn't really care. All I wanted was the food.

"You should see it." He moved so close that I could smell the tang of sweat and the alcohol on his breath. "I saw my sweet Shearjashub's face plastered all over the city. It's in every store, on every lamppost, posters of her absolutely everywhere. And blue ribbons. Thousands of blue ribbons. And the whole time I was walking around the city, seeing Shearjashub's sweet face looking down on me, you want to know what I thought?" He moved even closer in the darkness. "I thought to myself, I got the real McCoy. I get the most beautiful girl in the city. And that kind of makes me proud."

I stared at him, dumbfounded, trying to take in what he had said. Posters of me. All over the city. That meant that people were still looking. They hadn't given up. And it wasn't just my family. Other people were looking for me too?

"Beautiful posters everywhere," Mitchell seemed to sing, so proud of what he'd done. So proud of what he'd captured. So proud of what he owned. He reached into his pocket and pulled out a folded piece of paper. Holding it up to the light, I saw my smiling face. My name. A description and a hotline number.

My heart raced with anticipation. They were still looking for me! They hadn't given up yet. Maybe there was still hope.

I tried not to smile as my hopelessness was chased away. Mitchell watched me carefully, his eyes filled with lust and pride. Then he pulled out the food. Cheese and crackers. More raisins, carrots, and mayonnaise. There were even a couple sacks of cookies, something that was very appealing to a fourteen-year-old girl. It seemed like a massive amount of food. I realize now that it couldn't have fed us for more than a few days, but at the time it seemed like more food than we could eat in a year. I waited, my mouth watering, my instincts for survival kicking into high gear. I had to fight myself not to pounce on it, for I had already learned a hard lesson about patience and food. One morning, I had woken up and eaten a crust of bread before they had taken out the plates and blessed it. I had been severely chastised. Big trouble had come my way. So I knew I couldn't eat anything until they said the prayer. But sometimes Mitchell would pray for forty minutes. No way I was going to make it that long!

Mitchell laid out the food, arranging it carefully for us to see. The last thing he pulled out was a bottle of wine. I paid it no attention. I was focused on the food. "Can we eat?" I begged.

"Oh, you'll eat," Mitchell answered. "In fact, you can eat whatever you want. But first we're going to have the sacrament. We haven't had the sacrament for too long."

I glanced at him. A religious ceremony, up here, in the mountains, in the middle of the night, over a bunch of store-bought food . . . Okay. Whatever. As long as we got to eat.

He opened the wine and filled a pewter mug. The liquid reflected deep red, almost black, in the shadows of the flashlight. I smelled it and pulled away. This was the first time I had ever smelled alcohol. I remembered the label was a Merlot. He also had a bottle of white, Sauvignon Blanc.

After pouring the wine, he put the glass before him, took a slice of bread and broke off three small pieces, and placed them on a plate. He took out the scriptures and read a section that talked about the sacrament, then said a prayer. After all of this preparation, he passed me the bread. I took a piece of crust and ate it. It tasted so good. My mouth watered. I wanted more! He took the cup of wine and drank some, then passed it to Barzee, who took a drink as well. Then he passed the cup to me.

"I'm not going to drink it," I said.

The light was dim, the night dark, but I could see that Mitchell was smiling. *Not going to drink it? We'll see,* his dark eyes seemed to say.

"Drink it," he said.

"Drink it," Barzee urged impatiently. The last thing she wanted was to fuss about some wine.

"I won't do it," I said. "I can't. I won't."

"You will," Mitchell answered in deep anger. His voice was hard. Violent. Any good mood at the success of his plunder had been instantly wiped away. He reached over and filled the cup completely.

"You will drink it all and you will drink it right now. You're not going to eat until you do. You're not going to move. You can't go to bed. You do this, or you do nothing. You can sit here all night. You can sit here all day tomorrow and the next day, but you're going to drink it, and you will."

I stared at the cup of wine, feeling sick. He knew what he was doing. He knew how I felt about drinking. Mormons don't drink alcohol. This was a big deal to me. It was important.

He sat there and stared. "No food. No water. No sleep. Nothing until you drink it. You will do what I say, do you understand that, Esther? Drink. Work. Think. Sex. You will do everything I say. If I tell you to drink, you're going to drink it. Now, do you understand?"

I shivered as he spoke. There were so many reasons that I didn't want to do it. One of them was religious. I believed that my body was a temple and I didn't want to harm it. Part of it was the fact that I had made a promise to myself that drinking was something that I would never do. I didn't need it. I wouldn't do it. He was asking me to betray everything that I held dear. Finally, I was repulsed by the fact that it was bad for me. That wasn't anything based on religion, that was just a fact.

Now, I know that might seem a bit ridiculous, considering the circumstances I was in. I was being raped every day, sometimes multiple times a day, by a dirty old man who had only showered once in two weeks. I was going days without food. My water was being rationed. I had to wash my hands in a bowl of water that was so dirty it was as brown as earth. My only shower had been a thirty-second washdown with a single gallon of water from the stream. I was sleeping in a tent. I spent my days cabled between two trees. None of this was what you would consider a healthy lifestyle. There were lots of reasons why it was silly to worry about the unhealthy effects of drinking a glass of wine. But of all of those things that were happening to me,

I couldn't control a single one. But I thought I could control the things I ate and drank.

It turned out that I was wrong.

I sat there, defiant. He stared back at me. *As long as it takes,* the fierce look on his face seemed to say. Minutes went by, the two of us staring at each other. Five minutes. Ten.

Throughout this time, one thought kept rolling around in my mind: *Whatever it takes to survive.*

I wanted to live. I wanted to get back to my family. I wanted to be rescued. And one day I might be. But he wasn't going to let me eat or drink or sleep until I'd drunk the wine.

And so I drank it. And to this day, the smell of wine will almost instantly make me sick.

I sipped the cup and tried to pass it on, but Mitchell would have none of that. I had to drink the whole thing. And so I forced it down. I thought it tasted terrible. I gagged a bit, but finished the cup. He filled it up again. "This too!" he commanded. I forced it down as well. He filled it once again. I was forced to drink it down.

He knew that was enough. So he finally let me eat.

I dove in. I was so hungry. But the fog inside my mind was growing thicker. I was getting slower. A few minutes later, a little mouse snuck around the corner of the tent, casting a flickering shadow in the dim light. All of us turned to watch him. Mitchell picked up a piece of cheese and threw it to him. The little mouse cautiously approached it, sniffed, then picked it up and scampered back into the shadows. I felt angry. This was *our* food! I didn't want to waste it. I didn't want to go hungry ever again.

After eating, I felt exhausted. My belly was full of food and my blood was full of wine. I was so tired. I moved slowly toward the tent. The moment I lay down, I was asleep.

Soon after, Mitchell came in to rape me. I woke up and tried to fight him, but I was barely even conscious. I wanted desperately to stay within myself, to stay in my right mind, but it was too late, and he did what he did.

After, I lay on the mattress, feeling as low as I had ever felt. I felt terrible about the wine. I felt terrible about the rape. And as I lay there, I began to understand why some people might start to drink.

19.

Routine

―――――――

Although the days began to run together, I never lost count of them. The fourth day. The fifth. A week. The second week. I was aware of every minute, every hour, every sunrise and sunset. In some ways, it never really hit me that time was starting to pass by. Emotionally, I was in it for the long haul. Thirty years until he dies, was what I kept thinking at the time. Every day was long and painful. I was bored. I was scared. I was humiliated, homesick, and lonely.

All night long, Mitchell was in and out of the tent, constantly interrupting my sleep as he got up to exercise in the dark. He thought that exercise could heal pretty much anything, so he would get up and go outside and bounce up and down on one foot and then the other, then do a lot of deep breathing. He was always anxious, never able to relax, even in the middle of the night. Barzee didn't seem to notice that he was always up and down. At least, she never complained. I'm pretty sure she always slept through the night. After a while, I started sleeping through his nightly exercising too.

Every day was much the same. We would get up with the sun. After climbing out of the tent, the first thing we did was have a morning devotional. We'd start out with a hymn from Barzee's collection of religious songs. There was no "Onward, Christian Soldiers" or "Welcome to Sunday School" type of hymns in her collection. No, her songbook contained only hymns that were pointedly focused on God. We'd sing, then read from the scriptures or from Mitchell's book, which was considered scripture too. Then we'd pray. Oh, how we'd pray! Brian David Mitchell had more to say to heaven than any other man in the world. Forty-five minutes was the norm. Kneeling. Eyes closed. Head down. My legs would cramp and my knees would hurt. And I'd be bored beyond my own tears.

Maybe then he'd rape me. Or maybe he'd wait until the afternoon. Or maybe that night. Or maybe one and then the other.

"Shearjashub, you are so lucky," he would remind me after the abuse. "I brought you out of sin. I brought you out of the ugly world."

Having just lived through another rape, I found it very hard to feel grateful.

Over time, I learned about what they called the Seven Diamonds Plus One. The seven diamonds were seven books: the Bible, *The Book of Isaiah* by Avraham Gileadi, the Book of Mormon, *The Final Quest* by Rick Joyner, *Embraced by the Light* by Betty J. Eadie, the *Doctrine and Covenants*, and *The Golden Seven Plus One* by C. Samuel West, which is all about natural healing and health. Those were the seven diamonds. The plus-one was the Book of Immanuel David Isaiah. I don't know if you could really call it a book—it was only about forty pages of Barzee's handwritten calligraphy bound between card stock and stapled together. There was also a binder of Mitchell's personal papers: a collection of his blessings and revelations, his calling as a prophet and that kind of thing. These writings also contained the commandment that he was to take seven wives. It didn't specifically mention that they had to be young girls, but Mitchell made it clear that this was his intention. That was the only way they would be malleable enough for him to control them, he would later admit. Finally, Barzee had written a long journal that chronicled their travels and conversion. On those rare occasions when her husband wasn't talking, she would read out of this journal to me.

We always got up with the sun and went to bed when it grew dark. The weather was hot and monotonous. We were on the south face of the mountain and the sun bore down, cutting through the shade, making the afternoons very hot. All day long, we'd sit around in our linen robes, which certainly didn't resemble linen any longer. At night, when the sun went down, it quickly grew cold. We were high up on the mountain and the air was too thin to hold in the heat. To stay warm, we put on these gray men's shirts. They didn't have any buttons, you'd have to pull them over your head, and they were large and ugly, but I was grateful for something to keep the chill away.

We never built fires in the beginning. We didn't necessarily need one to stay warm, but a hot meal would have been nice every once in a while. We would eat granola and nuts for breakfast. A few vegetables and fruit for lunch and supper. The fresh food never lasted long, however, and soon we were spreading mayonnaise on tortillas again and eating those with crackers and not much else. We didn't eat well, that was for sure. It seemed I was always uncomfortable. Always thirsty. Always in pain. Mitchell seemed to be completely confident that he was never going to get caught, but he was still careful, so he rarely hiked down to the spring to get us water, not wanting to take the risk of being seen or meeting someone on the trail. Plus, he was lazy. It was hard work to hike down to the spring, and very hard work to bring a heavy container of water back up, as I would soon learn when they began to treat me like a mule.

Eventually, Barzee began to figure out exactly what a handmaiden was. If her husband was going to use me for his pleasure, then she was going to use me too. And putting me to work was a good way to get even for all of the attention that Mitchell seemed intent on showing me. She didn't let me prepare any of the meals—that was always just for her—but she made me do pretty much everything else. And it's amazing how much work there is to do when you are actually living in a camp. Once in a while, Mitchell would put me to work expanding the dugout. It was backbreaking work to shovel the dirt, but my cable would only reach partway into the dugout and pretty soon I had dug about as far as I could go.

When I wasn't working, the only thing I could do was read. During the first weeks I made my way through almost the entire Old Testament and some of the other scriptures too.

But I was bored. Oh-so bored. It was an impossible adjustment to make. I had been an active teenager. I was used to being involved in school and music and sports. I had a group of friends. My family and I always did things together. Now I was cabled between two trees. Twenty feet was as far as I could roam. I had the choice of listening to Mitchell talk or reading a few books, but that's all that I could do. When Mitchell wasn't talking, Barzee would be chatting in my ear. Sometimes it felt like I was being tortured by their voices. Tortured with boredom. Tortured with fear. Cabled. Humiliated. Taken from my home and family. It was no fun at all.

Mitchell never trusted me. He certainly never gave me an opportunity to escape. He and Barzee never left me alone a single moment. I slept within a few inches of them. We spent every waking hour within a few feet of one another. I was forced to use the bathroom without even the slightest hint of privacy. Mitchell never took me off the cable. I was nothing but a caged animal.

My faith was tested every day. And though I never really lost hope, as time went by I certainly began to recalibrate my expectations. I realized he was never going to let me go. I realized he was going to keep me cabled until he knew that he could trust me. Over time, I quit thinking or hoping that anyone would find me. Instead, I started thinking about the things I had to do in order to survive. I never quit thinking about my family, but I gradually began to accept that he would kill them if I ever left him or if I tried to escape. The only people I ever talked to were him and Barzee. Every day, it was the same thing. More threats. More fear. More abuse and pain. All this proved to me that Mitchell was a very dangerous man. Did I believe that he would kill me if he had to? Absolutely, I did. Did I believe that he would hunt me down and kill my family? There was no doubt in my mind. Did I think that he was capable of murder? It's hard to be tortured and raped every day and believe that the man who is hurting you is not capable of anything worse. Did I think that he had friends who were willing to help him? It sure appeared he did. In fact, it seemed that he got everything he wanted. It seemed that he could lie or manipulate his way out of any situation. So yes, after a while, I started to believe some of the things he told me. Over time, I slipped deeper and deeper into pure survival mode until I came to measure every situation by only one thing: Was it going to help me to survive? That was the only thing that mattered. Whatever it took to live another day.

For the first week or ten days, I cried and cried. I couldn't help it. The tears just flowed. It wasn't an all day and all night kind of thing—Mitchell would have never put up with that—but when I was not busy helping with the meals or cleaning up or doing the dishes, or whatever else Barzee wanted me to do, I would sit on my bucket and the tears would soon come. I tried to keep myself together, and sometimes I could, but many times, I simply couldn't help it. I cried for myself and the life that I had lost. I cried about the lost opportunities to be saved. I cried for my family. I cried for it all.

Finally, Mitchell had had enough. "Stop it!" he commanded. "You can't cry anymore!"

I looked at him, wiping my eyes in fear.

"And quit talking about your parents. I don't want to hear it anymore! Your parents or your family! I'm sick of it all. Yeah, yeah, I get it. We both get it!" He glanced angrily at Barzee. "You loved your parents. You loved your family. But this is your new life. You need to look forward and not back. So I mean it, I don't want to hear your constant sniffling anymore!"

I wiped my tears away, but inside I was crying even more. He was so . . . *heartless*. So cold and unfeeling!

I turned around to hide my tears. And as I did, I remember thinking of my grandfather.

He is with me right now.

I don't know where it came from, but the thought was crystal clear.

He is watching over me and protecting me. That is why Mitchell hasn't killed me. Grandpa is keeping me safe.

Once again, I felt a flicker of hope. If my grandpa was protecting me, there had to be a reason. He wouldn't have helped me come this far just to let me die after suffering through so much.

Soon after this, Mitchell told me he wanted to give me a blessing. He placed his hands on my head, called me by my real name, and said a prayer. He told me about my family. He said they were going to be okay. He mentioned my grandfather. He told me my dad was a good man but that my family had been misled.

All of this was intended to manipulate me and draw me in. All of it was intended to convince me that he was my friend. It was designed to tie me to him, to make me dependent on him for my hope and morale. It was designed to make me believe that he understood me, that he cared about me, and that he wanted me to be happy—that he *wanted* to trust me, but that I had to earn his trust. It was designed to make it harder and harder for me to remember my old life, to worry about my family, to care about him more.

None of that worked. There was no Stockholm syndrome going

on with me. I never formed attachments to my captors or bonded with them in any way.

And though I was young, I wasn't stupid. I knew the only reason Mitchell tried to comfort me through this blessing was that he wanted to shut me up.

20.

Cold Water

———

There's a story I know of a group of early pioneers who were trekking their way across the prairie to settle in the west. This group was one of the handcart companies, a collection of families who traveled with everything they owned crammed inside a small handcart. The poorest of the poor, their handcarts were so small that a single man could push them as they moved across the prairie and even up the mountains. There were no horses in the company. No ox-drawn wagons to help them with their loads. Things didn't go well for this group of pioneers. For one thing, they didn't start their journey until late in the season. Some people told them to wait until the next year, but they had nowhere to stay for the winter and so they pressed on. After their late start, they had a series of problems along the way. In October, they were still on the open prairie when an early winter settled in. It was bitter cold, with snow and freezing temperatures making travel almost impossible. They were already critically low on food, and completely unprepared to survive out in the open against the elements. They trudged along at a backbreaking pace, trying to make their way to the Salt Lake Valley, all the time getting lower and lower on food. The weather got worse. One by one, they started to freeze or starve to death. Every morning, it was the same thing: Wake up. Gather up those who had not made it through the night. Fathers. Mothers. Little children. Families were devastated, with broken dreams and broken hearts. The survivors would try to hack a shallow grave where they could bury their loved ones, but many times the ground was so frozen that it was impossible to dig. So they'd pile rocks over the graves in hopes of keeping the wolves and other scavengers away. Throughout the day, others would die of starvation or exhaustion. But the company could not afford to stop to bury them. Too many dead and too little time. In these cases, they'd be forced to leave the bodies of their loved ones underneath any kind of marker they could find: a lone tree, a bare shrub, a small pile of rocks—anything was better than leaving the bodies lying atop the bare ground.

Traveling in this company was a little girl whose shoes had completely worn out, leaving her to cross the prairie barefoot. Her frozen feet got so torn up that she'd leave a trail of blood in the snow behind her. She'd wrap her feet in burlap, old cloth, anything she could find to protect them. Night after night she'd pray for a pair of shoes.

One morning, she woke up to find a miracle on the ground beside her. Underneath a small bush, next to the place where she'd been sleeping, was a brand-new pair of shoes. Pulling them on her bloodied feet, she found that they fit her perfectly. But where had they come from? No one in her company had given her the shoes. Certainly, none of them had such a luxury within their possession and if they had, they would have given them to her already.

The little girl realized that she had been given a gift from heaven.

Now, I don't mean in any way to compare my plight to the horrible experience of this little girl. She was in a life-or-death situation and her suffering was much more acute than mine. But one night I had a similar experience. And it taught me an important lesson.

———

I'm not sure how long it was into my captivity. More than a couple weeks, but not quite a month, I guess. We had gone a long time without going down to the stream to get any water. Maybe Mitchell was just lazy, but I don't think that was the reason. I think something may have spooked him, causing him to be afraid to go down to the spring. Maybe he was worried that someone had become suspicious of him on one of his trips into the city. He might have seen someone down in the canyon. I don't know what it was, all I knew was I was thirsty.

Down in the valley, the search efforts were still under way. Though weeks had now passed, my parents were working hard to keep the story of my kidnapping in the press. They knew it was vital to make sure that people were still aware, to keep the search efforts going and my picture in the news. From what Mitchell had told me, my posters were still up everywhere. The first time Mitchell had seen these posters, it had made him very proud, but I don't think he expected the search efforts to keep going for so long. And though he tried to hide it, I could see that he was worried.

Which meant that we weren't getting any water until he was certain it was safe to head down to the spring.

Mitchell started to ration what little water we had left, but eventually we reached the point where we only had a few cups remaining in the bottom of one of the plastic containers. Mitchell drank, then poured a cup for Barzee, then poured the last few drops for me. Though it didn't even fill my cup, I drank it eagerly. The water was warm, having been sitting in the sun, and it tasted like melted plastic. I drank it in one gulp, then put the cup down.

And that was it. The water was gone.

I stared at the other water containers, but I knew they were empty. We had checked them several times already, taking off the lids and pouring out the last few drops. Still, Mitchell went over to shake them just to make sure that they were empty. He could do that all he wanted. There was no water in the camp.

It was the end of June, deep into the boiling days of summer. Utah is a desert, and it had not rained since the first week that I was captured. Temperatures hovered in the nineties, sometimes reaching above a hundred. A hot wind blew every afternoon, drying us like leather. My skin was dry, my throat, my eyes. I was so dirty and so thirsty that I thought I would die.

After the sun had gone down we sat around for a while to savor the cooler temperatures, but eventually we went to bed. I was always the first to crawl into the tent. Mitchell came in beside me, then Barzee beside him. Before we went to sleep, he always checked my cable to make sure it was secure.

Surely he'll go down to get water in the morning, I thought as we settled down in bed. It was the only thing that I could think of as I drifted off to sleep.

The night was long and restless. Morning came. Mitchell didn't say anything about going down to the spring. I asked him, but he refused to talk to me about it.

All day we sat and cooked in the summer heat. Mitchell checked the water containers once again, but all of them were dry. I had thought that being hungry was difficult, but it was nothing compared to this. Nothing compared to the burning in my throat. Nothing compared to the drive to find something to drink. And I wasn't alone. Barzee and Mitchell felt it too. I could see it in their eyes. I could hear it in the dryness of their voices. Whatever had driven Mitchell to stay away from the bottom of the canyon must have been very powerful indeed.

The day dragged on. Hot. Miserable. Dry desert heat. I was beginning to lose my energy. None of us wanted to eat. I begged Mitchell again to go down and get some water. I begged him to let me off the cable. I offered to carry the containers if he was too tired to carry them himself. I tried to understand why he couldn't go, but none of it made sense.

Evening came. We went to bed. I fell into a restless asleep.

I was awakened in the middle of the night. Sitting up, I looked around. The moonlight filtered through the nylon fabric, casting the inside of the tent in a pale, yellow light. Mitchell was asleep beside me. Barzee was lying next to him. Both of them were breathing deeply, Mitchell's throat rattling with every breath. I looked around in the moonlight. Something had wakened me. Turning, I looked toward the front of the tent.

There was a yellow cup sitting beside my pillow. I leaned toward it, checking it in the moonlight. It was filled to the very brim with water. I stared at it a moment, not believing it was real. I reached out to touch it. The cup was cold. I pulled my hand back and looked around. Was I dreaming? Was I crazy? I quickly turned to Mitchell and Barzee. Neither of them had moved. I listened. A gentle breeze blew through the tops of the trees, swaying in the night. I turned back to the water. Slowly, I reached out to touch it once again. It was cold as ice and filled to the top.

I picked it up and drank it. The water cooled my throat and filled my stomach. It was cold and clear and wonderful, the best-tasting water that I had ever had.

After drinking, I stared at the empty cup for a long time before laying my head back on the ground.

Where did the water come from? I have no explanation other than the water came from God. I know we didn't have a drop of water in the camp. I know that neither Mitchell nor Barzee would have wakened to give me any water, even if they had any left to give. And this water was fresh and cold, like it had just come from the spring.

I never told them about the water. I never talked about it at all. But over the next few days, I thought a lot about what had happened. Why did God do it? How did it happen? What was God trying to say?

Would I have died without the water? Certainly not. As thirsty as I felt, and as terrible as it was, I was not teetering on the edge of a life-or-death situation. And I was not alone. Mitchell and Barzee needed water too. Mitchell wasn't going to stay up on the mountain and let us all die of thirst. Eventually he would have had to go down to the stream.

So why did God send me the water?

Because He loved me. And He wanted me to know.

He wanted me to know that He was still near. He wanted me to know that He controlled the Earth and all the heavens, that all things were in His hands. And if He could move the mountains, then he could do this thing for me. To Him it was a small thing—a terribly easy thing to do—but for me it was as powerful as if He had parted the sea.

This experience reminded me once again that God had not deserted me, that He was aware of my suffering and loneliness. And that assurance gave me hope. It helped me to keep my faith and gave me the strength that I needed to go on.

It also gave me something else to think about.

At the time, I had pretty much conceded that Mitchell might kill me. And if he didn't kill me, then I was condemned to a life of suffering and captivity. But the appearance of the water seemed to indicate that God had another plan. It told me that the fight for freedom wasn't over. God knew the end from the beginning and there was still hope for me.

In my life, I have come to believe there are lots of examples where God provides us little miracles to give us hope. Most of these experiences are not as obvious as waking up and finding a cup of water. Some of them are much more subtle. We may even have to look for His miracles along the way. But they are there. And they're important when we are struggling with the challenging battles of this life.

21.

Happy Fourth of July

I spent more than six weeks tethered to the trees. Six weeks having a steel cable wrapped around my ankle. Six weeks of eating and sleeping and going to the bathroom with two people watching me. Six weeks of never moving more than a few feet beyond the center of the camp. That's a long time to not have so much as a moment of privacy. It's a long time to be cabled and raped every day by one captor while my other captor talked, sang, or read her scriptures nearby.

Once a week or so, Mitchell would uncable me long enough to allow me to go down to the spring to have the bucket of water poured over my head before being forced to carry the heavy containers of water back up the mountain. But that is the only time I was ever allowed to be free. And as soon as we got back to camp, it was *snap,* and I was cabled up again. Never would he reward me for good behavior or show me any sign of affection by allowing me to spend a single moment without being cabled to the trees. And even when I went with them down to get the water, I always had the ten-foot cable around my ankle, which meant he had complete control of me.

From the moment I was captured, I was a pawn in their hands.

Naked. Hurting. Terrified of what was coming. Terrified of the thought that it was thirty years to go before he died. I had no dignity. No freedom. No power over my body. No power over what I ate, what I drank, what I heard, or what I read. It was endless hours of indoctrination—hearing about their journey, hearing of their god, hearing how smart Mitchell was and how he was the chosen one.

I was a prisoner in heart and mind and soul.

There was no way I could have endured this abuse without falling under his control.

And the worst of his manipulations was the fear that he instilled. Always the same script.

"If you ever try to run, I'm going to kill you," he would hiss into my ear, his dry breath raising the hair on my neck.

"He'll do it!" Barzee would pipe in, ever eager to prove how deadly her husband was. "He's not kidding. He'll kill you in a heartbeat!"

Mitchell would pull me a little closer. "And if you ever get away, I will come and kill your family. I know where they live. I know all about them, just like I knew about you. Think of your little sister. What a cute little girl. How old is she . . . maybe nine? And the little boy. He's just a baby! Do you really think you can protect them? Do you really think the police can protect them? Sure, they might keep your family safe for a while, but they can't do it forever. Time will pass and they'll forget you. Other cases will come along. They have a lot to do. Eventually, they'll move on. They'll forget you and your family. But I won't forget you. I'll never forget your family. I'll be waiting for them, Esther. Me. My friends. We'll be waiting. Watching. Looking for our chance to kill them. And it will come. Sooner or later, it will come. And when it does, your entire family . . . every . . . single . . . one of them will be dead. And it will be your fault! Do you want that? Are you so selfish that you'd really kill your family just because you want to leave me? Think about that, Esther. Are you really that kind of person? Do you want their blood on your hands? If you think that you're unhappy now, wait until you have the death of your family upon your shoulders. Imagine the guilt. The shame. Your family wants to live, the same as you do, but you're going to take that from them, Esther, if you ever run away. I will come and kill them. And it will be *your* fault."

Day after day, week after week, I heard it again and again.

I can't even begin to tell you how demoralizing it was. It wore on me like a constant drip of emotional acid. And I became convinced that he would do it. I became convinced that even if he was captured, he had friends who would kill my family. He seemed to have a lot of people who would help him. How else could you explain his seeming ability to produce food and drugs and alcohol out of nothing? How else to explain his ability to go down into the city without fear of being captured? He had to have others who were helping him.

The more I thought about it—and I thought about it every moment of every day—the more I began to feel that my primary responsibility was to my family. I could not endanger them. I had to keep them safe.

It wasn't long before Mitchell started going down into the city three or four times a week. Every time he went down, he'd bring back alcohol. And never just beer. No way he was going to haul a couple of six-packs around. It was rum and scotch and whiskey. It was gin and vodka, too. Every time that he brought back alcohol, he forced me to drink it with him. Then he started rolling cigarettes and forcing me to smoke them. A couple times he forced me to smoke some of his dope, but watching me fail to inhale it properly, he decided to keep it for himself.

After a while, I began to realize that Mitchell had an inordinate interest in the "descending below all things" phase of becoming a great prophet.

I knew the fourth of July was coming. When every day is like a century, it has a way of making you acutely aware of the passage of time.

I had been begging Mitchell to let me go up to the top of the mountain to watch the fireworks. I was desperate for any kind of diversion from being cabled to the tree. More, I thought I might have a chance to escape. Maybe we'd meet someone on the top of the mountain who had hiked up to watch the fireworks as well. I knew it was unlikely, but I was desperate for any reason to have hope.

The day before the Fourth, Mitchell had gone down to the city to get supplies. Along with his usual assortment of alcohol and crackers, he also brought back a chicken for a special Fourth of July treat. It sat all day hanging in a plastic bag from a tree, and I imagined it being full of germs, but still my mouth watered at the thought of a hot meal. Real food. Warm. Seasoned. I could hardly wait. On the afternoon of the Fourth, we cleared an area in the brush right below the latrine and started a cooking fire, the first fire we had had since I'd been taken. Barzee brought out a blackened Dutch oven and placed it in the middle of the coals. I watched her pull the chicken apart and hand me the meat. I rolled the meat in flour and spices, then dropped the pieces into the oven. The oil popped and spat as the chicken began to cook. I watched it hungrily as it turned a golden brown.

The chicken couldn't cook fast enough for me. For one thing, I was hungry. For another, Mitchell was on one of his rants, going on and on about all the great food he and Barzee used to eat when she had a full kitchen to tend to. I had a hard time imagining her in a flowery apron, working over a stove. This was the woman who watched me get raped every day, hardly my idea of a happy homemaker. Soon, the lecture turned to another of his favorite subjects; the books of the Seven Diamonds Plus One. He went on about how fruit was the most perfect food on Earth. It was supposed to be the main thing that we ate every day, but the greedy processed-food producers and medical industry didn't want us to be well, so they kept pushing their nasty products and medicines down our throats. He told me that at one time, he and Barzee had eaten nothing but fruit for an entire year. They would go to the Dumpsters behind the local grocery stores and dig out the old fruit that had been thrown away. While they were on the fruit diet, neither of them ever suffered a single ailment. They had more energy. They never got sick.

I wanted to ask him why, if eating fruit was all it took to be in such miraculously great shape, they had abandoned the plan, but I didn't want to prolong the conversation. All I wanted to do was eat!

Later on, after more begging that we be able to go to the top of the mountain to watch the fireworks, Mitchell suddenly unlocked the cable, allowing me to walk free. He didn't announce anything; he just walked over to the padlock, pulled out the key from around his neck, and set me free. I still had the other cable around my ankle, but at least I wasn't tethered anymore. "Don't try to run!" he commanded after he had unlocked me. "I will kill you if you run. I will come and kill your family. You understand me?"

I nodded compliantly. I understood.

"Come on," he said.

I expected him to gather up the water containers and start walking down the mountain toward the spring. But he didn't. He started walking up. And for the first time, he didn't hold the other end of my cable in his hand. Then I realized that he hadn't given it the usual jerk just to remind me that I was an animal on his leash.

He started moving through the trees on the east side of our camp. Barzee followed him. She seemed . . . I don't know, I don't want to say happy—I don't think I ever saw her happy—but she didn't seem as angry as she usually did.

I watched them for a second, then started following them up the side of the mountain.

The forest was thinner above our camp, with occasional open meadows, or at least places where the trees were not as thick. The mountain dipped into a couple bowls where the terrain was not as steep. It wasn't an easy climb, but it wasn't nearly as steep as the route was toward the bottom of the canyon. As we climbed, I realized that we were not far from the route that Mitchell and I had taken on that first morning when he had led me into the camp. I flashed back to my red pajamas and white running shoes. I flashed back to my little sister lying beside me in bed. It seemed so long ago! A lifetime. Like it wasn't even real. Who was that little girl in the red pajamas? What had become of her? Who was the girl who was now living in her place?

Then I realized it was the one-month anniversary of the night I had been taken. One day short of my "wedding" anniversary. The thought made me feel sick.

As we climbed, I thought of my family, wondering what they were doing on this Fourth of July. Had they forgotten me? Were they going on without me? Had they given up on the search? Surely they had. What else could they have done?

I remembered that in years past, we'd go to the Fourth of July rodeo up in Oakley. I used to dream of being a cowboy princess, with a glittering tiara on my cowboy hat. I dreamed of carrying the American flag around the arena on the back of my horse. I knew that, it being the Fourth of July, my family would have gone up to my grandparents' ranch for a family party. I knew that the kids would be playing in the woods. I thought of my cousins. They'd be giggling in anticipation of playing night games, chasing one another around the huge yard. They suddenly seemed so young, so innocent and far removed from me.

I felt one hundred years old.

Surely my family would have mourned my passing, I thought. But just as surely they would have gone on with their lives. And they should have. It was the healthy and normal thing to do. My parents had other children they had to care for. It wasn't fair to them if my parents were obsessed with my loss. It was important to bring normality back into their lives. It had been more than a month. To me it seemed like years. It must have seemed that long to them as well. And there was no reason for them to believe I was alive, no reason to believe that I was ever coming home. They couldn't go on mourning my passing every day.

I pictured my mom again, still driving around our neighborhood and looking for any clues. I pictured my dad staring out the window every night. I thought of my family kneeling together to say their family prayers. Did they still pray for my safety? Did they pray that I'd return? Or did they pray now for acceptance and to get past the pain of losing me?

Whenever Mitchell went down into the city, he didn't talk anymore about posters or blue ribbons like he had before. No more search parties. No more airplanes or calling voices or helicopters hovering over the camp.

No, they weren't looking for me any longer. Everyone had moved on.

We walked up the side of the mountain. It took us about an hour, maybe a little less, to make it to the highest part of the ridge. There, the mountain opened up. It was an incredible view. I could see in every direction. The Wasatch Mountains continued to the east. Another canyon lay behind us, to the north. Looking east, I could see down into the city. Again, I was struck with how very close to home I was.

If I could fly . . . if I could fly . . . I would flap my wings and fly home.

Mitchell had one of his sacks and he opened it up and pulled out a rubber ball. He and Barzee started tossing it around. They invited me to throw it with them, which was difficult because of the sagebrush and weeds. In addition, the mountain fell away on all sides of us, so we had to be careful not to let the ball roll away. Still, I joined in. We threw the ball in a triangle. Wow! Isn't this great, I thought sarcastically. Here I am, playing catch with my new friends! I could have been down in the city, having a barbecue with my own family, looking forward to sleeping in my own bed, not worrying about getting raped that night. But instead, I got to be up here in a dirty white robe, throwing a ball around with two of the most evil people in the world.

Night came slowly. I was glad for that. I wanted to savor every moment that I wasn't tethered between the trees. We had a simple picnic up on the mountain, then sat down and watched the sun go down. It was the first sunset I had seen in a month. The orange globe faded toward the Great Salt Lake on the west side of the city until it eventually dipped into the desert on the other side of the lake. It grew dark. We waited, sitting on the dry grass on top of the mountain. Eventually, we saw the first of the fireworks go off. They seemed so far away, little balls of sparks and fire. They were too distant to hear the sound, though if I listened very carefully, and if the wind was just right, I could hear the faintest rumble from the cannonballs that blew up in the sky.

Watching the fireworks, I felt more homesick than I had in weeks.

Once the last of the fireballs had faded, Mitchell was suddenly eager to get back to camp. He quickly gathered up what little he had brought up to the top of the mountain and started leading us down, his flashlight illuminating the way.

I felt like I had just experienced a glimpse of spring in the dead of winter and now I was being yanked back into the black of winter again.

Happy Fourth of July, I said to myself as I followed him in the dark.

After we'd made our way back down to camp, Mitchell stirred the fire pit to rouse the flame, then we sat around the fire. I considered it a real treat to have its comfort and its warmth. Barzee started cooking popcorn in a wok with olive oil and salt. As we talked, Mitchell seemed to watch me carefully, measuring the conversation as if he were waiting to say something important. I sensed that something bad was coming. After being with him in the most intimate of conditions for every moment of every day, I had a pretty good feel for his moods and intentions.

He stood up to throw a small log upon the fire, then looked at Barzee. "I think the time has come," he said.

My heart sank. I had no idea what he was talking about, but I knew it wasn't good. And I couldn't imagine what could be coming that was worth the power of announcing *the time has come.*

Barzee started shaking her head. "Oh no, not this."

"Yes, it is time," he said.

My heart sank even further. I turned and studied his face. His dark eyes were sullen underneath his bushy eyebrows. His hair was long and greasy and parted in the middle, his beard full and powdered with tentacles of gray. It didn't matter. He was repulsive and ugly. Wild. Evil. Dark and menacing. He had taken on the image of his master and he looked like a devil now. And Barzee was no better. Her hair hung in strings at the side of her head. Her face was blotchy from the constant sun. Thick lips. Puffy eyes. Her eyebrows were almost gone.

Mitchell looked at Barzee, his eyes seeming to pierce the dark. Though he kept his face toward her, he was talking now to me. "The Lord has commanded us to do something. It is so hard for me to tell you, but it is time for . . ." He named a certain sexual practice.

My mind raced in panic. *What? What is that?* I had no idea what it meant. Then it hit me, my heart slamming in my chest as the most disgusting image crawled out from somewhere in the deepest recesses of my mind.

The words that he had spoken came again into my mind. *The Lord has commanded!*

What kind of god is this, I had to wonder.

In my darkest nightmares, I couldn't imagine anything that was worse than what I had been living through every day. But I guess that I didn't have a good enough imagination, for I had not imagined this.

Barzee shook her head again but then seemed to concede, her head slowly coasting to a stop. Having convinced her—a battle that had taken all of ten seconds—Mitchell turned his attention back to me. The shadows seemed to flicker from the fire, dancing images against the trees. Mitchell's face turned a shade darker. "Barzee and I are going down into the tent."

Yes! Yes! That's good. You two! Do whatever! I thought. Just please don't involve me!

"Then tomorrow we're going to demonstrate. And after that, you and I . . ."

I lowered my head and closed my eyes. I had never been to a slaughterhouse before, but that's exactly how I felt. I was nothing but a sheep being led to the slaughter. I wanted to die. I shook my head in despair.

Mitchell and his wife stood up and disappeared into the tent, leaving me to sit by the fire.

I felt as if I was completely alone in a world that had been turned on its head. I felt as if I didn't have a friend. I had reached a point where I wasn't able to fight them any longer. Whatever they told me, I simply did. I had lost every ounce of dignity. Every ounce of pride. Every sense of my inhibitions.

But not this . . . please, not this . . . I was praying in my mind.

Eventually they emerged from the tent. Mitchell looked at me hungrily. I shivered in my soul. "Go to bed," he told me.

I stood and walked toward the tent, my head down. Mitchell followed me into the tent to rape me.

It turned out to be a long night.

The next day, Mitchell got up and announced that he was going down into the city.

I knew what was going to happen to me when he got back. All day long I waited, feeling as if a guillotine were hanging over my head. I didn't eat at all that day. Not a thing. I knew from sad experience that the effects of alcohol would hit me much quicker if I drank on an empty stomach and I wanted my stomach completely empty when he came back.

Mitchell came stumbling back into camp about midafternoon. He brought food, and the regular assortment of alcohol, all of it the hard stuff.

"Drink this!" he commanded, handing me one of the bottles. "Then we're going to do that other thing."

I drank willingly. I desperately wanted the dulling effects of the alcohol to numb my senses before the nightmare began.

He watched me drink, then smiled. I don't know if he wanted to get me drunk, but I suppose he did. I think he knew it was the only way I was going to be able to do what he intended.

We finished half a bottle. He and Barzee started the demonstration. Then he forced me to do the same.

During this experience, the same words kept rolling around in my head: *Think about your family. Remember that they love you. Do whatever it takes to protect them. Whatever it takes to survive.*

Sometime later, I don't remember how long, it might even have been the same day, I finally got the smallest chance of revenge. He tried to kiss me and I bit his tongue. Bit it hard. He jerked back, furious. I thought he was going to hit me. He held his mouth and screamed in rage. Then he stared me down, his face contorted in pain. "If you ever do that again, I'll never have sex with you! You understand that, Esther? If you hurt me, I'll never have sex with you again. You'll be the most miserable woman in the world!"

I stared at him, utterly dumbfounded.

But that pretty much describes Brian David Mitchell's mind. That pretty much is a peek into his soul. In his opinion, I was the one who was getting the good end of the deal. I *owed* him for what he was doing to me. I was the luckiest girl in the world. I had the great pleasure, the great distinction, of having him abuse me every day. And if I ever did anything to make him reject me, I would be the most miserable woman in the world.

I can't even begin to tell you how messed up that is to me.

22.

Betrayal

"Why did you do this to me?" I once asked him after he had just raped me.

Mitchell looked at me, taking his time to answer.

"What did I ever do to you to deserve this?"

Mitchell remained quiet, thinking, which told me that a "prophetic" announcement was coming. I knew the routine now. When the prophet spoke, he spoke with authority, and it took a little time to generate an appropriately somber weight to his words.

It was early in the afternoon, mid-July, the hottest and driest days of summer. We were sitting around our camp doing pretty much nothing, which was pretty much what we did every afternoon. The air was calm and it was hot, the sky a reflective silver-gray. Dust and dandelion seeds floated through the trees. It was quiet. It seemed even the birds were too tired to chirp or move among the branches. I kept my eyes on him. I wanted an answer.

"I didn't deserve this," I said in a low voice, almost talking to myself.

"It wasn't me," he finally said.

I stared at him, defiant. *Of course it was you!* I wanted to scream.

Barzee lifted her eyes, paying close attention now. She liked it when I defied him, at least a part of her did. Sometimes she got tired of playing second fiddle, and I think she was hoping he would put me in my place.

"Why did you take me? Why do this to me?" I asked a final time.

Mitchell took a deep breath, as if he were forcing himself to be patient with a slow child. "We've been through this a thousand times before."

I slowly shook my head, which instantly made him angry.

"You are lucky, Esther," he sneered. "Don't forget that. God could have chosen another girl, but out of His great goodness He chose you."

It's a good thing that I didn't believe him or I would have hated God forever.

"You would do well to show a little gratitude," he sneered again.

I didn't know what to say. Moments passed in angry silence until he went on. His voice was softer now. "I didn't *want* to do this, Esther. I didn't want to take you. It wasn't my idea. But God spoke. I had to listen." He stopped a moment, his eyes looking down. "I am His prophet, Esther, his mouthpiece here on Earth. When He commands, I must obey. He could command me to move this mountain, and I would do it. He could command me to part the seas, and it would be done. Do you think I could deny Him if He commanded me to take a virgin and to save her from the world? I am nothing but a servant, and when He speaks I must obey."

He seemed to deflate, as if he were weary from carrying some extraordinary weight. His face sagged with sadness. "I didn't ask for this great calling, Esther. In fact, I tried to deny it. I begged God to let this calling pass. And for a time, He did. But the world has reached a point where God couldn't let me delay any longer. He has called me once again and this time I must reply.

"It's a heavy burden, Esther, a very heavy load. But you can help me. Do you see that? When you serve me, you're serving God. And think of that great honor. Out of the entire world, the Lord has called you. You are a handmaiden to the Chosen. That is such a blessing, Esther. You get to serve the servant of the Lord."

He fell silent, his statement of authority complete.

I was sitting on my bucket looking down at the tiny branch that was still struggling against the summer heat. I touched it with my fingers. Keep going, little guy! Don't give up, I thought.

"You know there are more to come," Mitchell said.

I lifted my eyes to look at him.

"I have been commanded to take seven additional wives. You are only the first. All of the others are young and malleable. Young girls that I can mold into proper servants. Believe me, I have learned that they can't be so old that they will fight me. They can't be so old that they will fight the will of God."

It was true. I wasn't the first girl Brian David Mitchell had decided he had to take. Neither was I his first attempt at having a second wife.

A few years before he kidnapped me, Mitchell had approached another woman about joining him and Barzee in their marriage. Of course, you don't jump into a long-term commitment like polygamy without taking each other for a little spin to test things out, so he ended up moving in with the woman, an African-American named Kelly. But Barzee finally put a stop to it when Kelly insisted on having Mitchell to herself. (The idea of two women fighting over Mitchell is so absurd that I can barely comprehend it, but such was the insanity that I lived with every day.) Worse than the fact that Kelly wanted Mitchell for herself was her refusal to honor Barzee as the senior wife, or to recognize her in her exalted role as the "Mother of Zion," whatever that meant. Angry at the lack of respect, Barzee had argued that Kelly was not chosen of God and demanded that Mitchell end the relationship. Her husband relented for a while but then snuck back to sleep with Kelly again. At this point, Barzee ripped Mitchell from the relationship. But after some pleading and praying and explaining, Mitchell convinced her once again that his relationship with Kelly had been sanctified by God. Willing to give it another go, and always wanting to please her husband, Barzee had agreed to go with Mitchell down to Kelly's apartment so they could invite her to come and stay with them up at their campground in the mountains. But their intentions hit a snag when they found Kelly with another man. Mitchell was furious that she would betray him. Barzee was furious that the other woman would show such disrespect to her man. Spitting with anger, they withdrew the offer of marriage and left.

So ended the sordid Kelly affair.

But Mitchell hadn't given up on finding another wife. Soon after, he received a new revelation. He was not to take one wife, but seven. And he was to focus on young girls, those who would be less likely to get involved with another man. And they needed to be pure. And from a Mormon home. Knowing what he wanted, but not having given any thought as to how he was going to get it, he simply found a young girl he fancied and followed her on the bus one day. Noticing that he was following her, the girl had waited until the last second at one of the bus stops, then suddenly jumped off, leaving him on the bus as it drove away.

After Mitchell had told me this story, I often thought of that girl. Good for you! I thought. You did the smart thing. I am glad you got away.

But part of me had to wonder why I had to be the one who was cabled to the trees.

I rarely got a chance to talk. Mitchell did all of that. Days. Weeks. Months of listening to him go on and on. But sometimes even he couldn't keep it up and there would be a lull in the one-sided conversation. Sometimes he would even ask me a question. It was extraordinarily rare, but sometimes I got to talk about something that I wanted to talk about. Which was always my family. It was the only thing I cared about. The only thing I ever thought about. I was desperate to keep their memories clear in my mind. Even if they had moved on—and I had accepted that they had—I had not moved on. They were my only hope. My only joy. The only thing I lived for was the thought that one day I might return to them.

But Mitchell hated it when I talked about my family. He hated it if I even mentioned them in passing. It was as if I were talking about something so foul and disgusting that it had to be avoided at all costs. (This from a guy who was pretty hard to disgust.) Whenever I mentioned my family, he would instantly get angry. "Get past it, Esther! You have to move on! This is your life now. You have to let your former life go! I don't want to hear about them, Esther. Not now. Not tomorrow. Never again!"

One day toward the middle of July, Mitchell was complaining about his mother. She had been granted a restraining order against him after he had pushed her down a flight of stairs, and it made him angry that he couldn't go near her anymore. As part of the conversation, he mentioned where she lived.

"My cousin Olivia lives in that neighborhood," I said without thinking. "She and I were very close." Realizing what I had said, I flinched against his coming anger at the mention of my family. But he didn't rip my head off like I thought that he would. I waited longer. He didn't say anything. I felt elated. He was going to let me talk! "We used to play together in her yard. She has a great swing in one of the trees in her front yard. And a small tree house in the pear tree. I loved being there. We'd have such fun together."

Mitchell seemed to think. "I know that house," he said. "It is very near my mom's house. Yellow paint, right?"

I was so excited to think about my cousin. "Yeah, yeah, the yellow house. Olivia and I were very close. We're the same age, you know. I would play with her and my other cousins all the time. In the tree house. On the swing."

Surprisingly, Mitchell allowed me to go on. It was like Christmas morning. I could talk about my family! I described the times that we had played together, the things that we would do, more about where they lived.

I had no idea that I had betrayed my cousin until the next day.

Mitchell came out of the tent in the morning. I was already up and so was Barzee. He wandered over to the small container we used to store our food and poked around inside but didn't take anything out to eat. Straightening up, he looked at me and forced a smile, which made me nervous.

"I have to tell you something, Esther."

I felt the familiar feeling of my stomach falling.

"You're not going to like it."

I was already braced. But the truth was, there was very little he could say or do to me that would have shocked me any longer. I didn't feel anything anymore. The soul that lived inside me had been pushed so far down that everything I did was simply going through the motions.

But even though I had retreated, I knew that something new was coming and I was sick with dread.

"The Lord has commanded me to go out again." He kept his snake eyes on me. "He has commanded me to go and take Olivia to be my next wife. I'm going to go and get her and bring her back here."

The blood rushed from my brain. I felt like I was going to fall over. I had to steady myself as I stifled a scream.

I had planted the idea. I had betrayed my own cousin by the things I had said.

I felt the crushing weight of utter despair.

Mitchell knew from experience that it was going to take planning and preparation to get what he wanted. He spent a week or so putting the plan in place.

He decided that he was going to kidnap Olivia on July 24, a state holiday commemorating the day the Mormon pioneers made their way into the Salt Lake Valley. He knew there would be lots of traffic and parades and parties and city fireworks that night. The police would be preoccupied, leaving him a little more slack to do his evil thing.

Thinking of what he was going to do made me sick with guilt. What would Olivia think when she was dragged into camp and saw me here? She would know I had betrayed her! She would know it was my fault. How could I ever face her? How could she ever forgive me? And if the police ever came to rescue us, would they think it was my fault too? Would I be sent to jail for helping Mitchell with this terrible crime? I know that sounds ridiculous, but I was young. And thoroughly brainwashed about how the safety of my family was my responsibility.

Then I had the worst thought of all: What if she was hurt, or even murdered, while Mitchell was trying to kidnap her? The fact that I had planted the idea in Mitchell's mind was almost more than I could bear.

But I have to admit that there was a tiny bit of me—a very tiny bit—that wanted her there with me. Together, we could find a way to escape! We would have each other. It wouldn't be so bad. But whenever I thought of this, I felt guilty. I knew my secret wish was incredibly selfish. There was no way I could wish this upon anyone.

———

The morning of July 24 finally came. Mitchell spent the day preparing for his crime. He packed his two green packs and tied them together with the same piece of dirty cloth that he had used on the night he came to get me. Although he didn't show me the deadly knife, I knew he had it with him. He ate and then rested, knowing he had a long, hard night ahead of him. First he had to hike down into the city. Then he'd take a bus to the southeastern section of the valley. After kidnapping Olivia, he'd have to climb up Big Cottonwood Canyon, a canyon that leads to some of Utah's most aggressive ski terrain. Big Cottonwood is also famous among mountain climbers for its steep granite walls. The canyon is rimmed with so many sheer granite cliffs that in most places it would be impossible to climb. And he'd have to do it with a terrified prisoner in tow. Olivia would be thinking of me. She would think I had been killed. Armed with that information, surely she would be more aggressive in trying to escape.

Once they made it to the top of the mountain, Mitchell would have to drag Olivia north across the ridgelines for . . . I didn't know . . . ten or fifteen miles. I knew how exhausting and time consuming all of this was going to be.

All morning, Mitchell tried to act as if a terrible burden had been placed upon his shoulders. *God has commanded me. I must obey. But it is so difficult. So difficult. Not what I want to do at all. But I must pass another test of faith, for I am the prophet of the Lord.*

But I knew it was all an act. And he was acting it very poorly. He couldn't keep the lusty smile from his face. It was obvious that he was keyed up and full of anxious energy. He was going to get another child. Another wife. Another toy. And as I watched him, I realized that he would never be satisfied. The evil that was inside him would always make him lust for more.

My heart raced as I watched him pick up the two sacks and

throw them across his back. *Olivia, I'm so sorry!* I was crying in my head. *Please, God, please protect her! Please, God, make him fail in this thing. I will do anything if You will spare her from what I am living through every day.*

All day long I waited. Too sick to eat, I sat on my bucket and prayed. I begged and cried and pleaded with God to protect my cousin. If Barzee was concerned, she didn't show it, though she did seem a little more terse than normal. She went about her daily routine, then sat and read and sewed and prepared a small meal. The day passed more slowly than any day in my life, the afternoon sun dragging across the gray sky. Afternoon passed, and then the evening. Night came. We waited. Barzee was getting nervous now. It grew late. Still no Mitchell. We waited. We went to bed. I didn't sleep. Midnight. The moonlight lit the trees around us in a pale, white light. Early morning came. We were in our tent. He's not coming back! I thought. He didn't get Olivia! He's been captured. He's is prison right now.

Lifting up on one elbow, I looked across the tent at Barzee, feeling suddenly terrified while imagining what might have happened. He got caught. But he isn't going to tell them about us. He isn't going to betray his wife. He'll be silent. He'll give her time to escape. He'll give her time to get out of town, to get on a bus and leave the state. He'll do whatever it takes to protect her. And he certainly won't tell the police about me! No way he'll volunteer the fact that he has me cabled up here in the trees.

And he has the key to my steel cable around his neck!

I almost panicked. Barzee would leave me here to die.

I lay my head back on the pillow and tried to go to sleep.

Early the next morning, I heard the snap of branches and the crunch of footsteps on dry leaves. Then I heard the soft sound of Mitchell singing as he walked up the hidden trail toward our camp.

My heart sank. He sounded much too happy. I slowly closed my eyes.

Mitchell sat on a bucket to tell us what had happened. He was alone. No Olivia. I wanted to cry with gratitude.

"She is not the one the Lord has chosen to be my next wife," he announced.

Barzee stared at him without reacting. I lifted my hand to hide my smile. *Not the one the Lord had chosen.* Okay. So he ran into a problem. Guess the Lord had changed His mind.

Mitchell went over and poured a long drink of warm water from one of the plastic containers, then settled down to tell his story. And because he liked to talk, he told it in great detail.

After hiking down into the city, the first thing he did was go to the nearest store and plunder a beer. He gulped it by the cooler, then plundered a couple more. Then he made his way to the bus stop. About this time, he needed to relieve himself from the quickly guzzled beer. With no restrooms around, he sat in the yard of the nearest house, slid forward so that his robe would not get wet, and urinated on the lawn. (Gross, but that was like him—part human, part devil, part animal.)

After getting on the bus, he took the long route to Olivia's neighborhood. By the time he got there, it was dark. Still, it was way too early to sneak into Olivia's house to take her. Slinking in the darkness, he made his way to his mother's house and snuck into her side yard, where he and Barzee had left their beloved "hand house," a tiny handmade house on wheels with a bar in the front so that two people could pull it. He and Barzee had pulled this hand house all over the Salt Lake Valley as they had journeyed for the Lord. He crawled into the hand house, slithered under a pile of old clothes, and waited until it was the dead of night.

When it was the darkest and quietest part of the night, he slid out from underneath the old clothes and headed to my cousin's house, a few blocks away. Circling like a wolf, he checked out the house, looking for the best way to get in. He checked all the doors. They were locked. He checked the windows until he found one that was open just a crack. Then, just like he had done at my home almost two months before, he took a patio chair and leaned it up against the side of the house underneath the partially opened window. Climbing onto the chair, he opened the window and cut a long slit in the screen. He stopped and listened. He waited. He heard nothing.

He reached his hand through the slit in the screen to push the blinds back. *CRASH!* Something fell off the windowsill and shattered upon the floor. He froze, not even breathing, his heart pounding in his chest. He listened. No voices or any footsteps. He took a deep breath, then pushed the blinds back once again. Another crash! He had knocked another decoration onto the floor.

Then he heard the sound of footsteps pounding down the hallway. The lights came on and someone started shouting.

Realizing that the Lord had *not* chosen Olivia to be his next wife, he turned and ran, the green bags bouncing like crazy across his back. Running as far as his breath would take him, he finally had to stop and rest.

It took him several bus rides to get back to our canyon, then a long hike back up the trail.

He never spoke of Olivia again.

23.

Barzee Takes Off

———

Mitchell and Barzee were always fighting. You would think that in such an austere situation as we were living in, there would be little to fight about, but they always found something. Lack of food. The condition of our clothing. Whether it was going rain. What to do and when to do it. When to pray and what to pray about. But the main thing they fought about was me. And the reason was pretty simple. Barzee hated me. And Mitchell was never going to let me go.

A few weeks after Mitchell's failed attempt to kidnap my cousin, he and Barzee got into a serious fight. After hours of screaming and cursing, Barzee finally took off, running down the side of the mountain.

We watched her disappear, the sound of her crashing through the brush eventually fading into the distance. I turned to Mitchell. "Will she come back?" I asked.

"Of course she will."

Silence for a moment. I wasn't sure.

"Has she ever taken off like that before?"

"Nope." Mitchell pretended he didn't care.

We waited and waited. No sign of her. I felt creepy, being with him by myself. As much as I hated Barzee, I hated being alone with Mitchell even more. It was like being alone with the devil. It made my skin crawl. Mitchell seemed completely unconcerned that Barzee had run away. Figuring he'd take advantage of the privacy, he took the time to rape me.

The afternoon passed. I could see that Mitchell was starting to get worried.

"Do you think she went down to the city?" I asked.

"Of course not." He brushed off my ridiculous suggestion.

We continued waiting.

Finally, Mitchell decided that we had to go and find her. He walked over to the cable to unlock me.

"Where are we going?" I asked, overjoyed to be free for a moment.

"She must have gone down to one of the other camps," he said.

Mitchell had spoken several times about these other camps. Apparently there were two of them. Both were down the canyon and much closer to the main trail at the bottom of the mountain. Both were outfitted with the necessary supplies; tents, water, tarps. He and Barzee had used them before they had kidnapped me, but never after. They were too dangerous, too close to the city and popular hiking trails.

Watching Mitchell unlock me, my heart started pounding with excitement. *I was going to be uncabled.* That alone was enough to make me want to cry with joy. After nearly two months of being treated like an animal, I can't begin to explain how wonderful it was to have a moment of freedom. And we were going down the canyon. Closer to my family. Closer to civilization. Maybe I would see someone who could rescue me. Maybe I would be found.

But I had already decided that I would never run away. I had tried twice already and both times failed with severe chastening and warnings.

———

Some people wonder how I could have become so subject to Mitchell's will, so utterly submissive and obedient. But when you consider my situation, it's pretty easy to understand.

For one thing, I was only fourteen years old. And I was as naïve as any fourteen-year-old girl could be. My innocence had been torn apart. And it seemed that Mitchell had done it with utter confidence and ease. He had shown the ability to get into my house. To pull me from my bedroom. To keep me in the mountains just a few miles from my home. Time and time again, he would hike down into the city with not a penny to his name, then return with all sorts of alcohol and supplies. He avoided the police. He avoided any suspicion. He seemed to move around the city without any fear at all. He may not have been omnipotent, but he seemed to get away with everything.

Physiologically, I was tattered. I had been tortured for months. Deprived of water. Deprived of food. Treated like an animal. No privacy. No hope. I lived in constant pain from being abused and cabled to the trees. I had been threatened and manipulated every second of every day. Mitchell was the master and I was the slave.

I was also terrified of making him angry. And I wasn't alone. His own family was afraid of him as well, to the point that they had disowned him. His own mother had a restraining order placed against him. He seemed to have lost all of the normal emotions that humans were supposed to feel. He abused me as easily as someone might flick an ant off the kitchen table. And Barzee was no better. She had voluntarily given up her children in order to be with him. She watched him abuse me without any compassion or any attempt to help me. To her, I was nothing but competition for his affections and I believed she would have killed me if he had given her the go-ahead.

And I felt constantly outnumbered. It was one child against two adults, both of whom were evil and full of darkness. But they were not stupid. Especially Mitchell. He was smart. And experienced at his craft. He had been lying and manipulating his way through life for many years now and I was no match for his distortions.

But none of these factors explains the main reason I was so obedient to his commands.

Fear was the reason.

Fear for my own life. Fear for my family.

Terror had been my constant companion from the moment that I opened my eyes in the darkness of my bedroom to see Mitchell standing there. Every moment of every day, I was sick with dread. After a time, that begins to change you. It changes the way you think, your expectations, the things you hope to get out of life. I *knew* that he would kill me if I tried to run away. Nothing could have convinced me that wasn't true. He'd kill my family. I wanted to protect them. *I felt driven to protect them.*

Mitchell would kill my family if I ran, so I wasn't going to run.

As we prepared to go down the canyon, I felt my only hope for escape was that we would, at some point, be put in a situation where someone else could save me. But that process had to be completely out of my control. It couldn't be my fault. I couldn't contribute to my own rescue in any way. Otherwise, Mitchell would blame me. Then he would kill my family, or tell his friends to kill them. And as horrible as my life was, it was far preferable for me to suffer than to hurt those I loved.

We headed down the mountain toward the stream at the bottom of the canyon. For a short time, we walked along the trail that ran parallel to the tiny stream, sometimes crossing back and forth to walk on dry ground. But after a while, Mitchell made us hike back up onto the side of the mountain, then track a different course to the canyon, making our way toward the lower camp. It was hard going, cutting through the mountain oak and brush. Eventually, we made it to the first of the lower camps, a small clearing surrounded by outcroppings of rock. It was almost completely hidden and we had to climb down the side of the sheer rocks before dropping into the camp. Mitchell quickly looked around, searching for any sign of Barzee. He grew very agitated when it became obvious that she had not been there. We climbed out of the camp and headed down the mountain again. It took some real bushwhacking to cut our way across the side of the mountain. I had on some old wool socks and from time to time I would stop and try to pull the burrs and stickers out of them, but eventually I just gave up. They were completely plastered. It didn't do any good. As we got closer to the bottom of the canyon, Mitchell became more and more angry, constantly cursing that we were getting so close to the main trails.

The second camp was located in a small meadow nestled on the side of the canyon. Surrounded by thick trees, this camp, like the previous one, was completely hidden from view. We stopped at the edge of the trees and Mitchell looked around, searching for any sign of trouble before he led me into the camp. The camp was pretty well supplied. A small tent. Water. A few tarps. A couple small plastic containers of camping gear. Mitchell searched through all of their belongings, looking again for any sign that Barzee, or anyone else, had been there. Finding nothing, he stood and looked around, his hands balled into anxious fists.

He stared down the canyon, then back up toward our camp. Then he made his decision. No way he was going to take me any farther down the canyon. It was time to turn around.

"Come on," he mumbled as he passed me. I turned and followed him as we started the long hike back to our camp. I kept my head low, my spirits deflating. Every step took me closer to my prison. Every step took me closer to a life that was killing my soul. Every step was like adding another rock onto an emotional backpack that was already very full.

We eventually made it back to camp. By then, it was getting very late, the last of the sunlight fading through the trees. The first thing Mitchell did was cable me up again. Then he started telling me—again—how each of us had a cross that we must bear, but how much God must have loved me to give me the opportunity to be his wife. While he was talking, we heard someone walking through the trees. Both of us turned to see Barzee emerge from the brush.

Though she didn't seem as angry as she had been before, there was a definite chill in the air. She and Mitchell talked. He reminded her once again that she was the chosen Mother of Zion. He reminded her that she was assured a position up in heaven at the right hand of God, a position right next to the Savior himself, if only she stayed faithful to what God needed her to do.

What a bunch of garbage! I thought as I listened to him talk.

A few days later, we were out of food again. Mitchell was preparing to go down to get supplies when Barzee confronted him. "Why do you get to go down and drink your liquor and get your smokes and do whatever you want to do while Esther and I are left up here to starve, waiting for your return?"

He glared at her but she stood her ground without flinching. "It isn't right. I'm tired of it. I'm not going to do it anymore."

He started to answer, but Barzee took a step toward him, her face as hard as ice. "I'm not going to stay up here and starve while you go down and party," she said with scorn.

And I could tell Mitchell was going to have to back down. Barzee didn't win very many of their arguments, but once she had made up her mind there was no backing down. She was tired of him going into the city and never allowing her to go. It had been going on for months now. Something was going to change.

Which was good. Really good. Because I knew there was no way they would leave me up at camp by myself. Seeing the opening, I started begging him to let me go down into the city too. My mind was racing with possibilities. Maybe someone would recognize me! Maybe someone would rescue me! Maybe Mitchell would, I didn't know . . . get captured . . . have a heart attack . . . decide he didn't want me . . . anything was possible.

I begged and I begged. But Mitchell was having none of it. Both of us were going to stay up in the camp.

"No, Immanuel. I'm not. I'm not going to do it anymore!" Barzee shot back.

It took a lot more pushing, but eventually Mitchell was forced to give in.

24.

Party in the City

Mitchell made me scrape off the nail polish that Mary Katherine had painted on my toes a few days before I had been captured. There wasn't much left, but he didn't want to take any chances. While I scraped the last of the blue polish off, he and Barzee worked together to sew veils that could be buttoned onto the sides of our headdresses. The veils were made of thick, white material and reached from just below our eyes to halfway down our necks, leaving very little of our faces exposed. After they were finished, Mitchell made me put the veil on so he could inspect me. Nodding in approval, he turned and started down the hill.

We made our way down the side of the mountain until we got to the trail, then turned west and started hiking down the canyon. Mitchell led the way, his two green sacks tied across his back. I followed immediately behind him. Barzee walked right behind me. My captors were never more than a few feet away. So close that I could smell them. So close that I could always hear them breathing. So close that, even if I had gathered up the courage, I could not have run away. It was hot, the sun beating through the branches on the trees. I felt like I was suffocating, the thick veil making it very hard to breathe. The heavy robe swished around my feet, kicking up dust that stuck to my clothes. The farther down we hiked, the clearer the trail became.

Crossing over two outcroppings of fractured rocks, Mitchell suddenly turned to the right. "Stay!" he commanded. Climbing to the top of a dirt embankment, he pushed a couple branches out of the way, revealing the "shoe tree." Hidden in a hole in the tree was a pair of sandals for him and a pair for Barzee. (Prophets didn't wander around in hiking boots, don't you know. They had to wear sandals to match their robes.) He and Barzee put on their prophet shoes, then he gave me Barzee's hiking boots and commanded me to put them on. Hiding his boots in the hollow tree, he covered the opening with the rotten sticks and we headed down again.

The canyon began to open up and the trail became well used and clear. Soon it intersected with the main path that ran along the foothills at the bottom of the canyon. This was Dry Creek, a very popular jogging and biking trail. We turned left and kept on walking. Parts of Salt Lake City came into view. My heart jumped in my throat. I was less than a mile from my home! Around a bend in the trail, a jogger emerged, running right toward me. *Look at me!* I was screaming in my mind. *Look at me! Don't you recognize me? Don't you know who I am?* Of course he didn't. He could only see my eyes. To him, we were just a couple of odd ducks dressed in old gray robes and veils. Not the kind of thing one expected to see on the mountain trail, but the scene didn't scream kidnapping! by any means.

The jogger drew closer. I stared at him, never taking my eyes off his face. *Look at me!* I kept praying in my head. *Think about what you're seeing! How many times have you seen this? Two women walking on a trail in Salt Lake City, their faces covered with veils. Look at me. Think about this! Look into my eyes!*

The jogger passed within a few feet of me then moved on, his attention always focused on the trail.

I felt myself deflate, the hope seeping out of my body.

A biker then emerged a little farther down the trail. *Look at me!* I screamed in my mind again. But he didn't. He kept his head down. The only time he even seemed to notice me was when he glanced up to maneuver his bike around us as he passed. He was so close I could have touched him as he rode by. But of course he didn't recognize me. I was nothing but a walking sheet and two eyes above a veil.

Up till that point, I'd had this fantasy that someone was going to see me and immediately scream out my name. Someone was going to rescue me. A cop was going to recognize me and come over and arrest Mitchell without me even saying anything. But I realized now that wasn't going to happen. No one was going to recognize me. No one was going to stop and talk to me. I might as well have been chained up back at camp as walking around, hidden underneath the veil.

As I looked at my captors, it hit me. Our appearance—the robes, Mitchell's wild beard, the veils—invited distance and mistrust. It demanded that we be given a wide berth. Everything about us begged to be ignored.

A little less than half a mile later, the trail broke into the open. The University of Utah campus lay before us. The hospitals and medical center were on our left. Downtown Salt Lake City was on our right. The Jewish Center was in front of us. We hiked through the center's parking lot toward the bus stop, where we caught the first bus and rode it downtown to 400 South. Climbing off the bus, I felt ridiculous. People acted like we were radioactive, staying as far away from us as possible. I shook with frustration. I was back in the city! This was my home. Didn't anyone recognize me? Didn't anyone remember all the posters with my face?

Mitchell stopped and leaned toward me as the bus pulled away. "I will kill you," he sneered as he stared into my eyes. "Remember that, Esther. I will kill your entire family! Your mom. Your dad. Your brothers and little sister. I will kill them all, slicing them with my knife. I will kill them if you try to get away."

Barzee moved so she could whisper in my ear. "He will do it!" she hissed. "You can't stop him. He is Immanuel."

They waited for me to acknowledge them.

Mitchell leaned forward once again. "I will chain you up forever if you don't do *everything* I say."

I slowly nodded. The threat was very clear.

Mitchell stared at me, trying to decide if he believed me. Satisfied, he seemed to smile. "All right then," he said. "The first thing we need to do is get some beer."

He led us to a small grocery store. Walking in, he seemed to know exactly where to go. He walked up and down the aisles, pausing to shove food into his bags. Crackers. Blocks of cheese. Cans of tuna. Cookies and beef jerky. Then he went to the beer cooler and shoved in a couple six-packs of Heineken. His sacks were almost full. I was amazed at how brazen he was about it. My heart was racing—I had never shoplifted before—but clearly Mitchell was not afraid. Grabbing a head of lettuce and a bottle of pickles, he walked up to the checkout counter. Barzee and I followed, never saying anything.

The young man behind the counter seemed to recognize Mitchell. He was a sketchy-looking character. Dyed black-and-purple hair. White skin. Thin as a skeleton. He glanced at the stuffed bags. If he knew that Mitchell had just shoved a bunch of food into his sacks— and he had to have known—he didn't say anything. In fact, he didn't even run the bottle of pickles across the scanner. The head of lettuce was the only thing he rang up. So this is how it works, I thought. Later, he would be Mitchell's source of marijuana—another step in my journey to descend below all things—but for now he was just a "generous" cashier who was willing to let Mitchell shove a lot of food into his bags. He and Mitchell exchanged some talk about a party that was going on that night and then we left.

Mitchell quickly led us toward a public restroom a block or so down the street. When we got there, he went in to make sure it was deserted, then pulled me inside. The restroom was dark and depressing, with black walls and a dark-green ceiling. It smelled of urine and rotting garbage—the perfect place to get me drunk. He forced me to drink a couple of beers. How can anyone drink this stuff for pleasure? I remember thinking as I forced the beer down. I almost gagged, coming very close to throwing up.

With a couple of beers inside us, it was time to get the real party going. Mitchell led us to the nearest liquor store. He went in while Barzee and I waited on the sidewalk. We must have looked ridiculous. *Nothing going on here, you know. Just the prophet's women hanging outside the liquor store while he goes in to get some rum.*

I screamed inside my mind at everyone who passed. *Look at me! Look at my eyes. Don't any of you recognize me?* But everyone was more than happy to ignore us and walk by.

Still, part of me was elated at being in the city. I was away from the camp. I was out in public. Anything was better than being cabled to trees!

Mitchell came out with his purchases stuffed in a bag. "We're heading down to Liberty Park," he said. "Going to drink a little rum and Coke."

We walked down to the park, where Mitchell began to survey his surroundings, looking for anyone he might know. While he checked things out, I sat on a nearby swing and started swaying gently back and forth. Mitchell moved closer to me. Barzee followed, moving to my other side. So there I swung, Barzee on one side and Mitchell on the other. I looked around at the children who were playing all around me. *You are so lucky!* I thought. A few of them seemed to glance at me. All of them were afraid.

Mitchell didn't like being around the other people. "Follow me," he said.

Walking toward the picnic tables, we crossed a small water park with spouting geysers of water coming out of the ground. I took off my shoes and started walking barefoot through the spouts of water, the cool spray upon my feet.

I am alive, but I'm not living, I remember thinking as I walked. I am the living dead. I am nothing but a shell.

I closed my eyes and imagined the water pulling me away, helping me to run away from Mitchell and Barzee forever. I felt the water running over my toes as it moved toward the drains. For a moment, I imagined it sucking the last of my spirit with it, washing my soul away. I wanted desperately to escape, to melt away with the rushing water, never to be seen again. I was a shell already. Why not let my spirit go? Why not let my soul escape into the nothingness that lay wherever the water went? Why not let my soul depart and leave my empty body to go through the motions of living in this world?

Mitchell and Barzee stood at the edge of the water park and watched me. I lifted my face toward the sky, wishing I could feel the sun upon my cheeks. I drifted back in time. I was with my family. I felt their love around me. I felt the peace of being in my home. I felt the comfort of an earlier day and time. Before Mitchell. Before the pain. Before everything that had left my empty body standing in the middle of the water park.

Thinking of my family, I resolved again: *Whatever it takes to survive this. Whatever it takes to live.*

Mitchell pulled me back to this world. "Esther!" he called impatiently. "Come on over here!"

I immediately followed.

He led us toward the nearest picnic table. A family that was close by quickly gathered up their things and moved on. Mitchell took out the rum and Coke and three plastic red cups, pouring us all a drink. And that's how we spent the afternoon. Pretty soon I thought I was going to be sick, and Mitchell finally quit pouring me any more. But he and Barzee kept on drinking, finishing the bottle off.

When the rum was gone, it was time to move on. We walked into the Hard Rock Café to use the lavatory. Because it was a public bathroom and people were all around, Mitchell couldn't follow me into the women's room. But Barzee could and she always stayed very close. Slipping into a stall, I had an idea. Part of my veil had been attached with a safety pin. Quickly, I unsnapped it and started scratching the word "help" into the paint on the door of my stall. My foolish hope was that someone would use the stall immediately after me, see the cry for help, realize it was me, and call the police.

It didn't work out.

Mitchell decided it was time to head back to our camp. We started making our way east, toward the trails. Getting closer to the university, he remembered that Daniel, the generous grocery clerk, had told him about a party that was going on that night. Realizing we were close to the location of the party, he decided we would go. By now I was exhausted. It was late and already growing dark. I hadn't eaten much of anything all day, and the rum was making me feel very drowsy and run-down. I could tell that Barzee didn't want to go to the party either, but she didn't object. She knew she was standing on thin ice and she was careful not to mess up Mitchell's fun.

We found the party house. It was a small brick and stucco structure in an old part of the city, surrounded by huge trees and other small homes set back from the road. By then it was dark, but the house was well lit. And there were lots of people. I mean *lots* of people. Lots of music. Lots of red plastic Solo cups. Lots of beer.

We walked into the house. It was literally body-to-body. There were people everywhere. It was heat and smoke and sweat. Laughter and shouting. Drinking. Smoking. Kissing. And lots of other things I had never imagined before. Things I *couldn't* have imagined. They were beyond my universe. It terrified me to see the underbelly of such a world. Then I had the most horrifying thought of all. Mitchell loved to be the big man, the man with all the answers and the power. What if he started passing me around? What if he shared me with the other men in the room? Maybe even the other women? I pressed against the wall, trying to make myself invisible. And for the first time, I was grateful to have my face covered with the veil.

Ever anxious to be the center of attention, Mitchell moved to the middle of the room and started preaching. Yes, he was a prophet, he told the people who were close enough to hear, but even God ate and drank among the sinners and he was happy to be among the lesser people of the world.

While Mitchell preached, I looked over to see the young man from the grocery store standing next to me. I reached up to lift my veil a little higher on my face. The young man studied me, then moved a little closer. "You have beautiful eyes," he said.

I wanted to faint. No one had ever said anything like that to me before. I realized that he was—I couldn't think of the phrase—coming on to me. I was shocked. For a moment, I wondered if he would have said what he did if he knew that I was only fourteen years old. Judging from some of the things that were going on around me, I don't think he would have cared. I backed away from him, or at least I tried, but I was already pushed against the wall. He leaned in to me again and started to say something when Mitchell suddenly appeared at my side, anxious to keep me under his control.

A glass jar full of a thick, yellowish-white fluid was being passed around the room. Mitchell turned, his eyes fixed upon the glass container. "Absinthe!" he said in glee. The word didn't mean anything to me, but it sure did to Mitchell. He pushed people aside to get in line for the drink. Grabbing the jar, he brought it to me.

"You've got to drink some of this," he demanded.

It looked horrible. Like rotten . . . I didn't know . . . like a mix of spoiled milk and orange juice.

"It's crushed from a special root," he explained, pointing toward the kitchen, where they were apparently crushing more. "You've got to taste it. It causes hallucinations."

I didn't even want to smell it, let alone put it to my lips.

He pushed the jar toward my mouth, passing it under my veil. The rim of the jar touched my lips. It was the most horrible thing I had ever tasted. Rancid as acid. Musky as rotten leaves. It made my lips burn and my throat tighten up.

Mitchell pulled the jar back and took a long drink. He definitely didn't want to share. I watched his Adam's apple bob as he swallowed the bitter liquid down. He drank much more than his share before passing it on, then stepped back to move among the crowd again. A couple of girls came up to talk to me. They seemed to be concerned. "Hey, how are you?" one of them asked, but before I could answer, Mitchell was back at my side. Pulling me to keep me close, he went back to preaching about God and how he had sent his prophet out among the sinners. A young woman with a sword tattoo in the middle of her chest seemed to tire of his preaching.

"Are you Jesus?!" she demanded sarcastically.

"No, but I am his prophet."

She studied his robe and slippers, casting a suspicious eye on me. "Am I a sinner, then?" She swept her arm around the room. "Are all of us sinners? I don't like being called a sinner. None of us do."

A few other people started gathering around. Mitchell, ever anxious for attention, began to preach even louder. An argument quickly developed until another woman stepped up and pulled him by the arm. She seemed to be in charge and she shoved him toward the door. "You are not welcome here!" she shouted, pushing him out of the house. "Go and do your preaching somewhere else!"

"You are my guardian angel!" Mitchell told her again and again. "You have saved me. You have delivered me from danger. You have saved the prophet of the Lord." She didn't seem to be impressed. She shoved him off the porch.

We stood in the front yard for a moment. It seemed that Mitchell was thinking of the next thing that we could do. Barzee was worn out and getting angry. "We're going back to the camp," she said.

Yes, yes, back to camp, I prayed. I was exhausted to the point of feeling sick. We had been walking and drinking all day, and it was very late now. I didn't know what time it was, but it was well past midnight and I was so tired that I could hardly walk.

"We're going back to camp," Barzee said again.

Mitchell only nodded at her blankly. I don't know if he was seeing leprechauns or unicorns, but it was obvious that he was not in this world.

We started walking, dragging our feet along. We got as far as Greek Row, where most of the fraternities and sororities are located on the U of U campus, when Mitchell suddenly sat down and said that we had to rest awhile. He was so drunk and out of it, he couldn't go on. Barzee was furious. For hours she had been trying to get him to go back to camp. She didn't want to go to the party. She didn't want to stay there so long. She didn't want to listen to him preaching, or watch him guzzle whatever concoction was in the jar. Now it was approaching morning, and he wanted to lie down on the side of the road and take a nap! She waited for as long as she could stand it, then stood up and yelled at him. "Immanuel, you are not acting as the Lord's servant!"

You're just noticing that? I thought sarcastically.

"You are not acting like a prophet of God."

Mitchell didn't move.

"Get up!" Barzee started screaming. "Get up, or I'm taking Esther with me and leaving you."

Mitchell looked at her with a drunken and dazed expression. Long seconds passed. He didn't move.

Barzee had had enough. "Esther and I are leaving!" she announced. She grabbed me by the arm. "Get up, you're coming with me." I struggled to my feet. She held my hand and started to pull me back up toward the mountains. We stumbled along, both of us exhausted. Too much walking. No food. Too many parties and too much alcohol. We made it to the main path, stumbling in the moonlight, then walked half a mile or so before turning up the narrow trail that led to our camp. I noticed that it was getting lighter now. Daybreak was not far away. I stumbled on, following Barzee in a stupor, too tired to think about anything but putting one foot in front of the other. Past both of the rock outcroppings. Past the spot where the stream crossed the trail. The eastern sky grew lighter, bringing on the gray light of dawn. We hiked a mile or so farther, then turned and made our way straight up the side of the mountain. There was no trail and we had to cut our way through the brush and trees, the dry leaves crunching under our feet. It was fully light by now. The mountainside grew steeper and I didn't know if I had the strength to climb any longer. Just when I thought I couldn't go on, we broke out of the trees. An open meadow lay before us. I immediately recognized that we were at one of the lower camps. Barzee marched over to where they had hidden their supplies, pulling me along. While she sorted through their gear, I fell in exhaustion on the ground, closed my eyes, and instantly fell asleep. Barzee kicked my feet. "Help me!" she demanded. Together, we set up the small purple tent.

The instant we were finished, I crawled inside and passed out from exhaustion.

I woke up to the sound of voices and a suffocating heat. Late-morning sun seeped through the tent, turning it into a greenhouse. It must have been a hundred degrees inside. I crawled out of the tent, stumbling with thirst. Mitchell and Barzee were talking in the center of the camp. I didn't know it yet, but a decision had been made.

The following day, we hiked up to our campsite, gathered up most of the essential gear, and took it down to the lower camp. Though we would hike up to the springhead almost every day for water, from that day until we moved to California, we stayed at the lower camp.

I was never cabled to the trees again. There was no longer any need. I had reached the point where I was being held captive by Mitchell's words.

25.

Too Scared to Speak

———

A couple of days passed after our first trip down into the city. We spent the first day recovering, then a day or two moving all of our gear down from the upper camp and setting things up in the new campsite. The new camp was much lower on the mountain—I guessed that it was maybe halfway between the city and the high camp—and it had a different feel. The trees were closer together and sometimes you could smell the salt that blew in from the lake. At night, you could see the city lights glow in the western sky and the wind was not quite as strong as it was up near the peaks.

For the first day or two in the lower camp, Mitchell seemed to be on edge, constantly looking down the canyon, his head cocked to listen against the wind. But after a while, he began to relax.

"The Lord had told me something," he announced to us one morning.

I immediately turned to him, my chest growing tight. I felt the adrenaline shoot through my body and my hands begin to shake.

Whenever Mitchell had an announcement, it turned out to be sickening news, and I braced myself for another catastrophe.

He took his time, letting the tension build. It was always the same. Whenever the prophet had received a revelation, it took a little effort to get it out.

I was sitting on the ground in the lower camp. We were sitting in a circle on gray tarp laid outside the tent door. It was midmorning and the sun was just beginning to warm where we sat in the trees. I didn't have the cable around my ankle, and I was grateful for that, but that wasn't enough to make me happy. I was still welded to Mitchell. I was anything but free. His words were stronger to me than any chains or cables ever could be.

While we waited for him to speak, I studied his face. His hair had much more gray in it. It was also growing thinner. So was his face. I turned to Barzee. Same thing. Strands of gray hair. Blotchy patches on her face. It was as if both of them were growing older right before my eyes.

Thirty years. I can outlive him. . . .

It was such a depressing thought.

Then I felt a shiver of warmth and heard a voice inside my head: *No. It won't be that long!*

The feeling took me completely by surprise. And the shiver definitely wasn't from something cold, but something warm. It seemed to seep into my soul, like warm water filling all of the emptiness that I had felt inside. I felt the power of my Heavenly Father near me. I almost started crying with relief.

It won't be thirty years. Stay strong. I haven't left you.

I closed my eyes, thinking back on the time I had stood in the middle of the water park and wished that my soul could slip away.

No. That's not the answer. I will provide a way.

I kept my eyes closed, then took a deep breath. Turning back to Mitchell, I waited for his announcement with new resolve.

"The Lord has veiled the whole of the city's eyes," he finally said. "He wants us to go among the people now. We are free to walk among them. We will rely on the Lord to keep us safe. We'll rely upon the Lord to take care of us and shield us from danger while He tests our faith."

If Barzee had been told about the decision, she didn't show it. In fact, she seemed to be a little surprised.

I stared at him. So he was going to allow me to go into the city all the time now? I almost shrugged. Stay here; go into the city; either way I couldn't run.

I suppose I was a little happy not to have to stay in the camp all the time. It would relieve a little of the boredom. But I hated the thought of having to walk everywhere we went. I hated the thought of going down and getting drunk every day, or going to horrendous parties and dragging home as the sun was coming up.

Mitchell watched me carefully. "All right, then," he said. "We are going down into the city. But you understand the rules, don't you, Esther? I don't have to review them for you, do I? I don't have to talk about your life or the life of your family. You're going to be a good wife, aren't you, Esther?"

I looked at him with blank eyes but nodded silently.

Stay strong. I haven't left you, seemed to roll in my head.

We started making regular trips down to Salt Lake. Sometimes we'd go every day. Sometimes a couple days would pass. Every trip was pretty much the same: drinking, plundering, walking down to either Liberty Park or the Artesian Well to eat whatever we had stolen and then hiking back to the lower camp again.

Every trip pretty much took all day. We were always on foot and even from the lower camp it was a long hike. Occasionally we would ride the bus once we got into the city but we almost always walked, which meant we were walking many miles.

Sometimes Mitchell would preach enough to get a little money. Almost all of it was spent on alcohol and dope, but there were a couple times that he let us go out to eat; once at Chuck-A-Rama, once at the Souper! Salad!, and once at a hamburger and ice-cream place called the Iceberg Drive Inn. I loved being able to go in and eat some real food. Something warm. Something that didn't come out of a cardboard box or a tin can. It was more wonderful than I can explain. But I hated the way that people looked at us; Mitchell in his wild beard and dirty robe, Barzee and me with our white head coverings that entirely hid our hair, our eyes peering above the veils, nothing but our hands exposed. Everyone thought that we were crazy, and they treated us that way. And how could you blame them? This was Utah, not Afghanistan.

Once or twice, someone would come up and ask what religion we belonged to. Mitchell always did the talking. A few of these people would look at me much longer than they looked at Mitchell or Barzee. When they did, I would stare back into their eyes, trying to communicate with them. *Yes! You are right. I am Elizabeth Smart!* But that is as far as it would ever go. Stares. Brief conversations. Nothing more.

Near the end of August, Mitchell started to talk about what we would do for the coming winter. He had started to build a dugout, but it was far from being ready and he didn't work on it any longer. Too much plundering, raping, and drinking to do. We knew we couldn't stay on the mountain. We didn't have any supplies. We didn't live day-to-day, we lived meal-to-meal; there was no way we could survive the winter in the unfinished dugout. No way we could hike up and down the trail every day for food. We didn't have any warm clothes, no winter supplies, no source of heat besides a fire. Utah winters were always brutal, with lots of snow and constant freezing temperatures, especially in the mountains.

Knowing we'd have to make a move before winter set in, Mitchell started talking about the options. He talked about renting an apartment. Wasn't going to happen. No money. And he wasn't going to get a job. He talked about going back to stay with a family whom they had lived with before, one of his friends who had taught him about the medical use of herbs, but quickly realized that wasn't going to work. Even if his friends didn't recognize me, how was he going to explain a fourteen-year-old wife? So he kept working on the problem.

"I thought you said the Lord would provide," I asked him as he debated all his options.

"Oh, He will," Mitchell shot back, "but He expects me to do everything I can to protect myself."

Which was kind of interesting. Mitchell relied completely upon the Lord for the things we needed to survive. Well, the Lord, and a little luck. And a lot of begging. And a lot of stealing. But when it came to any chance of getting arrested or having me taken from him, he wasn't quite as ready to rely upon the Lord.

Which left very few options.

Cold winter . . . lots of snow . . . no food . . . nowhere to live? What was the answer?

To go somewhere warm, of course.

Before we could decide where to go, we needed to do a little research. We needed to do some reading and study some maps.

The next day we headed down from the lower camp and went straight to the Salt Lake City Public Library. Walking through the front doors, I stopped to look around. It was the first time that I had ever been there, and I didn't know where to go. Mitchell seemed to hesitate as well. I glanced toward the ladies at the checkout counter. They tried not to stare, but it was difficult, and it took them a few seconds before they finally turned away.

A man was sitting at a table near the entrance. He stared at us as well. He looked to be in his mid-thirties, just a normal-looking guy.

Looking at me, he pulled out his cell phone and walked out of the library to make a call. I don't know if he was the one who called the police, but I have always thought it was.

Mitchell led us up the stairway to the second floor. He got us settled at a table that was out of the way, then went to work gathering up a series of maps and books for us to study. The library wasn't busy and it was very quiet. A few people climbed up and down the stairs. A young Asian girl, probably a university student, was the only other person in the map section and she paid us no attention once she got past her initial shock at our appearance.

Mitchell spread out a large map of California. Holding the corners, he studied it, moving his finger down the coastline, passing over one city and then another. He talked about each city as he moved his finger south. San Francisco. Sacramento. L.A. San Diego. He spouted a bunch of facts about each of the cities, but I don't know if he really knew what he was talking about. He studied the map a few more minutes, then tapped on San Diego. "Here," he announced. "This will be our new home."

I looked up to see a man approaching us. He was dressed in casual clothes and I thought he was a visitor to the library who was coming to ask a question. "Do you know where the bathroom is?" I expected him to ask.

But he didn't. Drawing closer, he pulled out a badge. "I am a homicide detective. I have a few questions for you," he said to Mitchell.

I thought my heart was going to explode. I turned to him and stared. I started shaking. My head was spinning. I was dizzy with hope and anticipation and gut-wrenching fear. Mitchell's words started screaming in my head. *I'll kill you and your family. I will cut them with my knife!* His threats were the only thing that I could think about, the only thing inside my head.

The officer glanced at me but kept most of his attention on Mitchell. "We've received a few phone calls suggesting this girl might be someone who has disappeared. If you could just allow me to remove the veil and see her face, then we can clear this up. That way, if we get any other calls, we can tell them we have already checked you out."

I felt a surge of joy so powerful I thought that I would cry. I wanted to stand up and run toward the officer. I wanted to jump into his arms. I wanted to rip my veil off and cry upon his shoulders. But I couldn't! I couldn't!

But it didn't matter anyway. He was here. He was strong. He knew what he was doing. He was going to save me now!

I kept my eyes upon the officer. This is it! I thought. Nobody is going to hurt me! No one is going to hurt my family! I didn't say anything. I didn't *do* anything. I've been quiet. I've been good. Mitchell has no reason to blame me. It's over! It's over! I'm going home!

Then I felt a hand clamp down on my leg, the dirty nails digging into my thigh. It felt as cold and hard and powerful as a metal vise.

Feeling Barzee's hand upon my leg made my heart stop. It was like I was instantly transported back in time. Every moment, every detail, of the past ten weeks flooded into my mind. The night that I had been kidnapped. Walking up the mountain. The first time that Mitchell raped me. Being chained up. Sitting on the bucket and crying until Mitchell finally screamed at me to stop. Hearing my uncle's voice calling my name. The helicopter above the trees. Ice-cold water being dumped on my head. Mitchell going down to kidnap my cousin. The taste of beer. The fog of alcohol. The threats against my family or anyone who tried to rescue me. Days of waiting. Days of praying. Months of indoctrination, being told that I came from a wicked and sinful world. Being told my family was paving their own paths to hell. Being told that I should consider myself lucky that I had been chosen to be his wife.

But above all else, I knew the hard grip was Barzee's way of telling me, *It doesn't matter what you say or don't say, it doesn't matter what you do or don't do, if we are captured, we will kill you. We will get you in the end.*

Another painful scene unfolded in my head. I flashed back to the first time that I had met her, the image playing in slow motion in my mind. The silver morning sky. The mountain air, heavy with the smell of pine. My red pajamas hanging at my feet. My heart beating like a hummingbird's. Barzee knew that her husband was about to rape me and yet she didn't care. She had walked up and put her arms around me, her hot breath against my ear. She had held me like a daughter. She knew that I was not a young woman. She knew that I was just a child! But still, she held me tight. And it was not an embrace of warmth or kindness. It was a wrap of power, its only purpose to instill a sense of dominance.

Reliving these emotions, I was overcome with fear. *I will kill you! I'll kill your family.* The words rolled around and around inside my head.

So I lowered my eyes and stared down at the table, never daring to look up at the officer again.

Every particle of my being was on edge. Could the officer protect me from my captors? Could he keep my family safe? I didn't know. I really didn't. He was just one guy against an evil man who seemed to have more power of deception than any other man in the world.

"All I'm asking is that you let me see her face," the homicide officer was saying.

"This is my daughter," Mitchell answered. "I can't allow you to do that. It is strictly forbidden by our religion. It would be against everything that we believe in."

The officer was silent as he thought. I felt his eyes boring into me. Though I kept my eyes down, my ears were fixed on every word he said.

"She is pure now," Mitchell went on. "She is innocent. That is important. Please, I know this must be new to you, but you must try to understand." I quickly glanced toward Mitchell. He was looking straight into the officer's eyes. His voice was calm. Tranquil. Pleasant. He was pleading in great humility. He was gracious to the core.

The officer seemed to be perplexed. "Could I convert to your religion just long enough to see her face?"

"No. It is impossible."

"We've had reports that she might be someone we are looking for."

"I assure you, sir, she is my daughter. I love her very much. I only want to protect her. I only want to keep her safe and pure."

Barzee kept her vise grip upon my thigh, her fingers biting into my flesh. I kept my eyes down, praying the officer would come and rescue me from the hell I had been living every day.

"Let me ask again. I could convert to your religion. All I want to do is to see her face."

I could hear Mitchell move toward me as if he was trying to protect me. "Even if you could convert, that wouldn't be enough. Only her family and her husband will ever see her face. And our religion is not something you can convert to in an hour. Our faith takes a lifelong conversion. Every day we are trying to do better, trying to be more humble and obedient. I am sorry, but your request is impossible."

"You have to understand. We are looking for someone—"

"But officer, if she were the person you were looking for, why would she just sit there?"

The officer paused. It was an impossible question to answer.

I was screaming in my mind: *Because I am completely overwhelmed with fear! Because I have to protect my family! Because I am nothing but an empty shell who can do nothing but what they tell me to!*

Later, there were times when I was angry with myself for succumbing to that fear. But those with shattered souls find it very difficult to speak.

They talked for maybe fifteen minutes. To me, it seemed like fifteen years. The detective asked a few more questions about who we were and what we believed in. Mitchell answered without any hesitation.

He was a wonderful missionary to his own religion when he wanted to be. If he was hiding something, he certainly didn't show it. He was open and sincere and appeared to be without guile. I couldn't believe it! This was the man who raped me every day! The man who stole me from my bedroom. The man who constantly threatened to kill my family. He was as evil and coldhearted as any man in the world. Now he appeared to be as harmless as a puppy, a simple man who was trying to live his religion in a threatening and judgmental world.

Eventually, the officer ran out of questions. He hesitated a long moment. It seemed he was unsure. Then he turned around and walked away, leaving me with the two monsters who had ripped my life apart.

As I watched him go down the stairs, every ray of hope that I had ever felt was instantly wiped away. Every ray of hope that I had for my future was swallowed up by an opaque blackness. I couldn't move. I felt I couldn't breathe. I felt as if every last shred of light had been sucked from my world.

Mitchell stuffed the map of San Diego into one of his terrible green bags, placed the other maps back on the shelf, then rushed us from the library, holding me with a steel grip.

If the officer had stayed around to watch us leave the building, he would have known. If he had seen the way Mitchell jerked me along, treating me like a slave and not a daughter, it would have been obvious. But he was gone. I was alone.

We walked back to camp without stopping to rest. All the way, Mitchell never stopped talking, his voice oozing with pride. "The Lord surely has protected me," he said. "He utterly blinded that officer's eyes."

I kept my mouth shut and kept on walking.

"This thin veil was all it took to hide my Esther." He laughed, flicking the veil before my face. "I am so smart. I am so clever. I told the officer that your husband is the only man who will ever see your face. But the funny thing is, it *was* your husband who told him that."

The farther away we got from the city, the more confident Mitchell became. "I stood face-to-face with a homicide detective," he sneered. "He is trained to look for signs of lying and deception. Yet he believed everything I told him. He looked into my eyes and I convinced him that you were not who they were looking for. I convinced him of that *while you were sitting there.* God has provided another miracle! And why did he do it? Because no one else will ever see my Esther's face until the Lord has called Hephzibah and my seven wives to testify unto a wicked world. Then I will call them to repentance! And that day is very near!"

Then he suddenly fell silent. We walked a few minutes in quiet as he thought. His mood seemed to shift. He was more sullen. He could bask in his own glory only for so long before it hit him. He was a breath away from having lost me. He was a breath away from having been arrested, a breath away from having to spend the rest of his life in prison. The reality seemed to sober him, crushing his mood. "What happened in the library had to be a message," he said. "Surely the Lord is telling me that the world is not yet ready to receive the light in my Esther's eyes. No, we can't take any more chances. We can't do anything so dangerous!" He turned and glared at Barzee, as if it were somehow her fault. "Hephzibah, from now on you and Esther have to stay in camp. No more going into the city. You have to stay up on the mountain until we move to San Diego."

Barzee grunted. She didn't like it, but she knew it had to be that way.

At that moment, I didn't care about anything anymore.

I felt like I was moving through a blur. Though I was walking through my own neighborhood, I saw none of it anymore. The things that used to make me happy, things that used to give me hope, all of these things were invisible to me now. The streets I used to walk on, cars like my family used to drive, flowers that reminded me of my mom . . . all of these things seemed to melt from my sight. I no longer kept an eye out for an opportunity to escape. I didn't even think about it anymore.

I felt nothing but misery. It was maybe the lowest that I had ever felt.

How could the officer have turned around and walked away? How could he not have known that I was the one he was looking for? How could I have been left to live with the devil and hell's mistress?

Hiking up the main trail, I felt like a prisoner walking back to her cell. I was in solitary confinement, with only my guards for company. And I was innocent. *I was innocent!* But no one seemed to care.

26.

California Dreaming

After the crisis at the library, Mitchell seemed to hunker down. Though his initial reaction had been an explosion of pride in his ability to manipulate law enforcement, as well as the realization that there was a certain sensitivity to people's religious customs that would allow him to hide me in plain sight, the reality quickly set in: *He had almost been caught.* Like the hit of a drug, the effect of manipulating the officer quickly wore off, leaving him paranoid and all the more anxious to get out of Salt Lake.

No more was I allowed to go down with him into the city. Neither was Barzee. She had to stay with me all the time, my personal prison guard. But Mitchell didn't back off on the frequency of his own trips into the city. He still had to plunder and minister for food. And he was working hard—okay, he was begging hard—to get enough money for the bus tickets to California. Plus there was the constant demand for alcohol. A few bags of dope from the generous grocer. Pornography. A certain amount of daily needs he had to fulfill.

So he'd go down and do his thing, leaving Barzee and me up at the lower camp by ourselves, where we did . . . well, pretty much nothing. All day. Every day. There just wasn't that much to do when you're confined to a tent and a small clearing in the trees. It was horribly boring. You can't even begin to imagine. We rarely cooked. There was little cleaning. I had read every book they had in camp, and I hated them all. I had read the entire scriptures by now, parts of them many times through. And other than reading, there was nothing else to do.

My life pretty much consisted of three things: getting raped, being forced to drink alcohol, and sitting on a bucket in a clearing in the trees.

But as horribly boring as it was to be left up in the camp, I was still relieved when Mitchell wasn't there. There was the obvious reason that it meant a few hours when I didn't have to wonder when I was going to be raped. Plus, I was just a little more relaxed when he wasn't around. I didn't have to listen to the sound of his constant preaching. His constant talking about himself. The constant singing of church hymns that once I thought were beautiful but now hated to hear sung in his voice. And Barzee was a little easier to live with when he wasn't around. She was always irritable and whiny and as pleasant as a thorn underneath your fingernail, but she was a tiny bit better when Mitchell wasn't leering at me or pulling me into the tent.

But I want to be clear. I never developed any kind of affection for Barzee. She was a monster and I knew that. She never showed me a single moment of kindness. She never demonstrated a single act of compassion or understanding toward me. If Mitchell was the devil, then she was his sneering sidekick. In some ways, I think that she was even worse. She was a *woman*. She was a *mother*. She knew what I was going through.

Still, of the two evils, I'd take Barzee over Mitchell any day.

And anyone who suggests that I became a victim of Stockholm syndrome by developing any feelings of sympathy toward my captors simply has no idea what was going on inside my head. I never once—

not for a single moment—developed a shred of affection or empathy for either one of them. There was no traumatic bonding. No emotional ties. The only thing there ever was was fear, and never anything else. That's the only emotion I *ever* felt toward them.

Sometime during the first week in September, the skies started to grow cloudy. It took a couple of hours for the billowing clouds to build, but they did, growing dark and menacing in the west. A cold wind suddenly blew down the canyon, bringing an instant chill. The clouds grew darker as they started to climb the mountain. The sky was shrouded in mist and the wind began to howl. Evening was coming quickly and the shadows were growing thick and full. Then it hit. Flashes of light. Deep thunder, the air shattered from its power. A hint of rain. And then the hail. Cold, hard, irregular chunks of ice falling from the sky. We ran into our tent for shelter. It was coming down so hard, I wondered if the hail was going to rip the tent apart. We huddled, the tent bent toward the ground, the hail beating down around us.

Once the storm passed, we climbed out of the tent. The mountain was white with a thin layer of hail, and the ground was wet and slippery underneath. And it was cold. It was as if nature had announced the end of summer with a single blow.

Mitchell looked at the sky. "We've got to leave for California soon," he said.

My heart sank, a crushing weight seeming to settle on my shoulders. I had been foolish enough to think that the time to leave for California wouldn't actually come. But it was here now. Soon we would be gone.

San Diego, California. Eight hundred miles from my home. It might as well have been in another universe. I'd be forever lost in California. No one had been able to save me when I was just a few miles from my home. What chance did I have once Mitchell had dragged me off to San Diego? I would lose all hope.

It took us a couple of days to get ready. There was a surprising number of things to do. First, we had to decide what we wanted to take with us and organize it for the trip. Everything we were going to take to California had to be packed in Mitchell's nasty green bags, including our bedding, clothing, the tent, the tarps, all of our food, utensils, and his books. It was not an easy thing to do. Then, once we had decided what to bring, we hiked back and forth between the upper and lower camp, storing all of the other stuff inside the half-finished dugout, trying to hide it from anyone who might happen upon the camp. We also had to protect it against the animals that would be digging around. Finally, we had to wipe away any of the signs that we had been in the camp.

As I watched Mitchell bury the last of our gear deep inside the dugout, I had to wonder, would I ever come back to Salt Lake City? Would he allow us to come back in the spring, or was he hiding all the gear because he knew he would never be back again? Was he hiding all the gear because he didn't want to leave a trail? Because he knew that he would never need it? Would I ever see these mountains or my hometown again?

That afternoon, Barzee and I had our final bath, Mitchell pouring bucket after bucket of freezing water over our heads. We washed our grungy robes in the stream, beating them upon the rocks to get them as clean as we could, then headed back to camp. We were working in the tarped area outside the tent when we suddenly heard voices. They were above us, a little higher on the mountain. And they were walking toward the bowl that hid our camp. Mitchell froze. Barzee's eyes went as wide as saucers. I didn't know what to do. I was so hopeless at this point, so far removed from thinking that I was ever going to escape, that I didn't even think about calling out.

Gathering his wits about him, Mitchell herded us into the tent, hissing at me to be quiet, then scrambled in behind us. He quickly jammed the zipper up, then released a corner of the flap that covered the screen and peered out from the sliver of an opening between the fabric.

Whoever was out there was close enough that we could now understand what they were saying. Two men. Apparently they were college students because they were talking about a test they had just taken. It sounded like they were out looking for some kind of animal bones to take back to the lab. They got closer, breaking from the trees where they could see into the bowl that hid our camp. Mitchell glared at me. I sat without emotion in the corner of the tent. Mitchell threw my headdress onto my lap and I reluctantly put it on. Barzee reached over and secured the veil in front of my face. Mitchell moved to the other side of the tent so he could see them through another slit in the fabric. I crouched and tried to follow him, hoping I could steal a peek, but he pushed me back, almost throwing me to the ground. "Shut up!" he hissed.

As though I had said anything.

I crouched in the corner and listened intently.

The voices suddenly stopped. They must have seen our camp. There was silence for a moment. "Hello! Is anyone home?" one of them called out.

Mitchell glared at me. Barzee moved a little closer. Mitchell pressed his thumb and index finger together then drew them across an imaginary blade, as if he were testing that it was sharp. I lowered my eyes and listened but didn't move.

"Hey there! Anyone home?" one of the young men called again.

Mitchell peered through the slit in the tent, tense as wire, his mind seemingly planning his attack if they were to come into the camp. The air was calm. Not a sound.

The young men started to walk toward the tent and then stopped. "Anyone home?" one of them tried a final time.

No answer. Only silence.

I could imagine what the students were thinking.

They must have felt like they were intruders, like they were trespassing on private property. The camp was well organized and well supplied. It had an air of permanence, like it was someone's home, not just an overnight camping location. If anyone was in the camp, they were obviously hiding in the tent. Clearly they could hear them, but they were not willing to answer—not a particularly friendly thing to do. And the camp was hidden in the trees a *long* way off the trail. Clearly, whoever lived in the camp had come there with the intention of getting away from people. Nothing indicated that they wanted to be disturbed.

Considering all of this, they young men did the right thing. Without saying any more, they turned and walked away.

It was the smart thing to do.

We waited a long time inside the tent, listening for the sound of voices or footsteps on the dry leaves. Convinced they were gone, Mitchell carefully unzipped the door and climbed out. Barzee and I followed. Mitchell stared at where the young men had been standing. No one was in sight. He waited another minute in silence. I carefully removed my veil.

"That was our sign," Mitchell announced. "The date that I have chosen is acceptable to the Lord. It is time for us to go."

Two days later, Mitchell had us up before dawn. We hiked down the trail in the darkness. All of us had to help carry the green bags, for they were bursting with our supplies. In addition, Mitchell had added a small supply of crackers, a bit of cheese, some water, a couple of plates, and a few utensils.

Is this the last time I will ever walk this canyon? I wondered as we stumbled in the dark.

Exiting the trail, we caught the University of Utah shuttle down to Rice-Eccles Stadium and walked downtown to the bus depot. Halfway to the bus stop, I was already very tired. And I felt ridiculous. Not only did I have the sheet across my face, but Mitchell had ordered Barzee to sew a thin veil in front of my eyes, leaving my face completely covered. I could see through the thin material, but only barely, and I felt claustrophobic peering through the veil.

It took us until midmorning to make it to the bus stop. We entered and moved toward a small bench along the far wall. Mitchell commanded us to stay there while he went to buy our tickets. The bus terminal was crowded with all sorts of people. Young and old. All sorts of nationalities. Most of them—no, all of them—were poor. Middle-class and rich Americas don't ride the Greyhound anymore.

Mitchell stood in line at the ticket window. Barzee didn't pay him any attention. She had been ambivalent about the move to California, and I think she was already tired of the work. Being out in public changed her relationship with me. Up on the mountain, I was her slave. She could boss me around, make me haul the water, cook, do most of the work. But she had to pitch in to help now and that bothered her a lot. Her body language was unmistakable. She simmered. Was it really appropriate for the future *Mother of Zion* to be hauling packs around?

While she seethed, I had time to look for any friendly faces in the crowd. When someone caught my attention I tried to stare at them, hoping I could communicate with just my eyes, even through the thin veil. I was still praying for someone to rescue me, for someone to recognize me and whisk me way. A middle-aged black woman seemed to look at me. I thought I caught a hint of a smile. Maybe she's a mother. Maybe she understands what trouble looks like? Maybe she will see the desperation in my eyes. I stared at her, praying she would recognize me.

Glancing at me, she got a sour look on her face. "What are you staring at!" she sneered. "Don't you know that's rude! And why don't you take that rag off your face!"

I looked away. I felt ashamed. I felt rejected. I felt my hopes were being shattered once again.

It was the last time that I ever tried to communicate with someone through my veil.

Mitchell came back to us with the bus tickets. He was so proud. His ministering had paid our way to California. The Lord had provided once again.

A few minutes later, we started boarding. There were only two seats on each side of the bus and Mitchell pushed me toward a window seat, then dropped into the seat beside me. Barzee sat in front of us with the green bag that held our meager supply of food. Mitchell didn't even wait until the bus pulled out of the depot before he reached up and took some of the food out of the bag and started stuffing his mouth with crackers and cheese.

I was worried. No, it was more than that. I was terrified.

I had already felt real hunger and I didn't want to feel it again. And at the rate Mitchell was eating, our food would be gone before we made it to Nevada. What would we do then? It had taken almost every penny that we had to buy the bus tickets to California. We were leaving the generous grocer behind. We were leaving behind all of Mitchell's friends. Mitchell didn't know a soul in San Diego. Where were we going to stay? How were we going to live? How would we get more food?

Mitchell must have been in an especially good mood that we were finally getting out of Salt Lake City because he passed me a few crackers and some cheese.

"Maybe it would be better if we didn't eat right now," I said. "Maybe we should save it until we really need it."

Mitchell and Barzee acted like I wasn't there.

I thought about trying to save some of the food, but changed my mind. Better to eat some while I could.

The bus was crowded. I thought it smelled bad, but maybe that was just Mitchell. The bus pulled out of the station, black smoke belching from the exhaust pipes underneath us. We rode south, through Salt Lake City and then Provo, seventy miles of nothing but cities and bedroom suburbs. On the other side of Provo, we started to hit the rural counties where there were miles and miles of nothing but sagebrush, juniper-covered mountains, and barren desert. Every passing mile took me farther and farther from my home. Farther from my family. Farther from the people I loved.

We continued through central and southern Utah. The great rock country outside of Zion National Park. We stopped in some of the larger towns. A few people got off. A few people got on. The ride seemed to take forever. The bus driver was a pleasant woman who would jump on the intercom from time to time to tell us bus jokes. I almost smiled. I didn't know there was such a thing as bus jokes. We passed over the Utah border. Will I ever be home again? I wondered. It was starting to get dark. We rode through a few miles of Arizona before the freeway turned west and dropped into Nevada. I leaned against the window and watched the passing terrain. Not much to look at. Nothing happening out there.

In the middle of the night, we stopped in Las Vegas to change buses. A lot more people got off the bus than got on. For the rest of the ride to California, I had a row to myself. I know it wasn't much, but I was grateful for the space. Mitchell, always a very light sleeper, seemed to jerk and wake up every time I even moved. No way he was going to let me slip off the bus in the middle of the night.

We finally made it to San Diego. It was still dark, but the eastern sky was turning a shade of gray. We stepped off the bus into a thick mist. I looked down the street. The roads were shrouded in heavy fog. Every streetlight formed a perfect circle in the yellow light, each one a little smaller the farther they were from me. I began to shiver. It was so clammy. So unfriendly and depressing.

Mitchell studied the metro map on the wall outside the bus stop, then pulled out the map he had stolen from the library, his eyes moving back and forth. Finally, he turned to us and said, "Lakeside is where we will go."

27

Fire Swamp

———

We boarded the metro and rode all the way to El Cajon, which was the last stop on the line. Watching the people, I realized I could expect the same kind of treatment in California as I had experienced in Salt Lake. The people stared at us, giving us plenty of space, pulling their children away. To them, I was just another stranger on the metro. Yes, I might have been a whole lot stranger than some of the others, but I was nothing they would remember. At the end of the day, they'd go home. They'd go on with their lives. But not me. I was trapped. I was never going home.

It took about two hours to get to the end of the line. It seemed like it took all day. After the all-night bus trip from Salt Lake City, we were all exhausted and mostly rode in silence. But it was obvious that Mitchell was in a good mood. The burden of the prophet was much lighter now that he had put some distance between himself and the law.

I couldn't help but see the symbolism in riding to the end of the metro line. That was exactly how I felt. I was at the end of the line.

So far from home. So alone and isolated. Already I was so homesick that I wanted to cry.

I hadn't realized how much comfort I had taken from the fact that, even if I was nothing but a prisoner, back in Salt Lake I was within a few miles of my home. I always had the hope that someone might stumble upon our camp and save me, that there were still some people looking for me, that somewhere I might be recognized and rescued. At one point—according to Mitchell, at least—there had been a huge effort to find me. Maybe there was a little bit of that still going on. Maybe I would still get lucky. But I knew that was infinitely less likely now that I was in California. No one knew me here. No one would recognize my face. I might as well have been riding the train to another planet.

After stumbling off the metro at the last station, Mitchell studied a map that showed the bus routes and got us on the right bus out to Lakeside. We bounced along for a while. Only a few passengers were on the bus. All of us were quiet.

Climbing off the bus, I took a look around.

Lakeside, California. My new home.

I didn't know it yet, but I was about to enter a new phase of my capture. Mitchell had never really cared if I was fed or cold or hungry, but he was about to set a new standard in neglect and abuse.

Lean days were coming. I was about to find out what real hunger was.

I stood on the road where the bus had dropped us off and took in my new surroundings as best as I could through my stupid veil.

I had expected to see a beautiful mountain lake surrounded by pine trees and white aspen. That was hardly the case. What I saw was a small man-made pond with a stubby boardwalk wrapped around it. A few ducks. A single black swan. A couple of people out for a walk. And we were hardly in the forest. Across the lake there was an old convenience store. Wrigley's was its name. Next to Wrigley's was a liquor store. Great. That was going to make Mitchell really happy.

Later on, I would find that the small town had a tiny library and an old grocery store that was run by a Muslim man who was always very friendly. I don't think he ever let Mitchell plunder like the guy back in Salt Lake did, but he was always kind to me, and he let us scavenge in the garbage for food. And he sold handmade tortillas. When Mitchell was flush with cash—meaning we had a couple dollars that he hadn't spent on booze—we'd go into the grocery store and buy some of his warm tortillas. I'd spread a little butter across the top and sprinkle on some sugar. I thought it was one of the best things I had ever tasted.

Lakeside had a couple fast-food places and, a little farther down the street, a much larger grocery store named Vons. And there was a small Protestant church. What a godsend! The people who ran the church were simply angels. Once they gave me some frozen tortillas. I was so hungry, I gulped them down like some kind of flatbread Popsicle. More important, behind their building, they had placed a worn-out plastic crate in which they left old bread they had gathered up from the local grocery stores so that people like me could have something to eat.

That first day, we walked over to the pond, our green sacks over our backs. We placed our belongings on the ground, then Mitchell turned to us and said, "I need to go and find a place for us to live. Hephzibah, you stay and keep an eye on Esther."

I remember watching him head off. How long is this going to take? I wondered. An hour? Ten hours? A couple of days? How does one show up in a new city, homeless and without any food or money, and find a place to live?

I settled onto the dry mud near the pond to wait, figuring it would be a while. It was a sunny day, warm and pleasant, and I was content to sit on the ground and watch the people go by.

I didn't have to wait very long. Maybe twenty minutes later, Mitchell came back. Seeing him walking toward us, I expected him to announce that this wasn't the place and that God had commanded him to move on. But as he got closer, I could see he was excited. "I have found the perfect place!" he announced.

We gathered up the green bags and started trudging after him. As always, I was walking in the middle, with Mitchell ahead of me, Barzee just a few feet behind. We headed up a hill and crossed the highway. We walked past the El Capitan High School, past the school's sports fields, and then a BMX bike park. There we came to an old sand levee with a spillway. Everything was covered with so much dust it almost made it hard to breathe. Mitchell ducked into some wispy willow trees that covered the steep embankment. The trees were so old, I couldn't tell if they were alive or dead. Cracked with age, their dry branches hanging down like bony fingers, they appeared to be completely leafless. Instead, they were covered with little hanging brown things that looked like worms. I reached out to touch one and it crumpled at my touch. It seemed that half of the wormy things fell off the trees as we walked underneath them, filling my hair with brown chalk.

I felt like I had entered the fire swamp from *The Princess Bride.*

This might be the only place on Earth that has never seen any water! I thought, already feeling homesick for our camp back in the mountains.

Mitchell led the way across the levee, then pushed us up the other side of the embankment where the ground was flat. More dead trees. More of the fire swamp.

"Here," Mitchell said.

It was incredibly discouraging to see the place that he had picked. There were so many branches, old logs, and twigs that I didn't know how he could possibly expect us to find a place to set up camp. But Mitchell was acting like a schoolboy at recess, smiling and so excited about our new hideout. He went to work, clearing an area of old branches and a million twigs, cutting away what he needed to in order to set up our tent. As he cut away the logs and branches, he piled them on the side of the campground that was nearest to the road, creating even more of a barrier to hide us. The road was only twenty or thirty yards away but, between the old trees and Mitchell's barricade, by the time he was finished we were completely hidden. After clearing away the debris, Mitchell got out his trowel and started digging, chopping at the ground to level it. Then he laid out two tarps, placing them so that they were slightly overlapping. He wandered off into the brush, looking for some branches that were not so brittle that they would snap in his hands. Dragging them back into the clearing, he started tying the branches together to make an arch. Then he made another. Once he had completed half a dozen arches, he drove them deeply into the ground, then took our largest tarp and draped it over the arches, creating a large tent that looked like a gray tunnel. He staked the tent into place. Even though the camp was bone-dry, Mitchell knew the rains would come, so he rolled up the edges of the tarps and jammed small sticks underneath them to form a lip just inside of the overhanging tarp. Then he dug a narrow trench around the outside of the tent to funnel the water away. Finally, he cut our last tarp in half and hung a piece at both ends of the tunnel.

Straightening up, he studied his work. Our new home was complete.

After clearing another space, he began to set up his own tent. When he was finished, he stood back and proclaimed his new temple. "This will be the Altar of Immanuel," he said.

The Altar of Immanuel. Wow! What was I supposed to think? It sounded like something out of a comic book. It was creepy and sacrilegious. It was arrogant and misogynistic and it made my skin crawl.

I noticed him steal a quick look at Barzee. She glared at him and nodded.

"Now that we have a new home, it's time to make some other changes," he announced. "From now on, we're going to stick to a schedule."

Apparently Barzee was angry (again) that he was constantly coming after me and ignoring her. Feeling forgotten and resentful, she had demanded that something change. No one asked me, or I would have desperately insisted that he should focus *all* of his attentions on Barzee. Cut me off completely. I'd have been the happiest person in the world. But no one asked me. And that wasn't Mitchell's intention.

Knowing he had to do something to pacify Barzee's wrath, he had come up with a plan.

"You're going to start taking turns sleeping with me in the Altar of Immanuel," he said.

I only have to sleep with you half of the time now! I thought. It was the greatest thing I had heard since the night I had been taken.

And that's what we did. For about two days. Then, to my utter disgust and disappointment, our schedule quickly migrated to where Barzee was "his" in the daytime, and I was "his" at night. But Mitchell was gone most of the day. Then, after a long day of plundering, ministering, and drinking in San Diego, he'd come home just in time to lead me to his altar, leaving Barzee simmering outside.

After a few weeks of this, Barzee demanded another change in the schedule. Mitchell promised to do better. But nothing ever changed. One way or the other, I was always in the altar, and Barzee was always left outside.

A day or two after arriving in Lakeside, we went to the local Walmart. Barzee and I were wrapped up in our robes and covered with our veils. Mitchell bought a few things and stole a few others: bedding, cheap pale green comforters and flannel sheets that were decorated with the image of a moose.

Across the highway from our new home was a small park where people would come to fly their model airplanes. Between the park and our hideout was an open patch of dirt with tons of cacti. One day Mitchell came back from his wanderings with a few prickly pears he had picked in the open field. Vicious little things, with tiny sliver needles that would stick painfully in your skin, they ranged in color from deep purple to yellowy-orange. None of us had ever eaten one before, so it took a little bit of careful prodding before we figured out how to cut them open and extract the fruit. The meat was slimy and filled with tiny seeds. I watched as Mitchell took the first bite, hoping it was poison. He chewed and swallowed without falling over. Bummer. But at least we had something to eat. He cut a piece for me and I ate it. It wasn't really good, but it wasn't terrible. For a long time, I tried to extract all of the tiny seeds and spit them out, but there were so many of them I eventually gave up and just ate them.

I turned to look at the field. It was full of prickly pears. But we didn't know how long the season would last, so Mitchell went out and picked as many as he could. Once I became accustomed to the slimy fruit and got over my objection to eating the seeds, I actually came to like them. We ate them a plateful at a time and, over the next few months, they turned out to be the main staple of our diet. The only problem was, no matter how careful I was not to touch the outer skin, it seemed like I spent half the day picking tiny slivers out of my hands.

Once we got set up in our new home, Mitchell really hunkered down. It became obvious that even though we were a long way from my home, and it appeared that no one was looking for me in California, the episode at the library had changed him. He was cautious to the point of being paranoid. Because of this, Barzee and I were only allowed out of our hideaway once a week. One day a week to leave my hot and dusty prison. One day a week to get away from the smell of blue plastic and warm water. One day a week to see someone besides my prison guards. My routine was very simple. Boredom. Hunger. Rape.

Sometimes Mitchell would bring us food, but it was sporadic and unpredictable. Soon, I was living with the pangs of hunger all the time.

I loved going out, not because I had any hope of being rescued but because I was desperately bored. Day after day, I sat and dreamed of getting out of the blue tent. I dreamed of getting out of the fire swamp, of seeing anyone besides Mitchell and Barzee. I desperately needed to be reminded that there was a real world out there. And even if I couldn't be a part of it, even if I couldn't do anything more than pass through it like a white-robed ghost that no one was willing to acknowledge, anything was better than sitting underneath the blue tarp day after day.

On some of the days that I was allowed out of the fire swamp, we would sit and watch the high school kids out on the sports fields. That should be me, I thought as I watched in misery.

But even though it was hard to watch the other kids, being in the world seemed to make me feel better. It reminded me that it was still there. And it rekindled the hope that one day I might actually be a part of it, not just someone who had to watch it from behind a veil.

Shortly after we arrived in California, Mitchell announced that our drinking days were over. Not a chance, I thought. And I was right. I don't think he went more than a day without drinking. It turned out that what he really meant to announce was that *Barzee's* drinking days were over. Every day he would go out and come back with a bottle of vodka, gin, or rum, but he always drank it by himself. Barzee felt this was ridiculously unfair. So she confronted him.

"You're either going to give up alcohol like you said we were, or you bring home enough for all of us!" she demanded.

There was no more pretense. No more submissiveness or piety. She wanted to get drunk and she wanted to get drunk all the time. Which showed that things had changed. There wasn't as much talk about being God's holy servants. Not as much talk about descending below all things in order to rise above all the sins of the world. Not that either of them had given up on the religion thing—the only subjects we ever talked about were religion, the impending end of the world, Mitchell being the "Davidic king," and Barzee's guaranteed place in heaven—but I think both of them just felt there wasn't as much need of pretending as there had been when we were living back in Utah.

A couple of nights later, Mitchell came home with a bag of Kentucky Fried Chicken and a twelve-pack of Steel Reserve sixteen-ounce beers.

I was about to find out that the beer in California was a lot stronger than the beer in Utah was.

We started passing around the chicken and the beer. Mitchell forced me to drink, making sure I swallowed every ounce of my beer. Then he passed me another can. I was already thinking that I was going to throw up. Meanwhile, he and Barzee were having a jolly time. Beer and KFC. The perfect night. I sipped, hating every swallow. Mitchell kept forcing me to swallow more.

By the end of the second can, I was in really bad shape. He handed me another beer. I knew there was no way I was going to get any of it down. I stumbled to the ground, and crawled off to a corner of the tarp. I laid there, listening to Mitchell and Barzee talking about how much more they liked California beer. They didn't even seem to notice that I was lying on the ground. After a while, Mitchell finally looked at me. Seeing I was sick, he threw me a metal bowl. I held it to my face. The metal was cool against my skin. It felt good. I waited, fighting to hold my stomach down. Mitchell must have decided either that I wasn't going to throw up or that he didn't want to get the bowl dirty, because he came over and took the bowl away. Almost immediately, I started throwing up. I wretched so long and hard that I thought I was going to die. Then I passed out.

I woke up late the next morning, facedown in my own vomit. It was the most horrible and disgusting feeling I had ever felt.

As a young Mormon girl from Salt Lake City, a young girl who had promised herself that she would never even taste alcohol, I had never imagined that I would find myself in such a degrading situation. If Mitchell wanted me to descend below all things, then surely I had done that. I was sick and devastated. Words can't explain how humiliated and disgusted I felt.

I used what little water we had to wash myself up. Mitchell laughed at me as he watched me trying to clean myself off. "You know, this is symbolic of where you are spiritually," he mocked with glee. "My little Esther, facedown in her own vomit! That is where you are now."

For the next couple of months, Mitchell would go into San Diego and "minister" almost every day. I don't know what he did with the money, I just know he never brought any of it home. He must have spent all of it on cigarettes and alcohol, because when he came back he always stank of both.

I do know that he didn't spend any of his money on food. The only thing we ate for months was the prickly pears, old bread from behind the church, and whatever food we pulled out of Dumpsters and garbage cans.

My mother always taught me that we needed to finish everything on our plates before we left the table. But I have to say that I am grateful for those people who threw away their food. Their scraps helped to sustain me for many months.

28.

Thanksgiving

———

Time moved forward one painful day at a time. Late summer melted into fall. The weather in Lakeside was generally pleasant, and I could see the wisdom in having left the mountains of Utah, which I knew would already be draped in snow. But I always felt homesick in California. I hated being so far from my home. And everything about our camp had an eerie feeling about it. The dead trees. The dust and cacti. The brown things that were hanging from all the branches. And I thought it was odd that there we were, living just a few feet off the main road and only a short walk from a large high school and the center of the town, yet no one seemed to know we were there, or if they knew, they didn't care.

As the days grew shorter, I realized that the change of seasons was under way. I thought back on the night I had been taken. June 4. It had been the beginning of the summer. I was young enough that three months of vacation felt like a *very* long time. I was looking forward to endless days of swimming with my cousins and jumping on the trampoline and summer parties with my family and celebrations on the Fourth of July.

All of it seemed so long ago. Another world. Another girl.

As Thanksgiving approached, I tried desperately not to think about my family. The only thing I thought about was that we might find a good meal.

Thanksgiving dawned gray but warm. Feeling magnanimous, Mitchell agreed to take us into the city. We got dressed in our robes and veils, then took the metro downtown. But we didn't go all the way into the city. Instead, we stopped at a metro stop on the outskirts of town. Mitchell had already scouted out our Thanksgiving meal. The HomeTown Buffet was offering a free meal for the homeless and the down-and-out. It was a traditional holiday meal: turkey, potatoes, gravy, and dressing.

I have never enjoyed a meal as much as the one I ate on the vinyl seats stuffed between other homeless people at the HomeTown Buffet.

For dessert, we took the metro to Lemon Grove and walked a short distance to a grocery store named Dave's. They sold a lot of health foods (images of the health-food store in Salt Lake City flashed through my mind) and were famous for their pies. Mitchell went in and bought a pumpkin pie for us to share. It was such a treat! Then we took the metro into San Diego and started wandering the streets. We didn't have anywhere to go, so we weren't in a hurry, and I was very glad to be out from underneath the blue tarp. We were walking along the boardwalk, the kind of place that families and tourists like to go, when I saw an old couple walking hand in hand. They smiled at each other and spoke in the short sentences that made it clear that they understood each other well. I couldn't help but stare at them. They seemed so happy. So in love. So *normal*.

I wondered what their story was. How had they fallen in love?

How many children did they have? Had they always been as happy as they seemed to be now?

A blanket of sadness hit me, settling deep into my soul. I'm never going to have such happiness, I thought. I'll never have such a life. I'm nothing but a slave to these two people who are keeping me so close. By the time I can get away from them, it will be too late. No one will ever want me. I will be too old. And after all the things that have happened to me, no one will be willing to give me a chance. I'll never have a real husband. I'll never have any children of my own.

Depressed by such thoughts, I put my head down and followed Mitchell. We walked downtown. It seemed like we ran into a lot of homeless people. I don't know why; maybe they were out for free meals or maybe Mitchell just had a way of attracting his kind of people.

"You know about the truck that's going to bring Thanksgiving dinner?" a homeless man said to Mitchell.

We didn't know. The old man told him. Mitchell was thrilled. More free food. He got the address and we started walking. Sure enough, not long after we got there, a large pickup truck with lots of silver containers in the bed showed up. But they weren't organized, there were no policemen or security, and it quickly turned into pandemonium: screaming, shoving, arguments that escalated into fights, people scrambling over turkeys, tearing them apart with their bare hands while others grabbed entire containers of food and ran. By the time we worked our way through the mayhem to the truck, the only thing that remained was a bunch of empty trays. I could still smell the fragrance of cooked turkey in the air. I could see white lines of mashed potatoes that had been spilled on the ground, kernels of corn that had been scattered everywhere. I was crushed. I had been so hungry for so long and for so often, the thought of a wasted meal was something that was hard for me to take.

It was starting to get dark. With no food to eat, and with nothing else to do, Mitchell and Barzee shepherded me back to camp.

That night, I lay atop my makeshift bed and thought, It's Thanksgiving. You're supposed to count your blessings. But did I have anything to be thankful for? I wondered.

At first, I didn't think so. Then I started to make a list.

I still believed in God. I knew He was the Savior of the world. And I knew that He was near, I felt His presence every day. He was the only reason I had been able to keep my sanity. He kept me strong and gave me hope. Nothing that Mitchell could ever do to me could take away my faith.

Yes, that was something to be thankful for.

I still had a family. I didn't get to be with them, but someday I thought I would.

Another reason to be grateful.

I was hungry, but I was healthy. And though I didn't get any dinner, I had been able to eat lunch at the HomeTown Buffet, which had turned out to be a really great meal. Millions of people around the world hadn't eaten anything all day.

My list went on. . . .

One day I would be able to get away from my tormentors.

One day I would be free.

The gray tent kept the sun off.

The trees around our camp kept the wind at bay.

I kept adding to my list of blessings until I eventually fell asleep.

29.

Another Girl

—

One day in late November, long after we had settled into a routine, Mitchell returned from ministering. He had that kind of evil look that I had come to know so well. Lustful. Entitled. Excited. "The time has come," he announced. "The Lord has prepared us. We are ready. I must go forth and obtain another wife."

My stomach dropped into my lap and I felt the blood begin to pound in my head. *Another wife. Another victim.* The thought made me want to scream.

Mitchell looked at me, waiting to see how I'd react. I stared at him in shock. What did he expect me to do? Smile and clap my hands? Agree with him? Encourage him? Did he think that I was like Barzee? Did he think that I was going to say it was okay! I couldn't meet his eyes, I was so angry! And in that moment, he knew he couldn't trust me. Which was perfectly fine with me. I hated this man. He was the devil. I didn't want to be trusted by him.

All of us were silent for a moment. Clearly, this was news to Barzee. But she didn't react. I thought it was incredible. It was as if Mitchell had come home and announced that he was going shopping.

Hey, I think it's time I got a new robe.

Hey, I think it's time I got a new wife.

It seemed to be about the same thing to her.

He watched me carefully, seeing the anger in my eyes, then went on. "She has to be a Mormon. And young and pure. I want her to be like you, Shearjashub."

I cringed at the name. They had started calling me Shearjashub again shortly after we'd moved to California. They knew I hated it. But they thought it would help me forget my old life and my home.

"I'm going to visit all the Mormon churches in El Cajon until I find her," Mitchell concluded. "Then I'll have to find out where she lives. Meanwhile, we'll prepare the same as we prepared for you, Shearjashub."

You might prepare! *I* won't prepare a thing! I thought.

"Why do you have to go all the way to El Cajon to find a wife?" I asked.

Mitchell looked at me as if I was stupid. "First of all, it needs to be far enough away that none of the searchers will stumble into our camp. Second, there probably aren't any LDS churches any closer than that. Like I said, she has got to be a Mormon. So that is where I will go."

The next Sunday, he got ready to go hunting.

I remember watching him search through the fire swamp for normal clothes that he could wear. Apparently God could command him to move mountains, part the seas, or call down fire from heaven, but He couldn't help to hide his identity when He sent his servant out to steal a new wife. That being the case, Mitchell knew he couldn't be kidnapping girls in his white robes. He would be way too easy to remember. Way too easy to identify. And it wouldn't do to show up in church dressed as an ancient prophet. Mormons weren't going to go for such a thing.

So he searched through our meager belongings for something normal that he could wear.

Over the past couple months, as Mitchell had wandered here and there around the city, he had stumbled on several deserted home-less camps. Rummaging through the junk and clothes that had been left behind, he had salvaged a few moldy blankets to hang in the trees around our camp. (Most of the little wormy things had fallen off the trees and we weren't hidden as well as Mitchell had wanted us to be.) Along with the blankets, Mitchell had scavenged some ragged khaki pants and an old purple shirt that was so faded it was the same color as the pants.

Mitchell came out of the Altar of Immanuel with his new clothes on. He had cleaned himself up as best as he could, tying his hair into a ponytail and twisting his beard into a braid that was wrapped right up to his chin.

I watched as he checked his clothes. Then he pulled the blanket back and walked out of the camp.

All day long, I waited for him to come back. My mind was in a panic, horrible thoughts racing through my brain: What will I do if he comes back with another young girl? What will I do when he tries to rape her? Will I be able to stop him? Will I be able to stand up to him and Barzee? Will the girl trust me? Will we be able to escape together?

Then I had the most sickening thought of all: What if I don't do anything? What if I just step aside and let him do to her what he did to me?

I couldn't stop the horrible thoughts going through my mind. By the time the sun went down, I was so sick with worry and lack of food that I almost didn't have the strength to stand.

A couple hours after sunset, we finally heard the sound of some-one winding through the fire swamp. The blankets were pushed aside and Mitchell was standing there.

I immediately recognized the smug look on his face.

He sat down to tell his story.

"I got to El Cajon and headed to the Mormon chapel. To my disappointment, the first congregation I went to was a Spanish-speaking group. And there were no young girls among them anyway. So I waited around until the next congregation came into the building." Mormon congregations are able to share the same buildings by starting their worship services at different times. "I went into the church and kind of looked around, like I was lost and lonely. Some people came up to talk to me. They invited me to the men's study group. All through the lesson, I almost had to laugh. They were treating me like I didn't know anything, when I am the Davidic king! The Lord's prophet here on Earth! What did they think they could teach me?

"Once that was over, I headed with the rest of the crowd to Sunday school, where the lesson was on Daniel in the lion's den. The silly little Mormon missionaries kept trying to pull me out of Sunday school to attend their special class but I told them I wanted to keep learning about Daniel. Those young fools. What do they know about anything?

"I do think, however, that the lesson was inspired. Is there any doubt that I was just like Daniel in the lion's den? There I was, all of these wicked souls around me, all of these wicked and nasty people who would have torn me apart had they known what I intended to do to one of their children.

"Finally, we went in to sacrament meeting. But again, I was disappointed. There were no acceptable young girls in sight! I started to think that maybe it was not the time yet. Maybe the Lord was just testing my faithfulness. Maybe it was a test like Abraham and Isaac.

"After the meeting was over, I was walking through the parking lot when a car pulled over and the window rolled down. A man who had sat by me in one of the meetings stuck his head out and invited me to come home to have dinner with his family. You should have seen the meal. It was beautiful! Chicken covered in almonds and sauce, green beans, mashed potatoes, and dessert!"

Mitchell stopped to look at us and gloat. He licked his lips for effect. "It was delicious," he said.

I turned and looked at Barzee. She was furious. And so was I.

Here we were, trapped in the fire swamp for weeks, sitting on buckets and homemade chairs, surrounded by filthy, smelly blankets and creepy overhanging trees. We had not eaten all day. We'd been eating poorly for months. The thought of a home-cooked meal sounded like a miracle to us. Barzee swallowed her anger and neither of us said anything.

Mitchell went on in his self-righteous voice, the voice he used after he had just talked to God. "I learned that they have a daughter. She will be my next wife."

Barzee stared at him in rage. "You ate without bringing us any food?" she hissed.

I shook my head at the bitter irony. Her husband had just told her that he had found another wife, and the only thing that she could think about was the fact that he had eaten without bringing her any food.

Mitchell looked at the ground in fake humility. "The Lord blesses those of us who are faithful. And because I was faithful, He revealed that their daughter was to be my next wife. Then, after I had received this revelation, the Lord gave me His approval by providing a sumptuous feast."

Barzee lifted her fist and cried, "Do you think nothing of me? You go out and stuff your face full of food and then come back and gloat about how good it was when you know I haven't eaten anything all day. I had nothing to eat yesterday! That's two days without food. We've been eating like mice for months now. *And you gloat because you got a home-cooked meal!*"

Mitchell smiled and moved toward her. He was so used to manipulating her, and she was so willing to be manipulated, that he knew exactly what to say. "Hephzibah, I love you. I always think of you. But the Lord has placed a heavy mantle upon me, even through my weaknesses. But then the Lord, in His great bounty, blesses me because He knows that I struggle under this great burden. To lighten my heavy load, He bestows great gifts upon me. The feast that I have eaten is one of those gifts. But it was also a sign that I have chosen correctly. All of these things were signs from God. It was like when the angel came to Joseph and told him that Mary was a beloved virgin and that he should still wed her."

Listening to him, I wanted to puke. *Blagh!* was the only thought that was going through my head.

After he had calmed Barzee, and after she had composed herself again, they pulled out their handmade calendar and started to go through the days, seeking revelation as to when he should "go forth" again.

They talked for a few minutes and then Mitchell announced, "January fourth."

They spent the next few weeks piling more branches and brush around our camp to conceal us a little better, obtaining an egg-carton case for the victim to sleep on and a few other things that were needed to get ready for the new wife. I wondered if he was going to cable her up like he had done to me, but Mitchell explained that he had reached the next level of faith and righteousness. Having reached this plateau of virtue, he'd be able to keep her in the camp by his pure force of will.

I was left out of the preparations. Clearly, they didn't trust me. Which made me very happy. No way was I going to help them. No way was I going to be a part of this. I would have felt like a cannibal preparing the fire for cooking their next meal if I had been forced to help them in their preparations for this despicable act.

30.

Throw Away My Christmas

—

Mitchell spent most of the next few weeks preparing for his new captive. It was all he thought about, all he talked about, the only thing on his mind. It drove me crazy how he always referred to her as his new wife. *She isn't a wife, she is a casualty!* I wanted to scream. Watching him, I was reminded again that the evil inside him would never be satisfied. He was fire. There was no water. As long as he was living, he would always want more. Someone new. Someone younger. Someone more beautiful.

December rolled along and pretty soon it was almost Christmas. For being such deeply religious people, Mitchell and Barzee didn't seem that excited about the birth of Jesus Christ. They did, however, view it as another chance for a good meal.

Christmas morning dawned cold and gray. Mitchell knew there'd be lots of people lined up for Christmas dinner, so we headed down to San Diego early. After stepping off the metro, we walked to the large convention center. It looked like every homeless person in the city had come for Christmas dinner. The line stretched out of the building and down the block. We got in line and waited. Thinking of the food, my stomach started growling. I was weak from hunger. I had been hungry since our arrival in California.

It never did warm up, and by the time we got into the building I was tired and cold. We continued moving along the line and eventually ended up in a large convention hall. We were greeted by one of the volunteers, who told us to sit down at one of the long tables. Looking around, I realized that most of the helpers were young women, many of them about my age. It was one of those moments that really struck me, sending a pain into my heart. What has happened to me? I thought. What has happened to my life? That should be me! I should be one of those girls who are serving the food, not sitting here at the table, waiting to be served. I'm not really homeless! I have a family. They love me. They miss me! They want me back!

I was glad that I had on my veil, for it helped to hide the tear that was sliding down my cheek.

A couple of the young women brought us our food. I was so hungry. I was so grateful. It was the best thing I had eaten since our homeless Thanksgiving meal. I ate until I was full, then watched Mitchell wolf his food down. He cleaned off his plate, scooping up every drop of gravy, then asked for more. I was kind of embarrassed, but Mitchell didn't care.

After dinner, we started walking around downtown. The streets were almost deserted and we didn't really have anywhere to go. I didn't care. I was just grateful to be out of the fire swamp. Rounding a corner, a young black man came up to us. "Merry Christmas!" he said as he handed each of us a small, handheld radio. Mine was pink with matching headphones. He smiled at me, then walked away. I looked down at my radio. I couldn't believe it! I thought it was the best present I had ever been given. Nearly overcome with joy, I put the earphones in my ears and turned the dial, searching for some music that I would recognize, something that would connect me to my former life.

I found a station that was playing Christmas carols: Karen Carpenter's "Merry Christmas Darling" and then "Winter Wonderland." Both of the songs reminded me of my mom.

Listening to the holiday music, I realized that the seasons had changed without me. The world had gone on. Things had changed. My school friends had gone on without me. Life had continued on without me. But still, I was so happy to have the music. I wanted to sing along, but I knew I couldn't. Mitchell would hate that. So I listened and enjoyed in silence.

Then I heard Mitchell's voice above the sound of the music in my headphones. "The world is so wicked!" He spoke so loudly that I couldn't tune him out. "The world is so wicked. And Hollywood is the worst. Singers and movies stars are the greatest tool of the devil. We must learn to tune them out. Tune them out of our lives. Out of our ears. We must learn to keep ourselves pure from their evil influence. How can we put God in our hearts if we put the devil in our ears?"

I tried desperately to ignore him. I knew he was talking to me but I didn't care. It was Christmas music, for heaven's sake! How evil could that be?

He moved closer to me and raised his voice. "Sure, their songs are easy and they may seem to make us happy, but they will grease our way to hell! They will kill and defile us! They will bring evil into our hearts. We have to deny them, don't we, Shearjashub?"

On and on he went. It was like listening to fingernails scratching down a chalkboard. He wouldn't shut up. He was like a whiny preacher intent on saving a sinful soul.

"Those who enjoy the sounds of Hollywood are enjoying the sounds of hell."

He jumped ahead of me to stand in my way, staring at me and not letting me pass. I returned his hard gaze, refusing to look away. For a moment, there was an unseen battle between us, a battle of souls and will.

You will do as I tell you! his eyes seemed to say.

I stared back at him. *I will do it for now, but not forever. One day I will defeat you. One day, I'm going to win!*

He seemed to grow a little darker, his lips tighter, his shoulders square. *I will always be the master. You will always be the slave.*

I dared to defy him only a moment longer before I had to look away.

I closed my eyes in sadness and frustration. As much as I wanted to just listen to the music, it wasn't worth it. As much as I wanted to hear the beautiful sounds and enjoy the wonderful spirit that the songs of Christmas brought, I knew it was impossible. Mitchell wasn't going to let me. He was going to make it more miserable to have the music than to not have it now. There was only one way to make him stop.

I took the headphones off and threw the radio away.

Mitchell watched me, then smiled an evil grin. We walked half a block in silence, then he took out his own radio, put the earphones in his ears, and started listening to the same music that I had been listening to.

I wanted to scream in frustration. I felt so betrayed. I felt so cheated. Barzee only laughed at me. She thought that I was such a fool. But at least Mitchell was not talking any longer.

We continued walking around San Diego. A couple blocks later, I saw a young man about my age. He was wearing a long-sleeved striped shirt, khaki shorts, and flip-flops. He wore dark sunglasses and had light-brown hair.

I watched him for a moment. (That was the only good thing about having to wear the veil; no one could tell if you were looking at them.) As I watched, I started thinking. I had never had a boyfriend. I had hardly even talked to boys. And though I was extremely shy, I had always looked forward to dating and having boyfriends. Like all young girls, I had dreamed of getting a new outfit and getting all dolled-up with my hair in curls and having makeup on! How exciting it would be to have a boy walk up to the front door with a bouquet of flowers just for me!

What if . . . what if . . . kept running through my mind.

About that time, we walked past a shop called Hustler. Mitchell tried the door, but it was locked. Disappointed, he turned and led us back to the fire swamp.

31.

Waiting for Disaster

———

Mitchell was nothing if not bold. I was constantly amazed by how brazen he was about the next kidnapping he was planning. He showed not a moment of fear or hesitation. If he ever thought he might get caught, he never showed it. And why should he? He had taken me. He'd been able to hide me just a few miles from my home. He'd been able to manipulate and lie his way out of every situation. Nothing in his experience gave him much reason to be afraid.

January 4—the day of the appointed kidnapping—finally arrived. When I woke up that morning, I felt like Judgment Day had come. But then I realized that this was worse. This wasn't a day to judge the guilty; this was a day for the innocent to get hurt.

Mitchell went through his normal routine, all the time trying to hide his excitement. Just like on the day he had prepared to go down to take my cousin, he put on an air of heaviness and persecution. So hard to be a prophet. Such a burden to carry out the work of the Lord. So difficult to be the Chosen. Glancing at Barzee, he tried to display a bit of sadness or hesitation. But none of it was real. He was nothing but excited. He was like an animal that was overcome by the smell of blood. He was driven by lust and nothing else.

He spent the day checking and double-checking the things he would need to capture his next victim. Then he made an important announcement. "My next wife will be called Maher-Shalal-Hash-Baz Rebeckah Isaiah," he said.

Holy cow, I thought. That's a worse name than Shearjashub.

"Maher-Shalal-Hash-Baz was a son of Isaiah," he explained.

Another boy's name for your new wife! I wanted to say. What is going on inside your head?

"It means 'plunder speedeth, spoil hasteth.'"

No, it only means you're stupid.

Mitchell waited as if he expected some kind of adulation for his excellent choice of names. Barzee didn't say anything. I just shook my head.

Late that afternoon, Mitchell got dressed in the same clothes he had worn when he had gone to church on that Sunday morning back in November to identify his next victim. But he also spent a long time packing the disgusting green bags. Dark clothes. Rope. Duct tape. His long knife. Fingering the knife, he turned to me and smiled. "Shearjashub, do you remember this?" he asked with a sickening laugh, his voice low and gutteral.

Of course I recognized the knife! How many times had he flashed it as he threatened me? How many times had he stroked its edge as he reminded me what he was going to do to my family?

"Do you remember what I said to you that night I brought you away from your family?"

Of course I remembered what he had said: *I have a knife at your neck. Don't make a sound! Get up and come with me.* They were the most terrifying words that I had ever heard.

He looked at me. I looked at him. He slipped the knife into his bag. Evening was coming on and it was starting to get dark. A night breeze began to blow and the willows bent and swayed, their bony fingers lifting with the wind. It was a hot wind. Dry. I wiped a bit of sand out of my eyes.

Mitchell waited a few more minutes for darkness to completely settle, then, sighing wearily, got up and said good-bye.

Barzee and I settled down to do what we did most of the time now, which was wait. The evening passed so slowly. Then the night. It was vey dark. I remember the moon and stars were obscured by dust and clouds. We went to bed. I didn't sleep. Hours passed. My stomach never settled. I was sick with dread. Then, very early in the morning, maybe just an hour or so before sunrise, we heard footsteps coming toward us. My heart beat wildly for a moment. What if Mitchell had been captured! What if he had told the police about me? What if I was being rescued?

The curtain parted and we saw Mitchell standing in the darkness. I quickly looked behind him. No one else was there.

"It is not time," he said to announce his failure.

I almost laughed with joy. He had failed! He did not get her! I was giddy with relief.

"Just like with Abraham and Isaac, it was a trial of our faith," he explained.

Barzee stood beside the tent, her face barely illuminated in the darkness. To me, she looked disappointed. She seemed to move toward him, but he walked past her and sat down. He placed his green bags on the ground and started pulling out some food. I was amazed. Every time I had food now, it felt like it was manna from heaven.

He placed a few sandwiches on the tarp. They were small and smashed from being stuffed in his bags. Looking at them, I knew they weren't going to satisfy my hunger, but still, I was grateful for anything to eat. Barzee and I made a beeline for the food and started eating hungrily. While we ate, Mitchell talked.

"I made it to El Cajon and walked slowly to where she lives. It was very late by the time I got there. I circled around the house, looking for a way in. No open windows. No unlocked doors. But I continued searching, knowing that God would provide a way. Finally I found a sliding door around the back that was unlocked. I started to slide the door back. When I had opened it just a crack, I stopped to listen. I thought I heard something inside. I listened for a few seconds, but it was gone. Slowly, I continued to slide the door back. Once again, I heard the sound. A low rustle. I didn't know what it was. But it went away again.

"I pushed the door back all the way and started to step inside. Suddenly, I froze. I realized what I was hearing. Snoring. A man was in the room! And he had to be a large man from the loud noise that he made.

"I realized I would never be able to find my new wife and get her past her father. So, knowing that God must have another plan"—and terrified at the thought of encountering a man much larger than you are, I thought—"I turned around and ran.

"But I didn't want to come back empty-handed. I wanted you to know that I always think about you. So I stopped by an all-night grocery store, dug around to find enough change to buy some ham and mayo, then stopped by the church and got the last loaf of bread out of the box they keep in back." He stopped and pointed proudly at the sandwiches.

I noticed there was not nearly a loaf of bread's worth of sandwiches left. Which meant he hadn't stopped to get us food because he was worried about us. He had stopped to get some food because *he* was hungry. And he'd eaten most of the sandwiches before he had come back to our camp.

"It is clear to me now," he concluded. "California was supposed to be a test of our faithfulness. But the Lord has other plans in store for me now."

God. Plan. Test of faithfulness. The whole thing was absurd! God wasn't testing his faith. There was no plan. There was no divine guid-ance or heavenly intervention. Mitchell was a dirty old man who wanted another child to satisfy him. That's the only thing this was about. He knew it. Barzee knew it. There was no godly mystery here.

Still, I didn't say anything. I was way beyond ever trying to talk to him, let alone ever trying to argue with him.

God bless that little girl, was all I thought.

32.

High Camp and *Hustler*

———

For the next two weeks we did pretty much nothing but sit around being bored and hungry. I was only allowed to leave the fire swamp once a week. It was a miserable time, Mitchell always talking, Barzee always whining about being confined to the camp, a constant hot wind, the creepy trees above us, the musky smell of old blankets around us. I felt like I had been completely forgotten by the outside world.

Then one day someone walked into our camp.

It was late afternoon. All of us were sitting outside our tents when I heard the crunch of footsteps coming toward us. I scampered toward one of the musty blankets we used for a barrier and pushed the corner aside. Mitchell was immediately at my side, his bad breath on my neck. A lone man was walking through the fire swamp toward us. Mitchell immediately pulled me back, almost pushing me to the ground. He dragged me back to the tent and hissed for me to sit down. Barzee followed, her face tight with fear. Mitchell made a lot of noise, rummaging through his gear. It only took a few seconds to find the knife and pull it out. Barzee did what she always did, which was to stand around and wait for Mitchell to tell her what to do. Mitchell peered out of the gray tunnel, his lips growing tight. He was standing right over me, peering from behind the tarp. Because I was on the ground, his hands were level with my eyes, and I noticed that his knuckles were white. He shifted the knife in his hand to put it in a better position to strike, then crouched down.

I don't know if the man heard Mitchell rummaging around, or if he saw the blankets that were hanging in the trees and thought he'd check it out, but for whatever reason he started walking toward our camp. As the sound of his footsteps got closer, Mitchell inched forward, ready to attack. I watched him intently. *Is he going to kill him?!* I wondered in horror.

The man came to a stop. "Hey," he called out. "Is anybody there?"

Mitchell glared at me and lifted the knife, moving it in my direction.

"Anyone there?" the man yelled again.

Mitchell put his fingers to his lips, then nodded at the knife. *As if he had to remind me what he would do if I were foolish enough to scream!*

"Anyone home?" the man repeated, though his voice was not as loud this time.

He waited, then started walking toward us again. We could clearly hear his footsteps across the leaves. He got closer. Closer. Mitchell was as tight as a wire. He held the long knife at his side, ready to spring at the intruder.

I wanted to scream!

The man continued walking until he was just a few feet from the hanging blankets. I could see his shadow through the thin barricade. He lifted his arm. He was going to push the blankets aside. He was going to see us. Then he was going to die.

Suddenly, the man stopped. He didn't move. He didn't say anything. All of us held our breath. No one dared to move.

I don't know what it was that made him stop. Maybe he was afraid. Maybe he started listening to that intuition that's inside all of us, that little voice that sometimes guides us when there is danger. Maybe his guardian angel was with him that day. I don't know. I only know that Mitchell showed every indication of intending to kill him. He was coiled like a snake and ready to strike. But the man never took that last step. He didn't push the blankets aside. He never said another word. He stood there a long moment, the tension sucking all of the oxygen out of the air, then turned around and walked away.

For a long time, none of us moved.

"We have to find another place to live," Mitchell said.

Mitchell was convinced that the Lord, in His great and manifest wisdom, had tried our faith and found us lacking. We were nowhere close to being worthy of accepting another wife. Nowhere close to being worthy of His constant protection. We had been tried and we had failed.

Which meant that something had to change.

"There's a story in the Bible," he explained. "The children of Israel are surrounded by the Syrians. Evil people. Really bad. They had a mighty army. A terrible and deadly scourge. But when the prophet Elisha stood up to face them, instead of seeing all of the Syrian soldiers that had surrounded them, he saw thousands of celestial soldiers that stood ready to defend the children of Israel. Chariots of fire. Angels with their mighty swords. 'They that be with us are more than they that be with them,' the prophet Elisha said."

Mitchell stopped and looked at us. Barzee nodded as if it were the most inspired thing she had ever heard. I looked at him as if it made no sense.

"You don't see it, do you, Shearjashub?"

I shook my head. I didn't.

"Just like with Elisha, the Lord could surround us with His angels. He could protect us so that no one would ever find us. But"—he paused and looked at me—"He can't do it if you're not worthy." He turned and looked at Barzee. "He can't protect us if you're not humble. He can't bless me if your faith isn't strong enough. He can't hide us. He can't protect us. He is bound by your weak faith."

He fell silent and thought a long moment. "We need to move to a more secure and hidden location. Tomorrow, we will go out and find our new home."

The next day, Mitchell made us dress in our street clothes, a bunch of filthy rags he had taken from the abandoned homeless camps. I wore a gray shirt and some oversize pants. Pulling them on, I felt so dirty. There I was, putting on a shirt that was so thin and filthy that a homeless man had thrown it away. That is what I had come to. I shook my head sadly and held my nose.

Once we were dressed, we headed out. It was my first time in public without wearing a veil. I felt uncomfortable. Vulnerable. I was surprised how much I'd grown used to it. And I knew it made Mitchell nervous to have my face exposed, which made me nervous too. Mitchell, of course, led the way. I followed. Barzee followed me. But we took a completely different route from any we had ever taken when exiting the fire swamp before. Instead of crossing the riverbed and climbing the small embankment, we turned left and crawled through a large irrigation pipe that crossed under the road. Emerging on the other side, Mitchell told us to be quiet and stay low while he checked it out. After a couple minutes of watching, he decided it was clear and we headed out again, following the dry streambed. We only went a couple of miles, but it seemed to take all day. It was hot and dry and dusty. When we couldn't go any farther, we climbed out of the ravine and found ourselves in an empty pasture. Again, Mitchell made us stay low while he took a look around. He was acting like a kid playing some kind of spy game, sneaking and creeping here and there.

But I knew it wasn't a game. It was dangerous. And I knew he had his knife.

While we waited, I sat down and put my hand into a patch of vibrant, green plants. I felt instant pain shoot through my hand and immediately jumped up. The stinging nettle was vicious and my hands were quickly covered with red blisters. Barzee watched me but showed no sympathy. "Spit on your hands," she instructed drily. "Dogs and cats lick their wounds. You're no better than they are. You should do the same thing."

I hated her reasoning but figured she might be right. I spat and rubbed it in. It felt a little better and Barzee seemed to puff a bit with pride.

Mitchell crouched toward our hiding place and pointed to a mountain about half a mile away. We would have to sneak across pastures and a narrow road to get there. Mitchell took off, leading the way. Trying to appear as inconspicuous as possible—something that was ridiculously difficult to do—we made our way across the pasture and road and started climbing the small mountain. It proved to be much harder than it looked from the bottom of the hill. It was steep and thick with shrubs and covered with huge rocks. We climbed slowly. I was already weak from hunger. Mitchell pushed us on, always talking. Barzee had taken to not saying very much anymore. I don't know why. She was just quiet now. It was slow and difficult work to climb the mountain. We had to scramble over boulders, pulling ourselves up by thorny bushes before dropping down on the other side. We had to lift and pull and help to catch one another. Sometimes we had to slip between tiny cracks between the boulders. As we climbed, Mitchell would point out how various rocks reminded him of sexual body parts and he would name the rocks with these names.

We finally made it to the top. But there was no place to make our camp. Mitchell looked around, then told us to sit tight while he looked for a place to pitch our tents. He scrambled off and I sat down, hungry and weak with exhaustion. A little while later, he came slithering back. Panting excitedly, he exclaimed, "I've found it! Come quickly! Follow me!"

We followed, fighting through scrub oaks and more boulders before dropping through a rock crevice that led to a small clearing. The north side of the clearing was backed by massive rocks that would be almost impossible to climb and far too dangerous to drop down from the top. The other side of the clearing was walled in by scrub oaks and then a sheer cliff. The left and right sides of the clearing were surrounded by prickly plants, scrub oak, and huge boulders.

Mitchell walked proudly into the clearing. "Shearjashub, Hephzibah, this is our new home."

I looked around. It was a huge improvement from the fire swamp. But it was also so remote, so very far from everything, that it made me feel even more isolated from the world.

"We will be safe here if we are only careful," Mitchell said. Then he stopped and looked at Barzee. "But we're going to have to act more wisely. Which means you aren't going to be able to leave the camp anymore. You're going to have to stay up here with Shearjashub until we are ready to move on."

Barzee scowled. I expected her to argue, but she didn't say anything. That's just the way it was now. Mitchell had essentially made prisoners of us both.

We hiked back to the lower camp, then spent all day packing up our gear, taking down our tents, and getting everything ready to move up to the new camp. Once it was dark, we started hauling things up to the top of the mountain. If I thought it was hard to climb the mountain in the daylight, it was nothing compared to hiking it at night with a good part of our gear slung over my shoulders and my bedding in my arms. I was terrified that I might fall. If I had, I didn't think I'd have the energy to stand up again.

We finally stumbled into our new camp. Mitchell made us help him construct a new tunnel tent, and the moment it was finished I crawled inside and immediately fell asleep.

I only slept a few hours. When I woke up, the sun was a quarter way up in the sky.

Mitchell figured it was a great time to do some exploring, so we spent the morning hiking around, checking out our new surroundings. At one point we came upon a tight crevice underneath a huge boulder that formed a sliver of a cave. Mitchell told me to slither underneath and see what was inside.

I lay down on my stomach and crawled into the narrow cave. I must be the first human who has ever been underneath this rock, I thought. Crawling a bit farther, I discovered I was wrong. A pair of old boots, a man's belt, and an old magazine were there. I wondered what would cause a man to take off his boots and belt. Then I picked up the magazine. Glancing at the cover, I let out a quick grasp and dropped it as if it were a spider.

After all that I had been through, I didn't think there was anything that could shock me anymore. But this was different. It was horrible. Mitchell had shown me pornography before, but he hadn't shown me anything like this. The horrible image was seared into my mind.

Hearing me gasp, Mitchell slithered into the crevice and maneuvered to my side. He snatched up the magazine and began greedily looking at the pictures. Then he stopped and stared at me. "We have made the right decision. This place has been sanctified of the Lord. The Lord has seen fit to bless His servant with this sign." He then inched a little closer. "Shearjashub, it's clear that your descent below all things is not complete. Who do you think you are to shrink from your brothers and sisters in this magazine? Do you think you are better than they are? Do you think you are more holy? More worthy of God's great love? It is clear that I must instruct you. When we get back to camp, I will."

I shook my head in dread. His instructions were always painful lessons. My heart sank in fear.

When we got back to our tents, he took the pornographic magazine and shoved it in my face. "Look at this!" he screamed.

I tried to fight him. I tried to close my eyes. But Mitchell grabbed my chin and turned my face toward the magazine. "Open your eyes or you'll regret it!" he sneered. "These people are more righteous than you are. They are more righteous than the rest of the world." He turned the pages, making me look at everything. "These people are showing more courage than you have ever shown. They aren't afraid of showing their true spiritual state."

I tried to look away, but he wouldn't let me. And it didn't matter. The images were already burned into my brain. I could never forget them. I felt as if my mind was scarred.

Then something caught his attention and he pulled the magazine away from me and started looking through it by himself. The images were a bright flame in the darkness and he was a mindless moth. It only took a couple seconds before he was completely engrossed. "My, my, look at this . . ." He started describing what he was looking at. He was graphic and detailed. Hearing the things that he was saying made me absolutely sick. I was so embarrassed. So shocked. I felt so slimy and scared.

He became so absorbed in the pornography that I think he forgot that I was even there. When he got to the last page, he looked up with his greedy, evil eyes. Then he stood up and walked toward me. The pornography had lit a violent flame inside him. And so he raped me.

And that was my first day in my new home.

33.

Hunger

———

Sometime in mid-February, Mitchell and Barzee got into a terrible fight. This wasn't anything new. They fought literally every day. Heck, they fought almost every hour. But this one was different. It was the worst fight I had ever seen. It was screaming and cursing and threatening with things that I couldn't even imagine. Finally, Barzee grabbed a kitchen knife and held it to her wrist. "I'm going to kill myself!" she screamed.

She had done this before, but this time I actually thought that she might do it. She pressed the knife against her skin. Mitchell didn't seem to care.

"I'm going to do it! I'm going to kill myself. I just can't take it any longer! You don't deserve me! I don't deserve this! I'm going to kill myself right now!"

Mitchell finally jumped toward her to pull the knife away. They tussled back and forth, and I wondered if one of them would stab the other. Finally, Mitchell emerged from the scrum, the knife in hand. But the fighting went on.

Listening to all of the screaming and ranting made me sick. It seemed to drive the very sunlight from the sky. It filled the camp with darkness and misery and a hateful, dreadful feeling that made me want to crawl away.

I crouched in the back of the tunnel tent. I didn't want them to see me, for I knew that if they did, one or the other would turn their rage on me. So I huddled out of the way, listening to the screaming while keeping my head down and staying out of it.

In a final fit of rage, Barzee stormed off, cursing everything about Mitchell that she could think of, which turned out to be a lot. I listened to her voice fade away as she wandered off into the dark.

She was gone all night.

It wasn't until late afternoon the next day that she came out of her hiding place in the rocks. As she stomped into camp, I could see that she was different. There was a renewed fire in her eyes. She was intense and animated. She was full of . . . I don't know, an evil energy that seemed to give her more nerve than she had ever shown before.

"Satan and his hosts surrounded and tortured me last night," she said.

For such a dramatic announcement, there was no drama or excitement in her voice. She said it matter-of-factly, as if she were announcing that it was cold or that it had rained.

Mitchell only looked at her. Devil or no, he wasn't ready to forgive or forget.

"They came and tortured me all night," Barzee went on. "Hours and hours of their taunting, their dark whispers, their rage and hate inside my ears. Then they tortured me. And I'm not imagining. It was very real. It was as if they placed a piercing laser at my feet and ran it up my body. It was pure agony. I've never felt anything even close to it before. Searing, burning pain. My body being cut in two. I can't describe it. It is impossible. I was cut from feet to skull."

I tried not to look at her. It was a horrible thing to say. Yet I almost believed her. If anyone could become a plaything for the devil, certainly she and Mitchell could.

Mitchell started to say something, but Barzee quickly cut him off. She was tired of him talking. She was tired of his preaching. She was tired of it all. It was her turn to talk and Mitchell was going to listen; that was clear from the fire in her eyes.

She swallowed, as if she were pondering her words. "I have something more to tell you. The fight is over for me now. My election to heaven has been made sure. It doesn't matter what I do now. I have suffered and bled enough. I have been measured and I am worthy. My place in heaven is assured. I don't have to follow you any longer, Immanuel. I no longer even have to follow in the footsteps of the Lord. I am going up to heaven. My place in the celestial world is guaranteed."

That must be pretty cool, I thought. Do anything you want? Still get to heaven? You're one of the few who gets that deal.

But of course I didn't believe it. She was just a sick and evil soul. She and Mitchell were nothing more than two malicious and self-serving people who justified their own behavior by twisting the truth.

Barzee squared her shoulders. "But you, Immanuel, you are not following in God's footsteps anymore." Her voice was high and piercing. She was more than full of fury; she was a cat trapped in the corner and hissing at a wolf. "You certainly aren't acting like the Davidic king. And worse, you're not treating me like the Mother of Zion that I am. I am tired of it and you must stop it. I'm not going to put up with it anymore!"

She stopped to take a breath, waiting for Mitchell to answer.

For a long time, he didn't say anything. Then he exploded in rage. And that started it off. It was the same thing as the day before, the same loud screaming and selfish arguments. After a few minutes, Mitchell stopped arguing, sat down, and started to pull his shoes on.

Barzee realized that he was leaving, and that threw more fuel on her rage. "You can't just leave me here again! You have to stay here! You're going to talk to me. You're going to face this now!"

But apparently he wasn't. Mitchell grabbed his handmade money-bag and the linen cap he only wore when he was going into the city.

Barzee kept on screaming. "The Lord has sent me to chastise you! You will not walk away!"

"I'm going into town," Mitchell said in a quiet voice. "I don't know when I'll be back."

He shoved the hat onto his head, then turned around and walked away.

I sank down in despair.

I knew it would take him until dark before he would even get into the city, which meant he probably wouldn't be coming back that night. That meant another day without any food. The only thing we had eaten all day was a small crust of bread with a tiny bit of mayo and the last remaining rings from a slice of an old onion. I had eaten maybe a couple thousand calories in the past week. It had been that way for months. My stomach was constantly aching. I was already weak and dizzy. The thought of going another day without anything to eat was almost more than I could bear.

Barzee stormed back into the tent, all the time ranting about Mitchell. All I could do was sit and listen, trying to stay out of her way. She went on and on. Hours and hours of her ranting. Sometime well into the night, she finally turned to me and said, "We have spoken long. It is late now. Let us pray and go to bed."

What do you mean by "we"? I wanted to say. I haven't said a word in hours. But yes, please, let's go to bed.

When I woke up, the first thing I thought about was food. I got up and searched through the camp for something to eat, but everything was gone.

Barzee picked up her ranting where she had left off the night before. By midafternoon, she was finally out of rage. There was silence for a couple of hours and then she said, "I'm sure he's on his way back. I'm sure he'll bring us water. I'm sure he'll bring us food."

I thought back on the single piece of crust and ring of onion I had eaten the day before. The day before that, I had eaten little more. I had been on a path of malnutrition for many weeks now, leaving me weak and vulnerable. I would have done anything for something to eat, I would have done anything for something to drink. I was beyond mere thirst and hunger. I was beyond misery and despair.

The day ended. Still no Mitchell. *Where is he?!* I was screaming in frustration in my head.

Day three came. Barzee seemed resigned to suffering through it, however it was to end. As quickly as she had gathered up the will to fight Mitchell, she had lost it now. If he had left us here to die, that seemed to be okay with her. We sat around in silence. We just didn't have the energy to talk. Besides, it hurt my throat to speak. I was as dry as bone.

I didn't think I was going to starve to death, at least not yet, but I knew that I could die of dehydration if I didn't get something to drink. My tongue was dry and swollen. My throat was as rough as sandpaper, not letting my thick saliva go down. Three days in the heat and dryness. Three days without food or water. My heart raced every time that I walked or even stood up. My body was on the edge.

That afternoon, I lay weakly on my bed and thought back on the miraculous glass of water that had appeared by my pillow on that night back in the mountains. It seemed so long ago. *Please God,* I started praying. It was hard to even form the words. *Please God, I need another miracle. I can't go another day without any water. If I don't drink, I'm going to die here. Please, help me find a way to go on.*

Weak, exhausted, and demoralized to the point of losing hope, I drifted off to sleep.

Shortly after, I awoke to a splattering sound on our tent. It took me a while to figure out what was going on. Then it finally hit me. Rain! It was raining! I was overcome with relief.

Then the words came very clearly into my mind: *I will not leave you comfortless. I will come to you.*

I closed my eyes to thank Him and then climbed out of the tent.

It was a fierce storm, rife with water, the rain coming down in enormous, drenching drops. Barzee jumped up and we worked together. We grabbed the spare tarp and tied it up to catch the rain. Then we put out every bucket, can, and container that we could find to catch the rain. As the rain pooled on the tarp, I poured it into one of the containers. Once I had a mouthful, I lifted it to my mouth and gulped it down. I let it fill once more and gulped again. I poured and gulped and poured and gulped until I started feeling sick. I was drinking so much water; I knew I had to quit.

Glancing over, I looked at Barzee. She was on her hands and knees, sucking water off the tarp.

Once we had quenched our thirst and filled every container that we had, Barzee told me to get the soap. "We're going to shower in the rain," she said. We scrubbed ourselves, then wearily went to bed.

The next morning came but Mitchell didn't. We lay on our beds all day.

"Is he ever coming back?" I asked Barzee.

"I don't know," she said.

"Has he ever done this before? Has he ever left you for so long?"

She slowly shook her head.

"Do you think—"

"I don't know!" she snapped at me.

Day five. No food. Hot and hazy. I hardly had the strength to move. Barzee and I sat around and talked, but only just a little. I felt too tired. Too weak. I lay in the tent and dreamed all day of food.

Day six. I felt so weak and dizzy it was almost impossible to walk to the bucket to get some water. I lay on my bed and stared up at the gray tarp. I felt like all my hope was slipping away. My life was nothing but sand through my fingers, water through my palms. I knew I had to eat or I would die, but I didn't know what to do.

On day seven, Barzee seemed to lose her mind. Struggling to stand, she walked over and pulled out the recipe book that she had painstakingly put together over so many years. She looked at it with dry eyes, then started to tear out the pages and shred them on the ground. I watched her curiously. She ripped and scratched until she had torn out every page. I looked at the scattered pieces, the perfect cakes and salads, the delicious pastas and desserts. I wanted to chew on every piece of paper. I wanted to stuff them in my mouth. But a sudden breeze came up and blew them all away. In final desperation, I crawled to the trash pile in the back of our tent and sorted through it one more time, looking for anything that I could eat. Every last shred of food was gone. I struggled back to my bed and collapsed.

I lay there, waiting. What I was waiting for, I didn't know.

Thinking of my situation, I almost laughed at the irony. After everything that I had lived through, the kidnapping, the knife at my neck, the daily rapes, the different moves, the months of abuse from my two captors, it seemed almost laughable that I was going to die of starvation in my tent.

For the thousandth time I wondered where Mitchell was. Was he ever coming back?

As I lay there, I started to wonder if this really was the end. Then I started to think about my family. No, that's not right, I thought about my family all the time. But as I lay there, I thought back on all the good things in my life, deciding that I had been very lucky. Almost all of my fifteen years of living had been about as perfect as one could hope for. Sure, the last eight months had been pretty terrible, but everything before had been near perfect. I thought about my beautiful mom and imagined how she would take care of me if she were with me then. I thought about my dad, who was strong and capable of fixing any problem I might have. When it came to a great family, I felt like I had won the lottery, and that included my brothers and sister, my grandparents, my aunts and uncles . . . I couldn't have asked for a more caring, loving family.

So I began to thank God for my life, my family, and the blessings that I had received in my short life. Then, not knowing if I could make it another day, I tried to think of things that I had done wrong and to ask God for forgiveness.

When I had finished my prayer, I lay still and waited to die.

It was in that moment that, far off in the distance, I heard singing. Had heavenly angels come to get me? No, this was something else. It was loud and off-key, and the melodies were completely mixed-up. It took me a second to realize that it was Mitchell. I was almost disappointed. He was about as far from a heavenly host as you can get!

Mitchell came panting and stomping into camp. Neither Barzee nor I had the energy to greet him. We waited until he stuck his head inside the tent. "Food?" we started begging.

He looked at us a moment. It must have been an incredible sight, the two of us lying on our sleeping bags, too weak to even move. But he didn't say anything. In fact, he didn't react at all. He didn't rush to Barzee's side, or jump around to get us something to eat. He didn't offer to bring us any water. He didn't even ask us how we were. Instead, he kind of smiled proudly. "I was walking through Lakeside when I passed the local KFC. They were throwing out their leftovers for the day. I asked if I could have them for my starving wife and daughter." He pulled out macaroni and cheese, chicken, a couple of biscuits, coleslaw, and potato wedges. I rolled onto my knees and reached out for the food, guiding a couple pieces to my mouth with shaking hands. I had thought that I could eat the entire bag, but after a few bites I started feeling stuffed. Another bite and I started feeling sick. Realizing it was going to take a while for my body to adjust, I quit trying to eat and lay back on my mat.

"Where have you been?" Barzee asked in anger. Her voice was dry and accusing.

Mitchell smiled as if he didn't have a care in the world and started to tell his tale.

The first thing he did upon getting to Lakeside was go into the convenience store to steal some beer. After gulping a couple of Budweisers in the aisle, he walked out of the store and saw a woman pushing a shopping cart while popping a few pills. "Ah," he thought, "the next step I must take in my quest to descend below all things." He went up to the woman and asked her for some of her pills. She refused, of course, so he grabbed her cart and started running. After getting away from her, he opened her purse and grabbed the prescription medication. Popping some into his mouth, he abandoned the stolen loot then turned and ran, the lady in hot pursuit. He jumped over a fence and kept on running. The drugs and beer, a really bad combination, started to kick in and he was getting wobbly. Soon after, he came to a church, the perfect place to spend the night. But all of the doors were locked. That wasn't right! He was the prophet of the Lord! And the church was nothing but an abomination, with evil people who went inside. Who were they to deny him access to his Father's house? So he found a brick and broke the window, then crawled inside and fell unconscious on the floor.

And that's where the police had found him.

He didn't remember a lot about being booked into jail other than the fact that he was able to flash a female officer from underneath his robe. He was really proud of that.

Seven days later, having given the police a fake name, and having told the judge that he had been clean for twenty years and how sorry he was that he had fallen off the wagon, and that, of course, he was willing to pay for the damages and do loads of community service, but that all he wanted now was to get back to his family, the judge had let him go.

He hung around the city for the rest of the day, then made his way back to camp.

"For seven days, you left us!" Barzee hissed like a snake. "Seven days without so much as a single scrap to eat."

"I thought you'd go down to Lakeside and get something," Mitchell answered without regret.

"For seven days, you were in jail. You got three square meals a day. We had nothing! You had a real bed with a pillow and soft blankets. We had this!" She lifted a finger to the gray tarps and the dirty bedding around us. "You had hot showers and a television and books and anything else you could desire. *We had nothing! We had nothing! You left us here to die!*"

Mitchell shook his head. "It was the Lord who called me to prison. I had seven days of preaching to the inmates, seven days of crying repentance to the sinful. All I did was serve the Lord."

Barzee lay back on her sleeping bag and closed her eyes.

I was about to point out that no one in the jail had been converted but decided there was no point in stirring things up.

A few moments passed. It appeared that Barzee was already asleep. Mitchell and I were alone together and I stared into his eyes. He looked at me and held my stare, refusing to look away. My unspoken words were very clear.

You tried to kill me. But you didn't. For all of your talk of being a mighty prophet, I am stronger than you are. One day, you're going to know that. One day, you're going to see.

The battle between us lasted only a few seconds. Then, for the first time since he had slipped into my bedroom, Mitchell was the first one to look away.

34.

Manipulating Mitchell

Mitchell was always driven by events. There was never a simple coincidence, nor did things ever happen just by chance. Everything that happed had to be a sign from God.

One afternoon near the end of February, a couple of weeks after Mitchell had abandoned us to our hunger, we were sitting outside our tents. Mitchell had decided he wasn't going to go and minister that day. Too much work. Much too hot. The Lord wanted him to stay in the camp. So he spent the day sitting around talking about his favorite subject, which was, of course, himself. Barzee was lapping up every word. I was hardly even listening. After eight months of listening to him every minute of every day, there wasn't a whole lot about him that I hadn't heard before. But I always tried at least to act like I was paying attention. There was a steep price to pay if he felt like I didn't give him the respect he thought he deserved. But I wasn't listening, I was daydreaming; about my family, about my friends, wondering if I would ever be able to go back to school. It was a sunny day, and the skies were clear. It was already getting hot and I wondered what the summers would be like in California. Was I going to spend the rest of my life here? Was I going to spend the rest of my life on the top of this mountain, miles from anyone and anything, surrounded by boulders and scrub oaks? Would we ever go back to Utah? I really didn't know.

Sitting there, I started to hear the low roar of helicopter rotors. The sound grew louder and Mitchell immediately stood up. The roar of engines and beating blades began to fill the air. Mitchell shoved me into the tent, then grabbed Barzee and pulled her in as well. Standing near the entrance, he jerked down the flap that we used for a door. The sound of the helicopter grew louder. It was coming right toward us. He motioned for Barzee and me to scoot to the back of the tent. I slid backward, keeping my face toward the door. The helicopter came to a hover right over our camp. There was a deafening roar of engines and the wind stirred up a terrible swirl of dust. The tarp tunnel was shaking so badly I thought it was going to be blown away. For a moment, I flashed back to the afternoon in the mountains over Salt Lake City, three days after I had been taken. But unlike that afternoon, this time I wasn't anxious or excited. Whoever was in the helicopter, and for whatever reason they had to check out our camp, I was pretty certain they weren't looking for me. I knew soldiers weren't going to rappel from the helicopter to save me. Still, I kept my eyes toward the sound. After all, you never know. . . .

The helicopter hovered a few minutes, then moved on. Mitchell made us stay inside the tent until he was certain it was safe. When he finally allowed us to come out, he was a changed man once again. Less confident. Not as cocky. Full of doubts and fear.

He looked at Barzee and said, "That is a sign from God. It's time that we move again."

I knew it wasn't a sign of anything. Mitchell was just scared the helicopter would come back or that the pilots would send police to investigate our strange camp.

Barzee looked at him but didn't answer for a second. I knew she hated this place. I knew she hated being stuck in the camp twenty-four hours a day. I knew she hated never being allowed to go into the city to party or to scavenge food or to see something besides the trees that were around us. I knew that, like me, she was desperate to talk to someone new. I didn't know what she expected out of a new place, but I suppose she thought it couldn't be worse than the situation she was in. So she hesitated only for a moment before she agreed, "Yes, God wants us to move on."

They started talking of all the places they could go, both of them getting excited about the possibilities. When you don't own anything, or have any family ties or friends, and when you don't really care where you end up as long as there's a place to beg for food, the whole world opens up. They talked about New York, Boston, and Philadelphia. They talked about a lot of other places too.

My heart sank. I felt a tinge of panic and despair. All of the places they were talking about were even farther from my home! I always assumed we would eventually make our way back toward Utah. It was my only hope of getting rescued. No one had found me in California, but no one was looking for me here. But if we could make it back to Utah, I might be recognized. Someone might see me and realize who I was. They might call the police and save me without me having to do anything that Mitchell could blame me for.

All of the places they were talking about were on the East Coast. No one would recognize me there. And I had seen how much effort it had taken to get to California. Months of planning. Months of ministering to get the money. It would be so much harder to come back once we had made it all the way out to Boston or New York. Once we were there, there was no way we'd ever come back west.

As I thought, Mitchell started talking about his quest to obtain the remaining six young wives that God had told him to get. In fact, he said, it had been revealed to him that he was supposed to take seven times seventy wives. But for the time being, he was willing to focus on just obtaining the initial seven. As I sat there listening to his drivel, an idea started forming in my head. I thought of all the ways Mitchell had justified what he did by using religion. I thought of all the times that he had gotten away with things by lying and manipulating people and their emotions. Down in the city, he used faith and scripture to manipulate people a dozen times a day. It was what he did to get everything he wanted. It was what he did to get away with everything.

At this time, religious discrimination was an especially touchy subject because of the 9/11 terrorist attacks. Yet Mitchell had even been able to turn that to his advantage. People were afraid of offending anyone, especially someone dressed in veils and robes, and Mitchell had been able to extract a lot of sympathy because of that. He had convinced a police officer not to even look at my face back in the library, all in the name of religion.

I knew it was wrong to try to manipulate people. As a young girl, the only manipulating I had ever done was when I tried to get Mary Katherine to brush my hair, or tickle my back, or make me a grilled cheese sandwich. Even then, it hardly ever worked. I was not good at manipulation. And I knew that it was much worse to use religion to manipulate people. But as I sat there thinking about it, I started to develop a plan.

But first I had to get things right with God.

I wondered if God would give me a one-time exception when it came to manipulation. Considering the situation I was in, I thought maybe He would help me out.

While Mitchell and Barzee were talking about all of the places they could drag me off to, I knelt down and started praying. I begged God to let this plan work just this once. I begged Him to help me, and if He did, I promised never to try to manipulate anyone ever again.

Once I had finished my prayer, I sat up and turned to my captors.

"I know this sounds crazy, but I keep having this feeling like maybe we should go back to Salt Lake City," I said. "I know that doesn't make any sense. And I know that God would never talk to me about this feeling, but it just won't leave me alone." I turned my eyes on Mitchell, my voice soft and sincere. "Do you think you could ask God if we should go back to Salt Lake? I know He will answer you! I know He will! You are His prophet! You are His seer. You are practically His best friend!"

I guess I stroked his ego just right, because Mitchell didn't immediately reject my suggestion. And I could see what he was thinking: Maybe my little Shearjashub is finally getting it. Maybe she's finally acknowledging that I really am the prophet.

So he agreed to pray about it. Then, just like Moses, he stood up and went up on the mountain to talk to God.

Sometime later he came back. "I think you are right, Shearjashub," he announced. "The Lord is beginning to work with you. That makes me very happy. We should go back to Salt Lake.

"Now we just have to find a way to get back to Utah. We could beg for money to ride the bus. We could buy a cheap car. We could take a train. We can't fly, though, That takes too much money, and we don't have any ID. . . ."

He muttered on, wondering about the best way to get back to Salt Lake.

I had an idea for that, too.

"You and Hephzibah always talk about your trek across the country," I said. "You talk all the time about how you used to hitchhike everywhere."

Mitchell stopped and stared at me with a look of surprise.

"I think we should hitchhike back to Utah," I said. "You and Hephzibah have hitchhiked all over the country. I never have hitchhiked in my life! My parents always dropped me off and picked me up! I think it's essential for me to experience that as well. I think it's an important part of descending below all things that I may rise above them all."

Mitchell's face changed from surprise to shock. Barzee seemed to squint, as if she was suspicious.

But I knew I had him. He was caught with his own artillery.

I didn't want to hitchhike all the way back to Utah, of course. But what I did want was to be in close contact with other people. Real people, not Mitchell and Barzee. If I could get close enough to other people, maybe there'd be a situation where I could be rescued or find a way to escape.

But Mitchell shook his head. He didn't like the idea at all. "Far too risky," he said.

He and Barzee started to discuss it. Surprisingly, Barzee agreed with me. It *was* something I needed to experience.

Mitchell finally gave in. But I could tell that he was suspicious of the idea.

I was so eager to get back to Utah! It was the only thing I could think about. I wanted to leave right away.

But there was a lot to do before we could be ready to go.

We had to get some money for the journey. That was going to take some time. We had to sort through all of our belongings, packing up those things that we intended to take with us. I had been through that before. I knew it was a lot of work. Mitchell said we also needed to plan an appropriate route back to Salt Lake City. We couldn't just stand on the side of the road holding a sign that read SALT LAKE CITY. We had to plan a route that took us from one small town to the next, eventually working our way back to Utah.

Which left us with one big problem.

Mitchell knew that people wouldn't pick us up if we were dressed in our strange-looking robes. Which meant we had to get some street clothes. But that included great risk, for people would certainly recognize me if they could see my face and hair. I would have to be well disguised or Mitchell would never go through with the plan.

Mitchell didn't know what to do. He said he'd have to think about it.

Still, I felt a wave of hope and excitement wash over me. After nearly nine months of being enslaved, I had shown that I was more than a bystander in my own life, more than just a puppet in his hands.

After months of grueling training and conditioning, I felt like I had finally kicked a goal.

35.

A Walk Through the Desert

Surprisingly, it only took us three days to get ready to hitchhike back to SLC. We spent the first couple of days sorting through all of our belongings, throwing some stuff away and deciding what things we would take with us on our journey. I was surprised at how much junk we had accumulated, most of it dug out of Dumpsters or from other homeless camps. We sorted and decided, trying to keep our sacks light, a goal in which we failed miserably. But it was no easy thing for three people to do, hitchhike for eight hundred miles while dragging along literally everything we owned.

After we had organized our things, Mitchell spent a little time ministering in the city to get some money. I never knew how much he collected—he certainly never shared that kind of information with Barzee or me—but I knew it wasn't much.

That afternoon, he sat and stared at me. "We need to cut your hair," he said. "Cut it really short and dye it too. That's the only way no one is going to recognize you."

I shook my head defiantly. I wasn't going to let him. He'd have to hold me down to cut my hair.

"Yeah, we're going to have to cut and dye it," he went on. "And you know what else?" He ran his fingers through his own hair. "I might have to dye my hair as well."

That didn't make any sense. He wasn't a fugitive. He hadn't had his picture pasted all over the country. No one was going to recognize him. But it made him feel important to think that someone might be looking for him too.

He turned and smiled at me. "Shearjashub, how do you think I would look as a blond?"

That one was easy. He'd look like an old man with dyed hair. He already looked like a cross between Rasputin and Osama bin Laden and I didn't think a little blond hair was going to change that.

Barzee jumped in. "I don't think you should make her cut her hair," she said.

I looked at her in surprise. In the nine months since she and her husband had kidnapped me, this was the only time she had ever interjected to protect me.

"A woman's hair is her crown," she went on. "It wouldn't be right to make her cut it. You need to find another way."

Looking at her stringy gray hair, I realized that all of this talk about cutting and dyeing our hair had bothered her. At the end of the day, she'd be left with a head of gray hair and she didn't want to be left out. Still, I was glad that she had said what she did.

Mitchell thought for a couple of minutes, unwilling to announce his decision. Then his face lit up like a lightbulb. "I've got it! We won't dye or cut her hair. We'll make her wear a wig instead." Relieved to keep my hair, I nodded eagerly. But it wasn't as if it was a stroke of genius. Wasn't getting me a wig an obvious answer anyway?

The next day, Mitchell took Barzee and me into El Cajon. We walked to one of the local strip malls and went into the dollar store. Of course! I thought sarcastically. The perfect place to buy a quality wig!

I stood quietly beside Mitchell while he and Barzee tried to find the right hairpiece, a decision that soon devolved into an argument. Looking at the selection, I had to cringe. The best way to describe them was "old-lady gray hair bubble." I rummaged around the rack, looking for one that was just a little less gray than all the others, finally picking out one that seemed to have a few more strands of brown. Turning it over, I read the style name: *Tiger Lily*. The irony was rich.

We selected that wig, then spent a whopping $1.29 on an equally stylish pair of sunglasses and walked out of the store.

After we had made our way back to camp, Mitchell made me put on my disguise. Then he looked at me and smiled. He was as proud as he could be. It was like, *voilà*! I didn't look like me anymore. But I knew the truth. I looked ridiculous. The shoddy wig hardly fit me and I constantly had to adjust it to keep from showing tufts of blond hair at the front of my head. The sunglasses were tinted green. We had found my pants alongside the road and my shirt had been taken from a homeless camp.

I looked down at my clothes and adjusted my wig, shaking my head in disbelief. *Really!* I thought. I was a fifteen-year-old girl in a gray wig and sunglasses so cheap they didn't even sit straight on my face. *Do you really think this is going to work? Who in their right mind is going to think it's normal for a young girl to be wearing a gray wig?* Not to mention the fact that it was already falling apart. If it couldn't even make it through a day, how was it going to look in a week?

But even though I knew I looked ridiculous, I felt like a princess compared to how I felt in the robe and veil that I'd been wearing for almost nine months.

The next day we woke up early. Our nasty green bags were packed and ready to go. I considered our belongings as we hoisted them on our backs. We had a small purple tent—and I do mean small; it was barely big enough for two small adults, let alone large enough to get abused in every night—a couple of blankets, Mitchell's collection of holy books, and a few kitchen items. A little food. A little water. Some of Barzee's clothes and personal belongings. A few of Mitchell's prized possessions, including his knife. Though it didn't look like much, it seemed to weigh a ton!

Slinging the heavy bags over our shoulders, we made our way out to the highway.

And so started a miserable, exhausting, and convoluted journey back to Salt Lake City.

It took us a long time to get a ride. The first people to pick us up were a kind man and his son who took us twenty or thirty miles down the road, then dropped us off at a campground, paid our camp fees, and even brought us some groceries.

The next day a young woman with two male friends picked us up. She spent a lot of time asking me questions, trying to figure out why I was wearing a gray wig and why I was with two misfits like Mitchell and Barzee. But Mitchell never let me talk. Whenever she asked me anything, he'd jump in before I had a chance to answer. Which was a relief. I could hardly even look at her, let alone answer any of her questions. I was so used to being alone, so afraid of making Mitchell angry, and so intimidated by human contact that it terrified me to be peppered with her questions. After nine months of constant threats and manipulation, it was impossible for me to talk to anyone besides Mitchell and his angry wife. So though we rode with these people a long way, I never said a word.

We spent that night on a hillside that ran beside the highway. All of our food and water was gone and I was hungry and exhausted. Cars were rushing by like crazy. Mitchell didn't want anyone to see us, but the hill was barren and there was nowhere for us to hide, so we got up very early in the morning, broke camp, and started walking before the sun came up.

We walked almost the entire day. It was hot and exhausting. I thought I was going to die from the lack of water and the heat.

Over the next several days, there were times when I felt like we were going to walk all the way to Utah. We got occasional rides, but many of them were only for a few miles and then we'd have to walk again. Miles and miles went by as we trudged along, the green bags slung across our backs. We hardly ate. We suffered without water. Wanting to stay away from the Highway Patrol, we kept to the back roads and little towns. Pretty soon, we found ourselves out in the California desert. It was a stupid thing to do, trying to hitchhike across the desert without anything to eat or drink.

At one point we were standing at a lonely intersection in an unknown town. There was a pie restaurant on the corner and a kind stranger took us in and bought each of us a slice of pie. I've never eaten anything so delicious in my life! After we had eaten the pie, Mitchell snuck around to the back of the store where they sold the pies in boxes to ship around the country. He bought a whole pie and ate almost the entire thing himself, leaving Barzee and me only a sliver of a piece to share.

With that little bit of nutrition in my belly, Mitchell herded us out again, heading north. My pack was so heavy, I was so tired, and the footing on the side of the road was so poor that I stumbled constantly. I'm not sure how far we walked but it felt like an eternity before we finally came to a barren intersection with a sign that pointed toward Borrego Springs. Once again, I didn't have any idea where we were. Mitchell was the navigator. I was the pack mule.

A woman in a station wagon pulling a small trailer stopped to give us a ride. As we climbed in, she said that she had never picked up hitchhikers before but for some reason she had the feeling that she should give us a ride. I was so grateful! I was tired, hot, and hungry. To me she was a saint. As we drove, she tried to tell us about her recent move to Borrego Springs, but Mitchell kept interrupting, telling her his story, how he was a servant of the Lord who had been chosen to preach repentance to the world. On and on he went. I started feeling sorry for her, having to listen to him for so long. She finally dropped us off at a small Mexican restaurant in another unknown town.

After she drove away, Mitchell walked toward the restaurant. "Let's eat!" he said. I was shocked. I had thought that we were out of money. We went inside and, for the first time, Mitchell let me order what I wanted. It was the first hot meal I'd had in ages! I ate until I thought that I'd be sick.

After eating, we walked along the highway until it grew dark, then left the road and headed off into the desert to set up camp. When we awoke the next morning, the sun was blazing hot, turning our tent into an oven. I crawled out of the tent, already very thirsty, and started packing up our bags. Looking around, I realized that we were literally out in the middle of the desert. The empty road stretched into the distance, the only indication of civilization that I could see. Nothing but desert and barren hills in every direction. No sign of life at all. I paused to listen. The stillness was absolute.

We started walking. The road seemed to grow gooey from the rising heat. After an hour or two, we ate the last of our food: old carrots mixed with vinegar and a can of black olives. We didn't have any water. We kept on walking. By noon, I was starting to believe we were committing suicide by thirst.

An occasional car sped by, but none of them stopped or even slowed down. I was as miserable as I had ever felt. But Mitchell seemed to love it. It gave him an opportunity to show his physical prowess. Plus, he loved the idea of suffering for the Lord. I could almost read his mind: *I'm just wandering in the wilderness and waiting upon the Lord. I glory in persecution. For when I am weak, then am I strong.*

Finally, some friendly Mexicans picked us up and took us a few miles to where there was a fork in the road. After they dropped us off, we stood at the intersection, waiting for Mitchell to figure out which way to turn. As we waited, a woman in a blue car stopped beside us. She had passed us before, then had gone into the nearest town, bought some hamburgers, turned around, and brought them back to us. I eyed the hamburgers hungrily. Another kind woman. Another saint!

After she left us, we started walking again.

It was at this point that things got a little strange.

As we headed into Blythe, or Brawley, or something like that, an old and cankered Winnebago went cruising by. Looking at the creepy motor home, I was glad it hadn't stopped. But all of Satan's children recognize their own and, as I watched the Winnebago speeding down the road, I was distraught to see it pull over, then turn around and come back to pick us up.

It took a long time before the door flew open. Then the driver beckoned for us to climb in. The interior was dark and eerie. I wanted to run away. I started to back up, but Mitchell pushed me forward and forced me to climb on board.

The interior of the motor home was as disgusting as I had imagined. For one thing, it was filthy. For another, every inch of the water-soaked walls was covered with cutouts of naked women. Alongside each picture, the driver had written what he wanted to do to that girl. To call it creepy was an enormous understatement. Mitchell, of course, felt right at home.

The driver looked at us and said, "It took me a minute to open the door because I had to take down some of the cutouts that would have been offensive to the ladies."

I looked around in disgust. *So this isn't offensive?* I wanted to say. I shook my head.

"You know that's why I stopped to pick you up," he said to Mitchell. "You have these two ladies with you." He was talking to Mitchell as if we weren't even there. I felt like one of Mitchell's cows or something.

And the driver never took his eyes off of me as they talked. It was obvious what he had in mind.

They kind of talked around it for a moment, but Mitchell made it clear that it wasn't going to happen.

The man nodded. Okay. No big deal. They could still be friends.

Soon after that, Charlie, the Winnebago driver, was telling us about a nudist camp that he was heading to. "Want to join me?" he asked. Of course Mitchell did.

Charlie drove us to a secret oasis in the desert where there was a warm spring. He kept staring at me, waiting for me to take my clothes off, but Mitchell wasn't going to share me even visually. Handing me a large T-shirt and some old shorts, he told me to put them on. The spring felt cool in the hot afternoon and there were lots of naked people around, the vast majority of them old and wrinkled as dry prunes. We sat in the cool water surrounded by palm trees until the sun had gone down. That night we set up the tent outside of the old Winnebago. Charlie tried one more time to make an agreement with Mitchell, but Mitchell continued to refuse.

The next day, Charlie took us to a small town outside of Las Vegas and dropped us off. But he kept turning his motor home around and circling back to pick us up again. Mitchell, wanting nothing more of Charlie, forced us to hide in the bushes along the road. "You're mine!" he proclaimed. "I'm not going to share you. I don't care if he gave us a ride!"

I felt my stomach churn. So he wouldn't share me for a ride. But what if he got a better offer? The thought made me feel sick.

After Charlie had finally driven off, we started walking down the road again.

Another ride from a nice man in another decrepit car left us at another intersection on a nameless road in the middle of the scorching desert. We started to walk again. No water. No food. The day passed with no one else offering us a ride.

The next morning came as hot as ever. We walked and walked, always hoping for someone to pick us up. But the cars kept zooming by. By then, my light skin had been sunburned to a painful cherry red. My cheeks and nose were blistered and bleeding. The sunburn was very painful, and having to carry the heavy bags across my sunburned shoulders only made it worse. Finally, I took one of Mitchell's undershirts and wrapped it over my head to protect my neck and face.

As evening approached, I was desperate for want of water. I really didn't know how much farther I could go. Suddenly a white truck pulled over. A young man jumped out and started handing us bottles of ice-cold water. He told us that he had passed us on the road and had gone up to the next town to buy some water, then circled back to give it to us. Another act of kindness! Another saint! A bit more strength to go on.

A few rides and a lot of walking later, we finally made it to Las Vegas. We immediately made our way to the nearest place to eat. While we were inside the Burger King, a lot of the people stared at us, always whispering to each other. Nothing unusual about that. But this was much more than the normal amount of whispering and pointing. Mitchell was starting to get nervous. He shifted anxiously in his seat, his narrow eyes darting around. His hands were always moving, flittering in front of his face. Seeing his growing agitation, I grew nervous too. What if something goes wrong? I thought. What if he blames me? What if he hurts my family?

The moment we finished our food, Mitchell got up and commanded us to go.

As we were walking across the parking lot, a police car drove up. The officers got out and started questioning Mitchell. I couldn't hear everything they asked, but Mitchell was always calm and cool. "We are ministers for Christ. This is my wife and my daughter."

One of the officers looked at me. I immediately dropped my eyes.

The officers questioned him a little longer, but there was nothing they could do. There were lots of strange people in Las Vegas. We weren't the only ones they would stop that day. After a few minutes, they got back into their patrol car and drove away.

Free of the officers, Mitchell was frantic to get out of Vegas. His face was tight with fear, and he croaked in fury as he turned to me. "Once we make it back to Utah, we will go to the upper camp. There, you will stay! You will never leave the camp until the Lord has said it is time to come out."

Until the Lord said it was time to come out? I knew that meant forever. I started shaking with fear and dread. That wasn't the reason I had wanted to go to Utah! I needed to be seen around the city if I was ever going to be rescued. No one would find me on the mountain. I closed my eyes and started praying. *Please God, help me find a way. . . .*

We walked toward a nearby gas station, where a bunch of semi trucks were fueling up. Mitchell went into the truck stop to use the bathroom. While he was gone, one of the truck drivers walked over toward Barzee and asked if we needed a ride. The driver was a little worried when Mitchell came out of the building and he realized that we weren't traveling alone, but he agreed to take us anyway.

We climbed into his truck. Barzee got in the front seat while Mitchell guarded me in the cab area where the man had his bed. Mitchell asked the man how far north he was headed. The man said he was going to Orem, Utah.

My heart started pounding! I would almost be home!

We rode in silence for most of the way. As night settled, Mitchell told me to go to sleep. The next thing I knew, he was shaking me by the shoulder, telling me we had to get out. It was either very late at night or very early in the morning. We climbed wearily out of the truck and thanked the man.

Inside, my heart was singing! I was back in Utah. I was almost home!

36.

I Am Elizabeth

The darkness was full around us. It was biting cold and I realized I wasn't used to the Utah cold weather any longer. I wasn't sure where we were, but I could hear the hum of the freeway to my left. The parking lot was dotted with yellow security lights and there was no one else around. I could barely make out the outline of the mountains to the east, dark shadows against the starry sky, their snowy peaks glistening in the night. I thought I recognized the distinctive peaks of Mount Timpanogos, which would put us somewhere south of Provo, but I wasn't sure. Looking at my surroundings, I felt a rush of joy. It was early March. I had been gone for almost six months. I was so glad to be near my home.

Mitchell looked around, his eyes darting here and there. He was very nervous. It was the first time I had been in Utah without my robes and veil. And this was deep in enemy territory, back in the very heart of the state. He stared at my ridiculous wig, the crooked dark glasses, and the clothes that didn't fit, then shook his head. *Have I made a mistake in doing this?* the uncertainty on his face seemed to say.

He motioned to a park on the other side of the highway. I thought I saw a sign that read CAMELOT, but it was very dark and I couldn't tell for sure. Mitchell started jogging toward it, picking up speed as he ran.

He is scared! I realized as Barzee and I followed him toward the park.

We crossed the highway and walked through the gate. As we got closer I was able to read some of the signs. We walked past King Arthur's Round Table and moved to the back of the park. Picking out a patch of grass beside a gentle river, we set up our small tent. A shiver ran through me from the cold, and I realized that my single blanket was not going to keep me warm.

Before we went to sleep, Mitchell raped me, as he always did.

It would prove to be the last time.

Mitchell woke us early. The morning was gray and cold, the grass thick with heavy frost. I could see my breath inside the tent and the sides of the fabric were dripping with condensation from our breathing. My body ached from the cold and being crammed inside the small tent with two adults who would just as soon lie on top of me as give me any room. We climbed out of the tent before it was fully light, Mitchell pushing us to hurry. He wanted to get out of the park before anyone saw that we had been sleeping there. I took the tent down as quickly as I could, but my fingers were icy cold and it was difficult to make them move.

After packing up our gear, we headed out of the park. We walked along the frontage road for a short distance before we came to a convenience store with a McDonald's inside. Food! I was so hungry! We walked in and placed our order. The woman at the cash register mumbled as she explained that it was hard for her to talk because she'd had her wisdom teeth out the day before. Mitchell kept asking her all kinds of questions, and it was obviously painful for her to answer, so she was happy to hand us our food and get us on our way.

We headed to a booth and stuffed our breakfast down in silence. As soon as we were finished, Mitchell herded us out of the restaurant.

Standing on the sidewalk in front of the store, Mitchell took a look around. It was still early and there weren't very many cars around. But there was a young man who was getting some gas and Mitchell walked up and asked if we could get a lift. The young man looked at us suspiciously. I knew that we looked like a bunch of dirty vagabonds, but he hesitated only a moment before he said, "Sure. Jump in."

We climbed into his car. As I got into the backseat, he looked over his shoulder. "Be careful, that door is broken. It might fall off in your hands."

I could see that the inside panel was barely hanging on, but I got the door shut and we took off. He took us to Orem, but that was as far as he could go. When I got out of the car, the door panel fell off in my hands. "I'm so, so sorry," I said as I tried to put it back in place.

"Don't worry about it. It's not your fault." He laughed.

I fixed the door as best I could, then got out and the young man drove off.

We headed toward the bus stop, which was not very far away. Tons of people were around. Most of them couldn't keep from staring at us, causing me the usual embarrassment and shame. We climbed on the bus, which was so crowded that many of us had to stand. I kept my eyes down, staring at Mitchell's feet. He kept very close, never more than a few inches away. His eyes were always moving, darting here and there. Barzee seemed withdrawn, as if she had resigned herself to whatever lay ahead. Since the night the devil and his angels had tortured her by cutting her body in two, it seemed she had lost a lot of energy.

Most of the people on the bus were either students or business-people heading into the city and we stood out among the well-dressed crowd. As the bus swayed along, I looked up to see a young man staring at me. I lowered my head again. I could still feel his eyes on me and my heart started racing. So conditioned was I to being alone, and so conditioned to feeling terrified of Mitchell's threats, that I immediately withdrew from any human interaction, even if it was just a glance.

After a few minutes, the man moved toward Mitchell and started talking to him. "Who are you?" he asked.

Mitchell didn't say anything.

"Where you headed?" The man was trying to be nice.

"We are ministers of the Lord," Mitchell answered.

"Ministers? Really! What do you believe?"

Mitchell obviously didn't feel like preaching. He answered the man's questions only briefly, not really saying anything. I glanced at the young man out of the corner of my eye. He nodded at me. "Why is she wearing a gray wig? Is that part of your religion?"

I glanced toward Mitchell, seeing the panic in his eye. "We believe many things," he answered curtly. He was very defensive. His voice was sharp and on-edge.

The young man didn't seem to care. He pressed a little harder. "The way she is dressed, the wig and stuff, is that part of some religious ceremony? She is so young. Is it designed to teach humility or something?"

Mitchell refused to answer. Taking me by the elbow, he edged me toward the front of the bus. The young man watched us curiously. We got off at the next stop, leaving him to stare at us through the dark windows as the bus pulled away.

Standing on the side of the road, Mitchell held my elbow in a painful grip. "Once I get you back to camp, you will *never* leave, Shearjashub! It is too dangerous! I will not lose you. I will not put myself in danger. I am too important to the world. You will go to the camp and stay there. That is the Lord's desire."

I thought back on the way the young man on the bus had looked at me, the way he had challenged Mitchell, the way he had kept his eyes on us while the bus had driven away. Mitchell had been shaken by his advances, but I would pay the price.

We waited for the next bus, then jumped on. I don't know if Mitchell even knew where the bus was going, he just wanted to get off the street. This bus was not very crowded and no one asked us any questions. We sat alone, surrounded by looks of disgust. But that was no surprise. We were filthy and we smelled bad. I wondered if I'd ever feel clean again.

We only went a couple of miles before Mitchell forced us to get off the bus again.

We had made it beyond the point of the mountain that separates the Salt Lake Valley from Utah County. I looked at the mountains on the east, recognizing their features. We were very close to my grandparents' house. Less than twenty miles from my home! I flashed back to summer afternoons, playing in their backyard that had been flooded by the irrigation ditch. Bobbing for apples. Playing with my cousins. It felt so good to be so close to home.

Then I thought of what Mitchell had told me: *You're going to spend the rest of your life up at the camp!* My heart sank again, my stomach tying into knots.

We were standing on State Street, one of the main roads that leads downtown. Mitchell started walking without saying where he was going. Barzee and I followed as we always did. He walked into a Walmart, where he stole some new hiking boots and some other things. Our green bags were bulging with the stolen items by the time we made it to the front of the store. Mitchell paid for a few things to relieve any suspicion, then we walked toward the door. People were always looking at us. We just didn't fit in.

Passing by the main entrance, I glanced at the wall with all of the pictures of the missing children. Am I up there? I wondered. I started walking toward the wall, scanning the photographs. Mitchell grabbed me firmly by the shoulder. A sharp pain moved up and down my arm. He squeezed tighter and leaned toward me. "You are not up there. No one remembers or cares about you anymore. You are mine. You'll always be mine. Your previous life is over. Now, come on! Let's go!"

He started to pull on my arm, but I pulled back, staring at the pictures of the children. I don't know why, I just couldn't seem to pull away. So many children. So many shattered lives. But I didn't see my picture, which meant that Mitchell was right. Everyone had forgotten me. I was not on the missing posters anymore.

He jerked on my arm again. "Quit calling attention to yourself!"

I turned around and followed him out of the store.

We walked down State Street toward the middle of the city. We were on 106th South Street. We had a long way to go. But I knew what was going to happen. We'd take another bus downtown, then walk east, toward the university, then up the canyon toward our old camp. Then I'd be in my prison and Mitchell would be home.

I walked wearily, dragging my feet. I felt like I was walking toward a penitentiary with my personal prison guards. I had felt this way before.

We had only walked two blocks when I saw the first police car. It came up and stopped immediately beside us. Mitchell cursed. Barzee sucked in a breath of air, her throat seeming to gurgle. We kept on walking. I kept my head down.

Another police car came up and stopped beside us, then another one in front. I heard Mitchell cursing once again. "We shouldn't have done it!" he hissed in fear. "We shouldn't have done this." His voice was tight with rage.

I felt sick. I felt elated. I didn't know what to do!

I thought about every threat that Mitchell had ever made about my family. I thought about the painful life that lay before me in the camp. Years of being raped. Years of hunger and abuse. Years of being trapped up on the mountain.

I thought of everything that I had gone through.

All I wanted to do was go home.

Then I thought about my little brother and sister. I loved them so much! I wanted to keep them safe!

The policemen jumped out of their cars and walked toward us.

Please help me protect my family! I prayed.

"Sir, I need to talk to you," the first policeman said.

Mitchell kept on walking.

"Sir, I need you to stop. I need to talk to you!"

Mitchell didn't answer.

An overwhelming feeling of panic swarmed over me. *Please, God, help to set me free!*

"*Sir!* I need you to talk to me. I need to see some ID!"

The officers became aggressive, all of them shouting now. Mitchell's eyes were wide with fear, his face draining of all color. He stammered once or twice, trying to get something out, but his voice seemed to crack. Barzee didn't say anything, holding close to her husband, her lips tight across her teeth. She glared at me, her eyes hateful and defiant. I flashed back to the scene at the library when she had pinched my leg underneath the table, her iron fingers digging into my skin, communicating all of the fear that I had been subjected to for months. I looked at her, then turned away, my mind a jumble of hope and fear.

Another policeman came toward us. His voice was firm. He seemed to be in charge. The other officers gathered around. Though they were talking to Mitchell, their attention was primarily on me.

"What is your name?" one of the officers asked me.

I felt almost dizzy. I was sick with uncertainty and fear.

"What is your name?" he asked again.

Was it Esther? Was it Shearjashub? I hadn't been called Elizabeth for so long.

The officer frowned at me. He didn't treat me like I was his friend.

I felt like I was falling over a waterfall. *Don't say anything. Don't give Mitchell a reason, or he'll hurt you! Don't give him a reason to hurt your family!*

"Hey, I need to know your name," the officer pushed again.

What will Mitchell do to me? What will he do to my family?

"Your name!" the officer demanded.

"Her name is Shearjashub," Mitchell finally answered.

The officer only glanced at Mitchell. "Is that right? Is that your name?"

I thought of the long black knife. I thought of the fact that Mitchell had never spent more than a few nights in jail. He seemed impervious to being captured. He would kill my family if I talked!

"Where are you from?" the officer demanded.

"We just got here from California," Mitchell answered for me. "We are preachers. We aren't doing anything but serving the Lord."

The officer ignored him. "Is that right?" he asked, looking into my eyes.

"She is my daughter."

"Where are you going?" the officer asked me, moving a little closer.

"We're heading to Salt Lake City," Mitchell answered for me again. "We're ministers. We've done nothing wrong." His voice was calm and cool now. There was no sign of panic or deception. He spoke softly and acted very confident and sure.

"I'm not speaking to you, sir, I'm speaking to the young lady." The officer stared at me, waiting for me to say something.

"She's scared," one of the other officers whispered from the back. "She doesn't dare say anything."

The officers huddled together, a couple of them keeping their eyes on Mitchell and me. Barzee seemed to have melted into the background. It was as if no one cared that she was even there.

"She's scared of him," the officer said to the others. "She's too scared to even answer. You've got to get her by herself."

One of officers walked toward me and put a gentle hand on my shoulder. I immediately flashed back to when Mitchell had grabbed me in the Walmart just a few minutes before. Mitchell's hand had been a death grip, like the Grim Reaper on my arm. But this was different. It didn't feel like the officer was going to hurt me. Maybe he could actually keep me safe.

He nudged me away from Mitchell, then leaned over and looked me in the eye. "What is your name?" he asked me gently.

I felt my heart racing in my chest.

More than anything, I wanted to tell him! I didn't want to stay with Mitchell. I didn't want to walk with him up into the mountains. I didn't want to be raped every day. I didn't want to suffer hunger anymore.

All I wanted was to be with my mom and dad. All I wanted was to go home!

But Mitchell's face filled my mind like a monster in a dream. I heard his voice. It was the devil. I had heard it so many times before: *I will kill your brothers and your little sister. I will kill your mom and dad. I will plunge my knife in and I will turn it! I will kill them all!*

The officer waited, then leaned toward me, looking me right in the eyes again. When he spoke, his voice was soft and assuring. "Are you Elizabeth Smart? Because if you are, your family has missed you so much since you were gone! They want you back. They love you. They want you to come home."

For a moment, my world seemed to absolutely stop. I looked at him. He looked at me. I felt calm. I felt assured. Months of fear and pain seemed to melt before the sun. I felt a sweet assurance.

"I am Elizabeth," I finally said.

37.

Mom and Dad

———

The officer turned me around and handcuffed me, then put me in the back of his car. This wasn't what I had expected, and I wondered what was going on. Staring through the window, I saw the other officers surrounding Brian David Mitchell and Wanda Barzee. I watched as they were cuffed, but then the officer started talking to me and I had to look away.

By the time I turned back, Mitchell and Barzee were gone.

It would be many years before I would see them again.

The policeman told me they were taking me down to the station. The police car started moving. I had never been inside a police car and I had to crane my neck to see out of the divider that separated me from the front seat. The cuffs were uncomfortable and it scared me, not being able to move my arms. I was feeling just as fearful as I had felt before. Why had they handcuffed me? What had I done wrong? Did they think it was my fault? Did they think I was a criminal like Mitchell?

We rode along in silence. "What's going to happen to them?" I finally asked.

I could tell by the look on the policeman's face that he thought that I was worried about them, like maybe I wanted to be with them, or that I wanted to make sure they'd be okay. Nothing could have been further from the truth. I was scared to death that they might put me in the same cell as Mitchell. I was certain he would kill me if they did. That was the only reason that I asked. I just wanted to know if they were going to keep me safe.

The officer didn't answer. So I stared out the window and wondered what was going to happen to me as we rode along in silence.

I was nearly overcome by everything that had just happened. I had gone from being a hopeless prisoner to being someone who would soon be free. But it hadn't hit me yet and I wasn't sure that it was real. I wasn't sure that something wasn't going to happen that would take it all away.

We drove to the police station, where I was uncuffed and led into a small room. There were no windows, only a shabby sofa, and all of the walls were bare. My heart was still racing. I had no idea what to expect.

"You can take off your disguise," a policeman told me before he left the room. I immediately pulled off the dark glasses and the nasty wig and dropped them on the floor.

I sat alone. No one came to me. Were they going to let me call my mom and dad? Were they going to send me to prison? Surely they'd let me talk to someone before they sent me away! Maybe they were going to let me go? But if they were going to set me free, wouldn't they have done it already? I wanted to stand and test the door to see if it was locked, but I didn't dare. I was terrified that I would open it and see Mitchell standing there.

I don't know how long I was in the room, but it seemed to be a lifetime. My heart was constantly racing. As I sat there, I kept thinking about being sent to prison. I decided that it didn't sound that bad. Compared to what I had been living through, it would have been a huge improvement. As long as they didn't put me back with Mitchell, it was going to be okay.

I leaned back on the sofa and tried to relax. Suddenly, the door flew open. Looking up, I felt my heart leap. My dad was standing there!

He looked at me as if he were seeing a ghost. His face showed absolute shock, as if I couldn't be real. The dead was living! His daughter had come home! I looked at him and waited. Time froze. My heart stopped. I don't know if I breathed. We stared at each other for what seemed like an eternity but must have been less than a second, then my daddy ran to me and grabbed me and started hugging me as only a father can. It was a grasp of desperation and giddy happiness and absolute disbelief. It was a hug of relief and happiness that is impossible to describe. But I felt it. And I knew he felt it. We held on to each other very tight. Then he pulled away and looked at me, staring into my face. "Elizabeth, is it really you?!"

It took me a moment before I was able to answer. "Yeah, Dad, it's me."

Both of us started crying, a swell of emotion that erupted from the very bottoms of our souls.

Then it seemed I heard a voice inside my head: *You are home. You are home. It's going to be okay.*

I leaned into my dad's shoulder and held on like I was going to drown.

Your dad is there. You are safe. He will never let another person hurt you. Your mom will always stand beside you. It is going to be okay.

We hugged and cried awhile, neither of us saying anything. Then an officer stepped carefully into the room. "We need to take you to Salt Lake City headquarters," he said.

My dad turned around to look at him.

"Mr. Smart, could you and your daughter come with us? We have a car waiting."

We were escorted through the corridors to a back door, where a maroon police car was waiting. We climbed into the backseat. One patrol car pulled in front of us, and another pulled in behind.

The moment we had pulled out of the parking lot, my dad looked at me and exclaimed, "We *have* to call your mom!" He pulled out his cell phone and started punching at the numbers. I could hear her phone ring and then her voice say, "Hello?"

My dad was shouting, "Lois, it's her! It's really her! She's alive!"

My mom started screaming into the phone.

"Yes, yes, it's true!" my dad shouted back. "No, I'm with her! She's alive. She's okay. I'm with her right now!

I could hear my mom's voice screaming even louder through the phone, "Let me talk to her! Pass the phone, pass the phone! Is she hurt? Is she all right? *Pass me the phone!*"

My dad handed me the phone.

"Mom . . ." I said, my voice barely more than a whisper.

"Elizabeth, is that really you? Are you okay! Is it true? Is that you? Are you all right?"

Her voice sounded exactly as I remembered it, and for just a fraction of a second I flashed back to those first days on the mountain, reliving the fear that I might forget the sound of her voice.

It's okay. You are home. It's going to be okay.

"Mom . . ." I started to answer when the cell-phone battery went dead. *Ahhhh!* Seriously! Of all of the things that could have happened! My dad looked at me sheepishly and tried to smile.

It seemed to take forever to get to the police headquarters, but we finally made it and I was escorted to another private room. My mom was waiting for me. Seeing her, I almost felt like I couldn't breathe. She looked just like an angel. Nobody could ever look as beautiful as she looked to me. She jumped up and ran to me and started hugging me so tightly I *really* couldn't breathe. She was crying. I was crying. It was the same thing as with my dad. We held on to each other like we would never let go. We cried and hugged and smiled and laughed. "Elizabeth! Elizabeth!" she repeated again and again.

She could hardly let me go when one of the officers came back into the room. "Elizabeth, we need to ask you a few questions."

I looked desperately at my mom. I didn't want to go. Why couldn't I stay with her? My dad was already gone, somewhere in the police station, talking to some of the other officers.

"Elizabeth, we need to talk to you," the officer pressed. Reluctantly, my mom let me go.

The officer escorted me into another room. A woman and a man were waiting there. They introduced themselves as investigators, then started asking me all sorts of questions. I answered as best as I could, but I felt overwhelmed. I was on the edge of breaking down. After everything that had happened to me, I just wanted to go home. "I just want to be with my parents," I finally cried. "I just want to see my family. Can't we do this later? Can't I please go home?"

My dad suddenly stormed into the room. They had no right to take me from them, and he was very mad. "We will do this later!" he demanded, his face red with anger. There was no way he was going to let them question me right then and there.

He pulled me from the room and out into the hall. Down the corridor we went, back into the same room that my mom and I had been in before. My brothers and little sister were waiting for me. It was all of the crying and hugging and laughing all over again. It was one of the rare moments that is pure and incomprehensible joy. Some people may live their entire lives and never feel what we felt in that moment. It was beautiful. It was magic. It was everything that I could have asked for.

All of our family was together.

I was really home.

We were safe. Mitchell wasn't going to hurt us.

I had my entire life before me.

Everything was going to be okay.

William, the baby, was four years old now. He didn't join in the hugging. Instead, he looked at me with great suspicion. I tried to pick him up, but he turned away and reached out for my mom. That broke my heart a bit.

I've been gone a long, long time, I thought.

"Don't worry, Elizabeth," my mom assured me. "He'll remember you. Just give him a little time."

Then my oldest brother, Charles, came forward and held me by the arms. "I have felt so terrible, not only because I wasn't there to protect you, but because the last thing I ever said to you was to tease you about some stupid little thing. I'm so sorry! I'm so sorry. But I promise, never again will I say good-bye without telling you I love you. That will always be the last thing that I say whenever we say good-bye again."

And he was right. He always says that now. It is one of the reasons that I love him and why I am so glad he is my brother.

Another officer stepped into the room. "We need to take you to hospital to do a checkup," he said.

Once again, I was separated from my family. But this time, my mom came with me. She wasn't leaving my side again.

We were rushed out a back door of the police headquarters and into a white van with darkened windows. I couldn't believe how many people were waiting, hoping to get a glimpse of me. There were hundreds of reporters and photographers and well-wishers along the road. I was shocked. It seemed incredible! All of them were there for me!

At the hospital, I was poked and prodded and tested in pretty much every way you can imagine. But I didn't mind so much because I was with my mom.

After the examination, I had to give up the clothes that I was wearing. The police wanted to keep them for evidence. I was more than happy to get rid of them. They were a piece of another life, another world. I wanted to put it all behind me. Besides, they were so filthy and disgusting—castoffs from a homeless camp—I hated to even touch them anymore.

But what was I going to wear out of the hospital? I couldn't leave in just a gown. My mom and a couple of the hospital staff rustled up a white sweatsuit and some white booties for my feet. The outfit was far too small, and I felt ridiculous, but there was nothing else to do.

Holding hands, my mother and I made our way to another private door on the back side of the hospital and climbed into the waiting police van.

On the way home, the officers were wondering how to get me into my house without subjecting me to the massive crowd that had gathered outside. They talked about driving into the backyard, but there was no way that was going to work. They eventually settled on just driving into my garage and not letting me get out of the van until the garage door had come down.

Turning onto the street that led to my house, I saw for the first time all of the media and other people who had come to celebrate my return. It was nearly overwhelming. Once again I had to wonder that all of those people were there for me.

We pulled into the garage and I waited in the van. But I could hear a hundred voices, shouting, crying, calling out my name. I shook my head in disbelief.

Walking into the house—my house!—I stood in the middle of the living room and took a long look around. It seemed like I had died and gone to heaven. The lights were so bright! The carpet was so soft! The furniture was so beautiful. My family stood inside the room and looked at me. To me, they were a vision. I was so glad to be home!

"Well . . . what do you want to do?" my mother asked.

The answer was really easy. I wanted to take a bath!

Mom took me upstairs and led me toward my bedroom. Walking

in, I was shocked to see that all my clothes were exactly as I had left them on the night I had been taken. I turned to my mother. "Mom, you couldn't even fold my clothes for me?" I teased.

She didn't laugh. She didn't even smile. She looked away, embarrassed, then turned back and wiped her eyes. "Elizabeth, I couldn't. I just couldn't." She had to pause to clear her throat. She shook her head sadly. "Every time I came in here to organize your things, I started crying. It was too hard. It was too painful. I simply couldn't do it. I don't know if you'll ever understand."

I reached out and held her. And as I did, a thought came into my mind: *Your mom did her best. She has tried so hard to be so strong.*

We picked up a few things in the room, then I took a beautiful bubble bath. It felt better than anything I had ever felt before.

By then, it was time to go to bed. My parents gathered us around to have our family prayers. There were plenty of thanks to be given. It was a beautiful thing. After prayers, I got up, said good night to my parents, and started walking up to my bedroom. Both of my parents just stared at me.

"We were thinking," my dad said with a bit of hesitation, "you know, maybe we'd pull your mattress into our bedroom and you could sleep by us on the floor."

I almost laughed. "No, Dad. No more floors for me. I want to sleep in my own bed."

They only looked at me. They were not satisfied.

"Mom, Dad, I promise I'll be here in the morning."

It turned out that I hadn't convinced them. I woke up several times that night to see them standing in the darkness, checking to make sure that I was safe.

The next morning, I woke up before my brothers or sister did. After struggling to find some clothes that fit me—I had grown a lot over the past nine months—I got dressed and went downstairs.

Coming down the stairs, I met my dad walking through the front door with a green teddy bear and a bouquet of chrysanthemums. "Wow, thanks, Dad!" I said. I thought he was being nice.

"They're not from me," he said. "Someone bought them to the front door and asked me to give them to you." But that was just the beginning. A few hours later, our house looked like a floral shop. Once again, I had to wonder, *All of this for me?*

Sometime in the early morning, my grandparents burst into the house. They were frantic with happiness and exhaustion. They had driven all night from Palm Springs to come to see me. I don't know for certain, but it seems they may have broken a speed limit or two to get there so fast.

Hearing all of the commotion from my grandparents' entry, the other kids woke up and came downstairs. We all stood in the middle of the room and hugged each other. To my great relief, my baby brother, William, joined in the hug!

I felt so loved. So safe. I had not felt that way in a very long time. *I am home. I am home. Everything is going to be okay.*

The only thing I wanted to do was to have another bath. Then, while the other members of my family were waiting in the living room, my mom pulled me aside at the top of the stairs.

"Before it gets too crazy, I need to tell you something," she said.

I turned to look at her. She was so beautiful to me.

"This is important," she started. I could see from the look on her face that it was. I listened as intently as I could. And I'm very glad I did, for what she was about to say turned out to be the best advice that anyone has ever given me. In fact, I would say it changed my life.

"Elizabeth, what this man has done is terrible. There aren't any words that are strong enough to describe how wicked and evil he is! He has taken nine months of your life that you will never get back again. But the best punishment you could ever give him is to be happy. To move forward with your life. To do exactly what you want. Because, yes, this will probably go to trial and some kind of sentencing will be given to him and that wicked woman. But even if that's true, you may never feel like justice has been served or that true restitution has been made.

"But you don't need to worry about that. At the end of the day, God is our ultimate judge. He will make up to you every pain and loss that you have suffered. And if it turns out that these wicked people are not punished here on Earth, it doesn't matter. His punishments are just. You don't ever have to worry. You don't ever have to even think about them again."

She paused, as if the next words were the most important. "You be happy, Elizabeth. Just be happy. If you go and feel sorry for yourself, or if you dwell on what has happened, if you hold on to your pain, that is allowing him to steal more of your life away. So don't you do that! Don't you let him! There is no way that he deserves that. Not one more second of your life. You keep every second for yourself. You keep them and be happy. God will take care of the rest."

It's been ten years since my mother said those words.

The years have proven she was right.

38.

Comfort in My Bed

———

That first night I lay in my bed. I found it hard to sleep. My legs were agitated and I felt restless.

The night was dark, and the yellow light from the streetlights filtered into my room. If I held still, I could hear the occasional sound of cars driving on the road behind my house. Tomahawk Drive. The road where Mitchell had forced me to hide behind the bushes while the police car had driven by. I lay underneath my soft comforter, my head atop my fluffy pillow. It almost felt uncomfortable, sleeping in a real bed.

For the first time in months, I was going to sleep without suffering from hunger. I was clean. I hadn't just been raped. I hadn't just been forced to do things that I couldn't even speak about. I was surrounded by my family. I wasn't thirsty or exhausted. I hadn't been forced to drink a cup of dirty rainwater to keep my thirst down. I hadn't been forced to drink so much alcohol that I was sick. I hadn't just had a pornographic magazine shoved in my face. I wasn't cold. I wasn't hot. I wasn't lonely. I didn't have to lie in bed and wonder, What are my mom and dad doing? Are they okay? Were they happy?

Did they think about me anymore? I didn't have to wonder, What will my future look like? How long was Mitchell going to live? Would I ever be free again? Would I ever go to school? Would there ever be anyone else in my life except for Barzee and Mitchell?

I had my life back. I had a future. Everything that had been stolen had been given back to me.

I thought back, my mind drifting into memories that were powerful and very clear. Waking up that night, right there in that very bed, the same yellow light filtering through the window and a long knife at my neck. Hiking up the mountain. Asking Mitchell that, if he was going to kill me, he do it near the trail where my body could be found. Walking into the high camp and meeting Barzee. Her cold smile. Her hard embrace. The white robes. The first time that he raped me, Barzee sitting passively outside the tent.

All of these memories came flooding into my mind.

But there were other memories that I lived through that night as well.

Memories that gave me hope. Memories that gave me comfort.

The constant feeling that I was not alone. That God had never left me. That He was as close as any prayer.

The assurance that my grandfather had been called back home so that he could walk beside me, my heavenly bodyguard.

The night I had been given a cup of cold water by my pillow.

The night that it rained.

The reassuring voice that I had heard when I was standing in the fountain, the cool water washing over my feet. Wanting the water to wash my soul away, I had resolved again, *Whatever it takes to survive this. Whatever it takes to live.*

The young man in San Diego who had brightened up my Christmas by giving me a radio, allowing me to hear some Christmas music, even if only for a while.

The people who volunteered to feed the homeless on a day when they wanted to be home with their families.

All of the people who had searched for me. I was only beginning to understand everything that they had done. They had kept the search alive. They were the key to finding me! Were it not for them, no one would have recognized me once we had returned to Salt Lake City. Were it not for them, I'd be confined up on the mountain instead of lying in my bed.

All of the people who had stopped to give us a ride, or give us food or give us a little water as we hiked back from California.

Yes, I had lived through many miracles. I had experienced tender mercies that literally kept me alive. I had been carried by the love of others, and in many ways I had been blessed.

Rolling over, I pulled the blanket around my chin and thanked God once again that I was home.

39.

Trial

———

November 2010

It had been almost eight years since I had seen Brian David Mitchell. During that time I had finished high school, pursued a degree at BYU in music performance, had a few boyfriends, been to a lifetime of receptions, got a new dog, enjoyed many nights with my family, and made a lot of friends. I'd been skiing and camping and riding on my horse. I had enjoyed picnics and vacations and warm summer nights in my backyard. At the time of the trial, I was living in Paris, where I was serving an eighteen-month volunteer mission for my church. I had been able to come home and spend a few days with my family during the trial, but I looked forward to going back and finishing my service to the wonderful people I had come to love in France.

During the same eight years, Mitchell had been locked up in jail. He had told a thousand lies and sung a thousand songs. He had pretended that he was crazy and manipulated a few doctors into believing that his insanity was real. He had continued to insist that he was a holy prophet and that he spoke to God. He had pretended that he was sick, sometimes dropping into seizures upon the floor. He had been betrayed by his own wife and faced a dozen different prison cell mates, none of whom appreciated what he'd done. He had become a media sensation, his bearded face and narrow eyes making him one of the most recognized criminals in the world.

Now it was time for him to face the law.

The Federal Courthouse is a large, tan, neoclassical sandstone building in downtown Salt Lake City. It has a fenced parking lot in the back, but all of the entrances are visible to the public. A large crowd had gathered outside the courthouse, many of them photographers and television crews who were frantic to get any kind of picture that they could publish in the press. I could hear them shouting as my unmarked van pulled into the court parking lot. Surrounded by my family and a few key supporters, including a young woman named Katy Lund who had served with me in France and had become my closest friend, I was escorted into the courthouse through a back door. Ducking out of sight, I tried to ignore the press.

We were taken into a private room to avoid the boisterous crowd that had assembled in the courtroom. Finally, and at the very last moment before the judge was to get the trial started for the day, I was taken into the courtroom. It was everything that you'd expect. A raised box for the jury. High ceilings. A beautiful wood dais for the judge. The courtroom was absolutely packed. I was led to a seat behind the prosecuting attorneys and their staff.

A few minutes later, a large door to the right of the witness stand was pulled open. Everyone waited, but no one appeared. Then I heard him singing. It was not a beautiful sound. It was sick and scratchy and the song was nearly unrecognizable. It seemed to take a long time, but he finally walked into the room.

And there he was in all his glory: Brian David Mitchell. Immanuel David Isaiah. The Holy Prophet of his God.

His eyes were almost closed and his head was tilted upward just a little bit. He was thin, his cheekbones sunken underneath his hollow eyes. He wore the same beard but it was fuller now and he had the same long hair. His hands were cuffed in front of him and another chain ran around his back, holding his arms to his sides. The chains around his ankles made it difficult for him to walk, so he waddled into the courtroom, the sound of his chains clinking through the quiet room. He wore a simple pale shirt and loose-fitting pants. He was completely surrounded by security guards but he seemed to ignore them. Walking into the courtroom, he kept on singing, an awkward and lonely sound. His guards escorted him to his seat at the table with his defense attorneys. The guards helped him to sit down, but with all of the chains around his hands and feet he seemed to fall into his chair.

And there he sat, his eyes closed, his head back, his voice filling the courtroom as he sang.

I didn't take my eyes off of him. I *wanted* him to look at me. But he didn't. He kept on singing, his eyes closed. But I knew that he knew that I was there.

I was anxious, mainly because I didn't know what to expect. Not on any level. I was walking into the dark. What was he going to do? What was he going to say? How was he going to react when he finally looked at me?

I thought he might stand up and shake his fist, telling me to repent. I thought he might scream out that I was an unfaithful wife who had betrayed the Lord's servant. I thought he might tell me that I had failed my earthly mission. I could imagine him doing any number of crazy things

But as I sat there, I realized I really didn't care.

Nine years had passed since he had snuck into my room to kidnap me. My life had gone on. And I had been able to do what my mother had told me. *Don't you let him steal one more second of your life. Not one more second! You be happy. You move on.*

He was a nightmare, but it was over. I had woken up and I was safe now. I'd never let him hurt me or steal another moment of my life away. Soon the trial would be over, then I'd never have to see him or hear his voice or think about him again. This chapter in my life would be closed forever. I would go on with my life. Mitchell would go back to jail. I would be happy while he'd be . . . what?

I didn't care.

The trial was long. It seemed that some of the testimonies sounded more like personal résumés of lawyers trying to impress the audience than anything designed to prove guilt or innocence. Some of the testimony made me mad. Some made me happy. Some of it bored me almost to tears. But there were parts of the trial that, even now, I can remember word for word.

At one point David Backman, one of the prosecuting attorneys, was questioning a defense witness, Dr. Stephen Golding, who was testifying that Brian David Mitchell was incapable of knowing right from wrong. Backman had a pen in his hand and he was walking toward the podium to write down some notes when he must have realized that he didn't need his notes to make his point. He threw the pen down and began:

"Dr. Golding, is Dr. Welner a psychiatrist?"

"Ah, yes, I think so."

"Dr. Golding, is Dr. Gardner a psychiatrist?"

"Ah, yes."

"Dr. Golding, are you a psychiatrist?"

"No, I'm not."

"No further questions, Your Honor."

At that moment, I knew Mitchell wasn't going to get away with it. He wasn't going to be able to convince the jury, or the world, that he was crazy. He wasn't going to convince the jury, or the world, that he didn't know what he was doing. He wasn't a prophet. He hadn't received any visions. He hadn't talked to God. All he was was a dirty pedophile who liked living on the streets.

And though he never looked at me, or spoke to me, or acknowledged me in any way, there was one time when we did have a final communication between us.

One morning, when things were not going very well for the defendant, Brian David Mitchell suddenly stopped singing, fell down, and started shaking on the floor. He was moaning and frothing and acting as if he were going to die. His attorneys fell beside him, cradling him in their arms. "Immanuel! Immanuel!" one of them cried.

Oh, come on, I thought. This is ridiculous! All of us know this isn't real.

The paramedics came running into the room and got him positioned on a gurney. It was then that Mitchell rolled his head to look at me. He stopped shaking. He stopped moaning. He looked me straight in the eyes. He seemed to smile an evil grin. It was almost as if I could hear him talking, the look on face was so clear: *See! I have won, Shearjashub! I have won! Even now, when I am chained, I can do exactly what I want to do. If I want to finish this trial, I can make it end for the day. God has protected me. God will always protect me. I am His servant. And you are my wife!*

But even as horrible as he was to look at, nothing in that moment scared me or made me flash back. It didn't make me shrink away. It didn't make me cower. I wasn't afraid of the present. I wasn't afraid of what might come. I knew that I could stand on my own two feet. I knew that Mitchell would never hurt me again.

So I returned his cold stare, never looking away. *No, Brian David*

Mitchell, I am stronger than you. I'm not afraid of my future. And I'm not afraid of you. Not another second will I give you. I will live and I'll be happy. That is how this story ends.

We seemed to stare at each other for a long moment and then the paramedics wheeled the gurney away.

40.

Gratitude and Faith

———

When I go around the country and talk to different groups, I always get asked the same questions. "How did you survive?" and "How did you overcome what has happened to you?"

The answer to first question is pretty simple. The main reason I was able to survive is because of my God, my family, and my community.

The answer to the second question is a little harder to explain.

I think a few people might look at me and almost not believe what I say. Some of them might think, given the fact that I haven't received any professional counseling, that something must still be wrong with me, that I'm hiding my wounds or putting on a happy face. Some might think that I'm carrying a bit of baggage, or that there are certain things that I'm not ready yet to face.

But it's very important to stress that every survivor must create their own pathway to recovery. What works for one might not work for another. Therapy, medicine, and counseling might be the right path for some people, but not for others. The fact that I chose a pathway to recovery that worked for me is not to suggest that it's the best path, or that it's the only path. The only thing it suggests is that I found the path that worked for me.

My parents made it very clear that they would do whatever it took to help me. Every option was on the table. Counseling. Therapy. Doctors and medication. Whatever it took to secure a happy future. But while we talked about the possibility of therapy or counseling, I never felt it was the right thing for me.

So how was I able to get past all of the horrible things that happened?

First, I want to remind you of my mother. There are certain pains that only a mother can really feel, exquisite and intense, and my mother endured them all. She endured them day and night. She endured them for nine months. She wondered if I was dead. It's one thing to lose your child, but it's something altogether different to have your child stolen our of her own bed. She endured months of bitter scrutiny, with some of most horrible things being said about her family. In her darkest hours, she imagined all of the suffering that I might be going through. And now she knows about it, the pain that I endured and things that I was forced to do.

But she didn't let any of these things stop her. She remains the strongest woman I have ever known. She is full of faith and hope and optimism.

So you see, I come from a very strong mother. In fact, I come from a long line of strong women. Maybe I inherited a little of their stock.

And there is also significant historical precedent that indicates that what I've been able to do is not terribly unusual.

The truth is, history is replete with stories of human suffering. The world has been full of brutality and abuse and suffering since the beginning of man. There are examples of those who suffered abuse as I did, maybe in different forms, or from different sources, but I am not the first one to suffer at the hand of an evil man. And there were other kinds of challenges. Some of my own ancestors were early pioneers. They faced suffering and starvation, the loss of their children, the loss of other loved ones. They too endured the gamut of emotions, from utter devastation to lifesaving miracles. But the human spirit is resilient. God made us so. He gave us the ability to forgive. To leave our past behind. To look forward instead of back. I'm not the first one who has ever done this. People have been doing it for generations. Since the beginning of time, men have found ways to heal.

So what I did may not be so exceptional when you consider the entire scope of human experience.

But there are some things that helped me.

I have always loved horses and horseback riding. Even as a young child, I would much rather watch *Black Beauty* or *Wild Hearts Can't Be Broken* than anything else. For me, there's something very special about these wonderful animals. Their strength. Their power. The way they learn to trust you. The way you can learn, even as a child, to control them. The way they learn to depend on you, to treat you as an equal even though the fact is that in many ways, you are not. I loved riding before I was kidnapped, and I loved it even more once I got back.

But horses aren't like cars. You don't just get on, throw the horse into gear, and go until you stop. Even a good horse might spook at a shadow, a tree, or a rock, even if they have walked down the same trail a hundred times before. Maybe this time the sunlight hits an object a little differently, or maybe there's a different scent in the air, a different wind, or maybe you are sitting a little forward in the saddle. You always have to be on your toes with horses, never taking them for granted, and for me, there is just something therapeutic about being around them. Riding them. Feeding them. Brushing them and currying their manes. Going into nature and forgetting all the worries of this life.

I also think that if you take care of your horses, and are gentle with them, and work with them through their moments of fright, horses become a pretty accurate mirror of what kind of person you are. I have learned that a horse isn't going to treat you any different than you treat them.

So I have always loved horses. But more than anything else, I loved riding with my Grandpa Smart.

Grandpa Smart, despite being an oncologist, was a true cowboy. Not the city kind, with smooth boots that had never stepped in a corral and button-down denim shirts. He was the real kind; the kind who grew up taking care of animals, who loved them and related to them. If some men are all hat and no horse, my grandpa was all horse and a well-worn hat.

I loved riding with him, but it was always a challenge. He'd lead me bushwhacking through the forest, over the face of what felt like sheer cliffs, wading through ice-cold rivers. There was something simply wonderful about horseback riding with him. And we did a lot of it after I got back.

Grandpa never pushed me or pried. He simply brought me along to enjoy the ride. He used to say that some people talked too much. *Ride more, talk less.* That was his approach to life. Going with him, you always knew you were in for an adventure. But at the same time, you knew you would be left alone to your thoughts.

From him, I developed a true appreciation for the beauties of nature, silence, and being able to step away from the immediate and look at the big picture. This helped me to make decisions, and to see my life, and to see my problems with a little more clarity.

And again, I'm not alone. Horses, and riding, have been credited with helping many others through some of life's most difficult challenges, including serious illness. Ann Romney said that horses gave her the energy and strength to get out of bed, helping her to deal with her multiple sclerosis. Other treatment programs have been designed around the care of other animals.

I suppose that riding was my therapy. And it was very effective.

My Grandpa Smart passed away in January of 2006. I miss him a lot. But the things that he taught me absolutely changed my life.

I had another source of therapy that has helped me throughout my life.

One December when I was five years old, my mom took me Christmas shopping. While we were downtown, I saw a huge Christmas tree with an angel on top that was playing the harp. I remember looking up and thinking, "I want to be put on the top of a Christmas tree! I guess the only way to do that is to play the harp." That was the beginning.

I can't say that I was the perfect student who lived to practice, because I wasn't. There were plenty of times that my mom or dad had to physically come in and sit with me for the duration of my practice session. But I got pretty good. And I developed a great love for playing music.

When I came home, nothing could speak my feelings better than the harp. I know this sounds clichéd, but I think that every musician feels the same way. Music is the unspoken language that can convey feelings more accurately than talking ever could. So playing the harp became extremely therapeutic for me. If I ever felt sad or angry or frustrated, I would sit down and start playing. Once I had submerged my heart into my music, my feelings evaporated and I could go out and face the world again. Besides that, if you have ever heard the harp, then you understand that it is not possible to stay upset for long while playing such a beautiful instrument. Clearly, there is a reason that heavenly angels are depicted playing harps!

All of these things have helped me. But ultimately, to get better, I simply made a choice.

Life is a journey for us all. We all face trials. We all have ups and downs. All of us are human. But we are also the masters of our fate. *We* are the ones who decide how we are going to react to life.

Yes, I could have decided to allow myself to be handicapped by what happened to me. But I decided very early that I only had one life and that I wasn't going to waste it.

As of this writing, I am twenty-five years old. I have been alive for 307 months. Nine of those months were pretty terrible. But 298 of those months have been very good. I have been happy. I have been very blessed. Who knows how many more months I have to live? But even if I died tomorrow, nine out of 307 seems like pretty good odds.

Looking at it that way, I don't think I have much to complain about.

People sometimes ask me if I am happy. Have I truly been able to move on with my life? Have things turned out okay for me? I want you to know that they have. I am happy. I am fulfilled. I am satisfied and at peace with myself and the life that I have built.

I once heard an old saying: *I never said it would be easy; I only said it would be worth it.* I think that's about right. Like everyone, I have my challenges. But I have learned from them and they have helped to make me better.

There is one other very important explanation for why I've been able to overcome what happened to me.

I believe in gratitude.

When I first got home from being kidnapped, I was so grateful to be back with my family, so grateful that they cared and had not given up on me. I was so grateful for a roof over my head, a bed to sleep in, and hot water to take a bath. I was so grateful for food to eat, for shoes that fit, for clean cloths. I was grateful for literally everything.

Then, when my mom shared her advice with me, I made the firm resolution that I would always be grateful and never feel sorry for myself. I resolved that whenever I might have any doubts or moments of weakness—and I knew that they would come—I would tell my-self, *Elizabeth, you have everything back now! But you remember all those hard times, right? And because you remember all those hard times, you can remember the depth of your gratitude.*

And I have also learned that my challenges can help me reach out to others with more empathy and understanding than I could ever have had before.

When we are faced with a challenge, it is very easy to be mad or upset. But when we have passed our great test, we are then given op-portunities to reach out to other people. We are able to effect change in a way that otherwise we wouldn't have been able to.

Because of the things I have lived through, I can help other people now. I can reach out to other victims and help them to learn to be happy. Because I have actually lived through these experiences, I am able to be a voice for change. If I hadn't had this terrible experience, I'm not sure that I would have cared enough about these issues to be-come involved. And even if I did become involved, I wouldn't be able to do many of the things that I've been able to do. I'd be just another young girl who doesn't really know what she's talking about.

I am grateful for these opportunities that I've had to help other people. They have blessed my life.

Gratitude has also helped me to keep a healthy perspective.

One of my favorite movies is *Ever After* with Drew Barrymore. For those of you who have not seen it, it is another version of *Cinderella*. One of my favorite lines from the movie is when the evil stepmother tells Cinderella, "We mustn't ever feel sorry for ourselves, because no matter how bad things are, they can always get worse!"

Now, I know that sounds kind of pessimistic, but when I was being held captive, every time I thought that things couldn't get any worse, somehow they always did.

So instead of looking at the evil stepmother's words as being cold-hearted and mean, I now translate them to say, "We always have something to be grateful for because there will always be something that could make your situation worse."

The first time Mitchell made me go naked and said we were playing "Adam and Eve in the Garden of Eden" I didn't think anything could be worse.

Now I look back and I am grateful that I wasn't being filmed and then exploited and traded through the Internet like so many other children have been. I'm so grateful that my captors were strangers and in no way connected with me. I don't have to go home every night and see them, or see pictures of them hanging on the wall, or know that even though my family is so upset with what they might have done to me, there is still a piece of their hearts that cares and loves the abusers because they are their children, or parents, or brothers and sisters.

And there were other examples too.

Just when I thought it couldn't get any worse, Mitchell made me do something that made me sick. Just when I thought it couldn't get any worse, I went seven days without anything to eat. Just when I thought it couldn't get any worse, Mitchell made me drink until I woke up in my own vomit.

Knowing it can always get worse, I try to be grateful for whatever good I have.

I also believe in faith. Faith in a loving and kind Heavenly Father who will always care about me. Faith that my worth will never be diminished. Faith that God knows how I feel and that I can depend on him to help me through it all. I believe that God not only suffered for me, but that He will make everything up to me in His own time and

His own way. That gives me the peace I need to feel like justice will win out in the end.

That is why I could eventually forgive my captors. That is *not* to say that I want to ever see them again, or that I would ever invite them to Sunday dinner! Believe me, I don't! Every life that they have ever touched, they did their best to destroy. But that is not for me to judge. I don't have to spend even a second of my life worrying about what happens to Brian David Mitchell or Wanda Barzee.

The morning after I was rescued, I was able to write a message to the world. I don't have it anymore, and I don't remember every word, but this is essentially what it said:

I want to thank everyone for what they did for me. I consider myself the luckiest girl in the world. I am so grateful for everyone who prayed for me. I am so grateful for everyone who searched for me, or followed my story, or did everything they could to try to bring me home. Your efforts all made a difference and I want to tell you thank you.

Even now, after all these years, I still feel the same way. So I'll say it again. To all of you who helped me or prayed for me or tried to bring me home: Thank you. I will always be grateful. I love you for what you've done.

Epilogue

———

Elizabeth Smart is now a nationally recognized advocate for children's rights. She is president of the Elizabeth Smart Foundation, which advocates for change related to child abduction and recovery programs and legislation. As well as being involved in the Elizabeth Smart Foundation, Elizabeth has helped promote the National AMBER Alert, the Adam Walsh Child Protection & Safety Act, and other safety legislation to help prevent abductions. She also helped to develop a survivors' guide titled *You're Not Alone: The Journey from Abduction to Empowerment* to encourage children who have gone through similar experiences to not give up and know that there is life after tragic events.

Elizabeth met her future husband while serving her LDS mission in Paris, France. Elizabeth describes Matthew Gilmour, who was a fellow missionary from Scotland, as the nicest, most genuine, and most honest person that she has ever met.

On February 18, 2012, they were married in the Hawaiian LDS temple, starting their very happy lives together.

———

On May 21, 2010, Wanda Barzee was sentenced to fifteen years in federal prison for her role in the kidnapping and sexual assault of Elizabeth Smart, as well as one to fifteen years at the Utah State Prison for the attempted kidnapping of Smart's then fifteen-year-old cousin. The sentences are to run concurrently.

On May 15, 2011, having been convicted of kidnapping Elizabeth Smart at knifepoint, holding her hostage for nine months, and subjecting her to horrific abuse, Brian David Mitchell was sentenced to life in federal prison.

Under the federal system, he has no chance of parole.